I0200081

This book is dedicated
to the memory of

Keiko Kawamori

(October 19, 1948–December 27, 2002)

Managing Director – International Naginata Federation
Managing Director – All Japan Naginata Federation
Director – Japan Olympic Committee
Honorary Naginata Hanshi
4th Class Order of Merit

By the age of 54, she had done so much for so many, and being in her prime, had so much more to do. Her untimely death was a great tragedy for the Naginata world. She led by example, and it is for us to continue developing what she worked so hard for.

Recommendation

This long-awaited revised English language publication is the result of many years of research by Dr. Alex Bennett, and has become the standard reference for all people learning Naginata outside of Japan. The International Naginata Federation is unreserved in recommending this important volume.

As a non-Japanese who has studied traditional Japanese culture extensively, and who possesses a deep understanding of Japanese budo, I believe that Alex's insights gleaned through years of actual experience will serve to facilitate the spread of Naginata internationally. Possessing a profound knowledge of Japanese culture, Alex is able to convey the technical aspects of Naginata, as well as the important spiritual and historical elements in a way that is accurate and easy to follow.

In my capacity as president of the International Naginata Federation, I am honoured to recommend this wonderful publication, and am confident that it will be an indispensable reference for instructors and students alike. It is my hope that it will be utilised to its fullest to aid in the understanding and enjoyment of Naginata, and for learning the fundamentals of the art true to its beautiful form.

Kumiko Hashimoto

President
International Naginata Federation

NAGINATA

HISTORY AND PRACTICE

Alexander Bennett

ISBN 978-4-907009-20-5

For further information on this and other martial arts books please visit us at:

www.kendo-world.com

CONTENTS

Introduction

I had only just turned twenty when I first became involved with the creation of the International Naginata Federation (INF). As a young lad from New Zealand with a passion for learning Japanese budo, I was employed by the All Japan Naginata Federation in 1990 to assist in preparations for creating an organisation to oversee the spread of Naginata internationally. It was a dream job for me, and apart from liaising with Naginata enthusiasts around the world, I was also tasked with translating *Illustrated Naginata*, the first English language textbook on the art. My lack of ability in Japanese at the time, not to mention my limited experience in Naginata made it very challenging work indeed.

Throughout my short tenure at the AJNF, I was made to feel as though I was playing a meaningful role within the "Naginata family". I was indulged by such great women as Shizuko Konishi, Chiyoko Tokunaga, Takeko Mitamura, and of course Keiko Kawamori, whom I affectionately referred to as "Boss". All of these women have sadly passed away, but I will never forget how they helped me adjust to life in Japan. Looking back, I feel immensely privileged to have known them, and to have been involved in the creation of the INF.

The first overseas Naginata leaders that I met through my work were Helen Nakano and Dorothy Ichiyasu from the United States, and Tadahiko Kondo and Simone Charton from France. The United States and France were the first two countries to actively encourage Japan to establish an international federation. The United States actually became provisionally affiliated with the AJNF in 1973, followed by the French in 1982. It was not until 1988, however, that measures were taken to actively promote Naginata internationally.

A department tasked with international promotion was created in the AJNF for this purpose. Keiko Kawamori (Japan) headed the department, and Tadahiko Kondo (France) and Hatsuko Mochidome (America) were appointed as committee members. Acting as president of the European Naginata Federation, Mr. Kondo made an official request to the AJNF to establish the International Naginata Federation. AJNF Chairwoman Shizuko Konishi agreed to the proposal, and preparations were made. Hence my employment.

The International Naginata Federation INF was officially inaugurated at the

Hotel Grand Palace in Tokyo on December 8, 1990. The first affiliates were America, France, New Zealand, the Netherlands, Sweden, Belgium, and Japan. The elected officers were President Kakuji Yanagawa (Japan); Vice Presidents – Tadahiko Kondo (France), Dorothy Ichiyasu (America), Takeshi Shimoyama (Japan); Standing Director – Shizuko Konishi (Japan); Directors – Simone Charton (France), Helen Nakano (America), Alex Bennett (New Zealand), Shizue Funahara (Japan), Yasuko Kimura (Japan), Takiko Kozawa (Japan), with Keiko Kawamori appointed Secretary General.

On December 9, 1990, the 1st INF Friendship Tournament was held at the Nippon Budokan in commemoration of the federation's formation. The first seven affiliate nations were represented, along with the four non-affiliated countries of Great Britain, Australia, Canada and Brazil. The tournament was followed by an international training seminar at the Nippon Budokan's Training Centre in Katsuura City, Chiba Prefecture.

Since then, the World Naginata Championships have been held in Japan (1995), France (1999), America (2003), Belgium (2007), Japan (2011), and Canada (2015). Japanese competitors used to dominate the events, but the level of international competitors has improved dramatically in recent years. There are now 14 countries affiliated to the INF (as of 2015) with a growing number seeking membership. The INF continues to sponsor international training seminars on an annual basis hosted by a different affiliate each time.

Shizuko Konishi, the key instigator in the creation of the INF, died on September 20, 1992, a year after the federation was created. Ten years later, her daughter Keiko Kawamori also passed away before her time on December 27, 2002. On June 26, 2004 the INF's first President Kakuji Yanagawa also died. He had been at the helm of the INF since its inception. These people have been sorely missed in the INF. From the 3rd WNC in San Jose, the presidency of the INF was filled by Mrs. Kumiko Hashimoto. A graduate of the Sacred Heart School in Japan, the same school that Shizuko Konishi and Keiko Kawamori attended, Mrs. Hashimoto was also the wife of the late Ryutaro Hashimoto, the former Prime Minister of Japan.

Although the INF has now been operating for a quarter of a century, Naginata is still a relatively minor budo discipline in terms of population and exposure with many logistical problems hindering effective international dissemination. For example, practitioners who wish to take examinations for ranks 5th Dan or higher must come to Japan to do so. This is costly, and the opportunities are few and far between. There are a handful of high-ranked instructors living outside of Japan such as the wonderful Helen Nakano, who was awarded the "Order of the Rising Sun" in 2009 by the Emperor of Japan for her services to Naginata, but we need more. Procuring equipment is also a problem. Then there is the issue of training competent referees and certification. All of these matters are being dealt with, but progress is inevitably slow.

Perhaps one of the most pressing issues is the need to create more teaching resources. Compared to other budo disciplines, there is a noticeable dearth of reference materials for Naginata in Japanese let alone any other language. Most practitioners outside Japan have to make do with interim instruction, and are left to their own devices until the next regional or international training seminar. This means that bad habits and mistakes in interpretation go unchecked, and some practitioners even lose enthusiasm and give up altogether.

Of the miniscule number of books on Naginata that do exist, most are prewar Japanese textbooks that are, for the most part, irrelevant to the popular form developed from the 1950s. Postwar Naginata books are scant, and usually only cover the same basic techniques. Very little information is offered with regard to the cultural, historical, and spiritual aspects of Naginata. To date, apart from a few journal articles, there are virtually no references in English or any other language. Practitioners around the world have been left almost completely in the dark about how modern Naginata actually evolved in a process that spanned over a millennium.

I wrote this book with these points in mind. This volume is a complete rewrite and revision of my previous book, *Naginata: The Definitive Guide* (KW Publications, 2005). I understand that enthusiasts have flatteringly been calling the original book "The Naginata Bible" for some years, but I am not presumptuous enough to rename revised edition with this title. I hope, however, that this vastly improved and updated version will continue to provide the enthusiast with a solid base for further research into the history of Naginata and budo culture. It should also serve as a reference for both instructors and beginners in the techniques of Naginata.

Much of the technical information is based on my previous translation of *Sports V Course Naginata* published by the AJNF. I have also added more detail to the original text, including explanations of concepts found in the *Naginata Handbook* (revised edition 2013), a pamphlet published by the

AJNF for people taking examinations. Furthermore, the appendices at the end were included to assist middle to high ranked practitioners for reviewing refereeing, promotion examinations, Kata, vocabulary, and so on.

I would like to thank the following people for their help in bringing this book to fruition: Taishukan Publishing for allowing the use some of the photos, diagrams, and text contained in *Sports V Course Naginata*. Yasuko Kimura for her technical guidance and support. The students of the International Budo University Naginata Club for serving as models for many of the technical photos. Masashi 'Kan' Shishikura for the many hours spent editing photos, and Baptiste Tavernier for his technical assistance. Thanks also to Yulin Zhuang, Bryan Peterson, and Hamish Robison for their proofing and editing expertise. I am also indebted to INF President Kumiko Hashimoto, Fumiko Nagahama, Helen Nakano, Katsuko Tamaki, and the other officers for their support in this project. Finally, I would like to thank my place of employment, Kansai University, for providing the resources that have enabled me to finish this book whilst on sabbatical.

Alexander Bennett Ph.D.
International Naginata Federation Vice President
Kaikoura in New Zealand, 2015

Introduction

Conventions

Inevitably in a book of this nature there are many Japanese terms. Most Japanese words are italicised, however, I have refrained from using macrons except in the glossary of terms at the back. All of the budo arts mentioned in the text are treated as Anglicised words, and "*naginata*" in italics refers to the actual weapon. Any Japanese noun that is capitalised indicates that it is an official set of techniques, school, organisation, or title. For example, "Shikake-Oji" refers to the actual predetermined set of eight set forms, and "*shikake*" and "*oji*" refer to attacking and counter-attacking. Similarly "*kata*" refers to the generic term for set forms, and "Kata" to the official All Japan Naginata Federation forms.

CHAPTER 1
WHAT IS NAGINATA?

A scene depicted in "Ishiyama-dera engi emaki" (1324–1326).
(The illustrated scrolls of the founding of the Ishiyama Temple.)

Part 1: The History of Naginata

1. Origins

The word *naginata* first appeared in historical documents around the mid-Heian period (794–1185). For example, in *Honchoseiki*[1] the *naginata* was written phonetically using the characters "奈(*na*)木(*ki*)奈(*na*)多(*ta*)". Other texts such as *Wamyosho*—a Chinese-Japanese dictionary compiled by Minamoto-no-Shitagau in 934—mentions the *naginata* using the characters "長刀" (long sword). Toward the end of the Muromachi period (1333–1568). The glyphs "薙刀" (mowing sword) were used more frequently, and represented the sweeping motion of the *naginata* when employed to slash at human foe, or the horses they were riding. These characters were also utilised to make a distinction between actual "long swords" in vogue at the time.

Waka sansai-zue (Japanese-Chinese illustrated assemblage of the three components of the universe) was an encyclopaedia edited by an Osaka physician, Terashima Ryoan (dates unknown). It was completed in 1712 and makes mention of the *naginata* using yet another set of phonetic glyphs "奈(*na*)伎(*gi*)那(*na*)太(*ta*)", although this is extremely uncommon.[2]

A scene from the Go-sannen-no eki.
(Tokyo National Museum.)

Chapter 1: The History of Naginata

It is difficult to ascertain exactly when and why the *naginata* came into existence, but picture scrolls (*emaki-mono*) show that they were used by warriors in the *Go-sannen-no-eki* (Later Three Years' War). This was a military campaign in which Minamoto-no-Yoshiie subdued the wayward Kiyohara family of north-eastern Japan between 1083 and 1087. In these scrolls, warriors can be seen flailing weapons that look similar to swords, but obviously have longer and wider blades with greater curvature. They also had long shafts, and were used to cut, mow, and thrust with both ends. The fact that they are depicted in pictorial records of these battles suggests that they had been around for a while before the eleventh century.

Although some scholars believe that the *naginata* probably derived from the Chinese glaive (*guang-dao*), there is no solid proof to substantiate this.[3] Most Japanese weapons experts conclude that the *naginata* is indigenous to Japan, although there are differing theories of exactly how it evolved. The earliest known prototypes were the *tsukushi-naginata* from the northern Kyushu region. These were simply curved blades (approximately 58 centimetres in length) attached to wooden shafts. Another early prototype, although extremely rare, was the *nata-naginata*. Again, this was simply a blade attached to a wooden shaft. These early examples look like agricultural tools rather than weapons *per se*, and they probably served a dual function for farmer-warriors who had to contend with raiding bands of Emishi—the aboriginal tribal peoples of Japan who were forced to retreat northward around the eighth century after military invasions by the Yamato state.[4]

Another possibility, although difficult to prove, was that the *naginata* evolved from the *teboko*, a weapon developed during the Nara period (710–794). *Teboko* were relatively short weapons in which oddly shaped blades were inserted into thick wooden shafts. There are few examples left in existence, but five are stored in the Shosoin in Nara. It is unknown whether they were designed for combat or ceremonial purposes.

Perhaps the most plausible theory for the development of the *naginata* suggests that they were improvised weapons made by simply attaching a *tachi* (sword) onto a shaft, or possibly a broken spear (*hoko*). It is a simple concept, but extremely effective for slashing and stabbing at horses from a safe distance or from behind a barricade.

Whatever the origins, the use of these Japanese glaives had become widespread by the middle of the eleventh century, particularly among warrior-monks

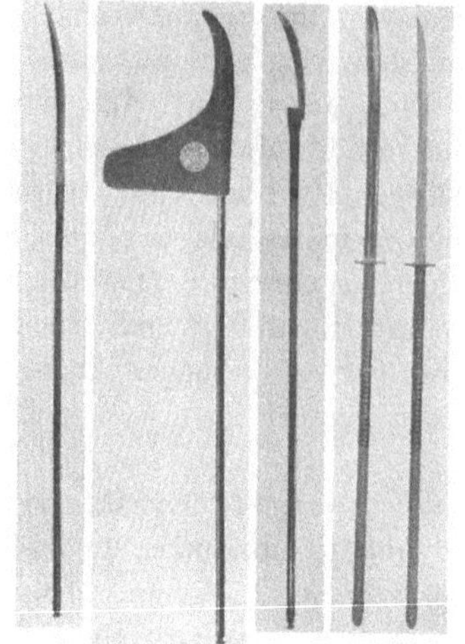

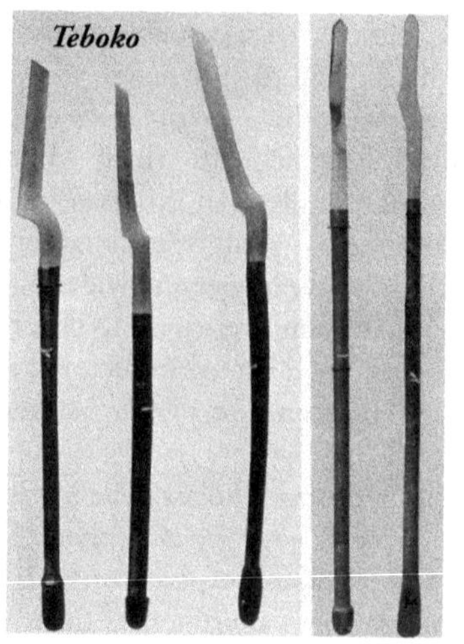

Nata-naginata

Tsukushi-naginata

Naginata and shafts from the Kamakura period

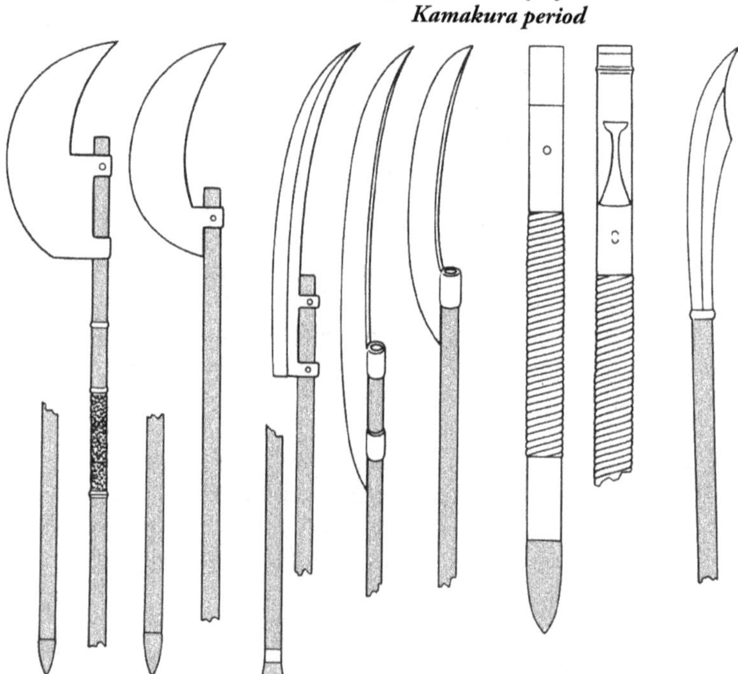

Mitamura Kunihiko "Dai Nihon Naginata-do Kyohan" (1939).

(*sohei*), and foot soldiers. Furthermore, by this stage the *naginata* had developed into a sturdy weapon with good balance and a superb tang-blade forged in the same fashion as swords of the day. The shafts were generally 1.2 to 2.4 metres in length, and the curved blade usually 30 to 60 centimetres long. The tangs were inserted in the oval oak shafts, secured with bamboo pegs (*mekugi*), and then bound tightly with cords and metal rings.

The butt end of the shaft was also an important feature of the *naginata*'s effectiveness. Known as the *ishizuki* (stone stabber), the butt was often capped with metal in various shapes and sizes, and this served as a kind of bludgeoning device, particularly lethal to unhorsed warriors trying to get to their feet again. Thus, the *naginata* was used in two ways: to slash at the legs of horses and stab the riders with the blade from a relatively safe distance, and also for close-quarters fighting and downward thrusts on fallen foe with the *ishizuki*.

Early *naginata* had relatively straight, thin blades, but they became increasingly thicker and longer with more pronounced curvature. In the fourteenth century a similar weapon, the *nagamaki*, came into use. The *nagamaki* had a longer blade than the standard *naginata*, but a shorter staff. Although close in form to the *naginata*, it is considered to be a different weapon. It is a sword with an very long *tsuka* (handle) as opposed to a blade attached to a shaft.

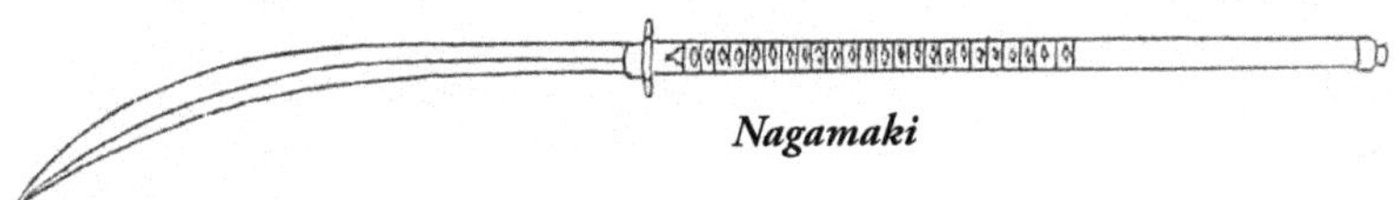

Nagamaki

From the fifteenth century onward, we see the addition of *tsuba* (sword guards) to *naginata*, and shorter but wider blades. The shafts, however, were lengthened making the weapon longer and heavier than its predecessors. This was the period in which "*naginata*" generally came to be written with the characters depicting "mowing sword". It was also from this time that the *naginata* became increasingly ornate with lavish cord-work and metal designs on the shaft, sometimes even inlaid with mother-of- pearl. We also see some *kagi-naginata* from this period with special perpendicular blade-stopping bars at the top of the shaft.

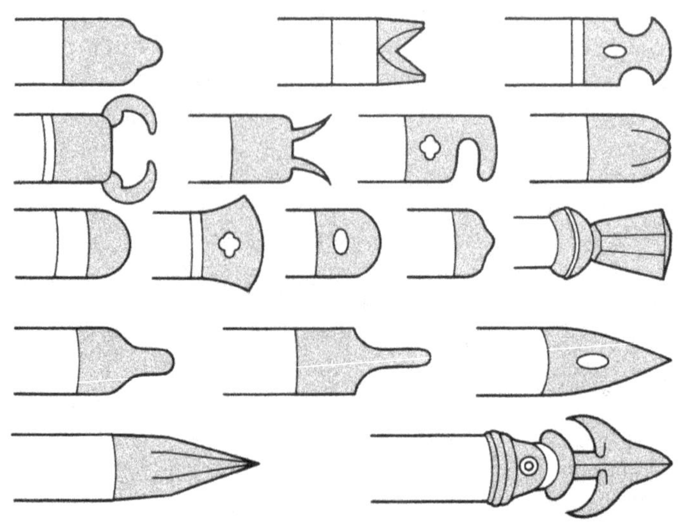

Various styles of ishizuki (Mitamura Kunihiko)

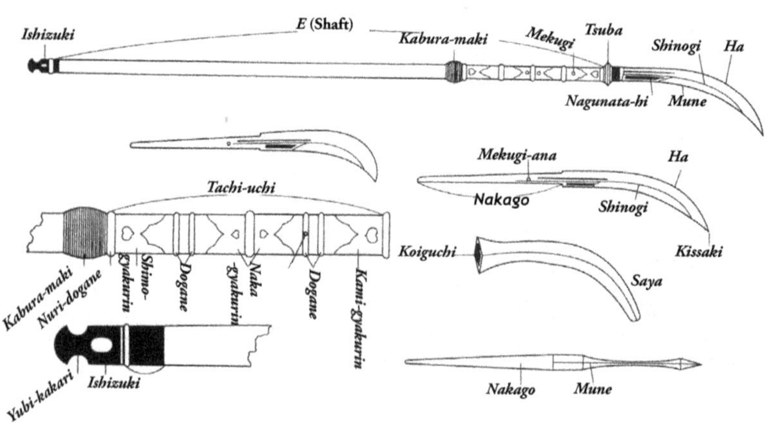

The parts of a naginata.

2. The Naginata in Battle

Despite the continued evolution of the *naginata* over the centuries, its heyday as a battlefield weapon was during the Genpei War (1180–1185)—a conflict between the two warrior clans of the Taira and the Minamoto—and the turbulent times immediately before and after. The extent to which the *naginata* was used is evident in warrior literature such as the *Heike monogatari* (*Tale of the Heike*).[5] This is one of the most well-known medieval war tales, chronicling the rise and fall of the Taira clan (Heike) in the twelfth century. The narrative contains many thrilling scenes of battle depicting the valorous deeds of samurai who prized honour, loyalty, and valour above life itself.

The following excerpt is from "The Battle at the Bridge" (*Hashi-gassen)* in Helen McCullough's translation of the *Tale of the Heike*. Note that she refers to *naginata* (長刀) as "spear" in her translation.[6] I took the liberty of changing it back to *naginata*:

> Jomyo Meishu of Tsutsui, one of the worker-monks, was attired in a dark blue *hitatare*, a suit of black-laced armour, and a five-plate helmet. At his waist, he wore a sword with a black lacquered hilt and scabbard; on his back, there rode a quiver containing twenty-four arrows fledged with black eagle-wing feathers. Grasping a lacquered, rattan-wrapped bow and his favourite long, plain-handled spear, he advanced onto the bridge and announced his name in a mighty voice.
>
> "You must have heard of me long ago. See me now with your own eyes! Everyone at Miidera knows me! I am the worker-monk Jomyo Meishu from Tsutsui, a warrior worth a thousand men. If any here consider themselves my equals, let them come forward. I'll meet them!" He let fly a fast and furious barrage from his twenty-four-arrow quiver, which killed twelve men instantly and wounded eleven others. Then, with one arrow left, he sent the bow clattering away, untied and discarded the quiver, cast off his fur boots, and ran nimbly along a bridge beam in his bare feet. Others had feared to attempt the crossing: Jomyo acted as though it were lchijo or Nijo Avenue. He mowed down five enemies with his *naginata* and was engaging a sixth when the blade snapped in the middle. He abandoned the weapon and fought with his sword. Hard-pressed by the enemy host, he slashed in every direction, using zigzag, interlacing, crosswise, dragonfly reverse, and waterwheel manoeuvres. After cutting down eight men on the spot, he struck the helmet top of a ninth so hard that the blade snapped at the hilt rivet, and slipped loose into the river. Then he fought on desperately with a dirk as his sole resource.[7]

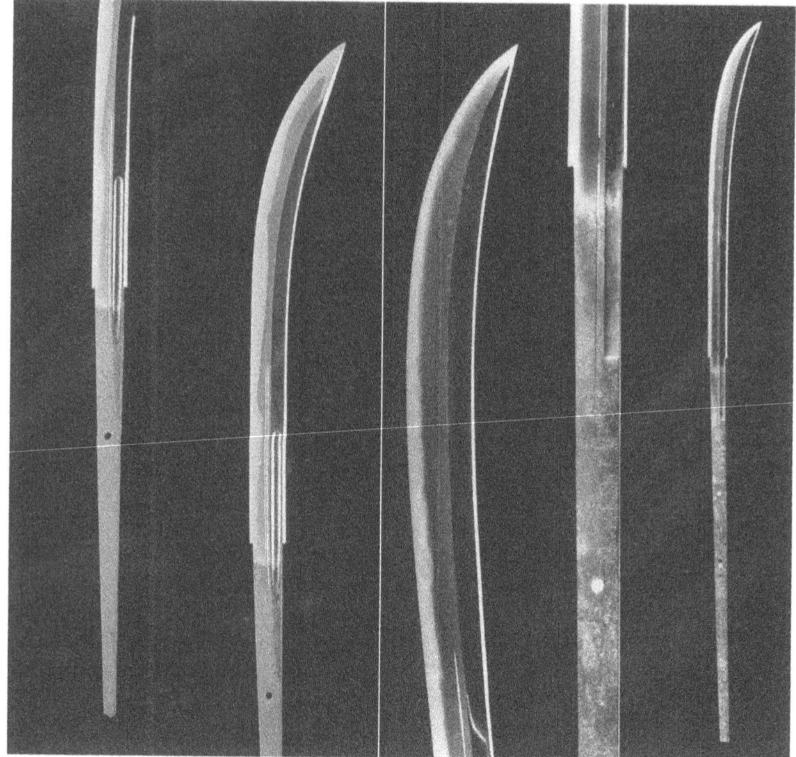

Kamakura period naginata blades.

Although many warriors of the period used the *naginata* in battle, there are a few historical figures who have remained synonymous with the weapon. Of them, undoubtedly Musashibo Benkei (?–1189) is the most celebrated. He was a legendary warrior-monk and loyal retainer of the tragic hero Minamoto-no-Yoshitsune. Although a historical figure named Benkei is briefly mentioned in the text *Azuma kagami* (ca. 1266–1301), the only detailed accounts of his life are almost entirely fictional.

According to the stories, however, Benkei was an extraordinarily cunning man, who was physically domineering and highly skilled in the martial arts. Benkei, armed with his trusty *naginata*, accompanied Yoshitsune through the campaigns of the Genpei War. Fearing his brother's popularity as a threat to his hegemony after the Taira were vanquished, the paranoid Minamoto-no-

Yoritomo turned against his younger brother, Yoshitsune, who was forced to flee with Benkei. When they were finally surrounded, so the story goes, Benkei fought valiantly to the death while buying Yoshitsune enough time to commit suicide rather than be slaughtered at the hands of his enemies. Benkei's faithfulness and courage are celebrated in several Noh and Kabuki plays, and television dramas, and he remains an immensely popular figure to this day, being seen as embodying the virtues of valour and loyalty.

BENKEI'S LAST BATTLE.

From James S. de Benneville's 1910 publication, "Saito Musashi-bo Benkei".

Although Naginata is widely recognised as a martial art predominantly studied by women, it is difficult to find any reliable historical documentation portraying women actually using the weapon in combat. Although factually

Tomoe Gozen.
(Tokyo National Museum)

questionable, the war tales do mention a couple of exceptional women warriors: Tomoe Gozen and Hangaku Gozen (sometimes referred to as Itagaki). Gozen literally means "one who is in attendance before an august person". The title could be applied to a noble lady of a good family, or possibly to a "singing girl". Interestingly, the *naginata* did not seem to be the main weapon for either of these women.

Hangaku Gozen is recorded as having been a tremendous archer. When trapped in a besieged fortress in 1201, Hangaku reputedly slew countless enemies by shooting from a tower above the fortifications. There is no mention whatsoever of Hangaku ever having ridden in battle, or wielding a sword or *naginata*.

According to *Tale of the Heike*, Tomoe Gozen accompanied Yoshinaka when he took flight to Kyoto in 1184. When Yoshinaka was in danger of capture by his encroaching enemies, Tomoe was urged to leave to spare him the embarrassment of having a woman with him. Tomoe refused to go until she had taken an enemy head, and prove that her martial prowess was equal to that of any man. Eventually she escaped, and is said to have remarried, or lived as a nun.

> ...Tomoe was especially beautiful, with white skin, long hair, and charming features. She was also a remarkably strong archer, and as a swords-woman she was a warrior worth a thousand, ready to confront a demon or a god, mounted or on foot. She handled unbroken horses with superb skill; she rode unscathed down perilous descents. Whenever a battle was imminent, Yoshinaka sent her out as his first captain, equipped with strong armour, an oversized sword, and a mighty bow; and she performed more deeds of valour than any of his other warriors." (*Tale of the Heike*)

There is no reference to her using a *naginata* here, even though many illustrations portray her holding one. The Chofukuji Temple in Nagano prefecture owns a *naginata* which it claims belonged to Tomoe. This is highly unlikely and is refuted by most scholars, but the temple continues to strongly promote the artefact as genuine. Only Tomoe would ever know! If any of the stories of the legendary Tomoe are even remotely true, she would have been a formidable foe regardless of what weapon she used.

3. Naginata in the Warring States Period

The Muromachi period (1333–1568) was an era of both great cultural achievement and widespread social disorder. During the latter half of the Muromachi period, a time referred to as the Warring States period, use of the *naginata* waned with the introduction of more regimented fighting strategies utilising *yari* (spears), and also the introduction of firearms.

Chaos engulfed the country for over a century and a half. Fortune or failure was a mere backstab away. Needless to say, the "art of war" burgeoned in this violent period as daimyo honed their skills and resources for maximum destructive effect. Different to the small scale battles of the Kamakura period where highly extroverted individual samurai sought to make a name for themselves through feats of bravery, war became highly regimented. Thousands of beleaguered peasants were drafted as lowly infantrymen into armies (when they weren't growing rice). They did not receive the training professional warriors had in bladed weapons or bows, but with introduction of comparatively easy-to-use pikes (*yari*), peasants provided a formidable ingredient to the ever-expanding warring armies as *ashigaru* (light foots). Medieval warfare was not centred on the clash of steel blades as it is often portrayed.[9]

As the *naginata* was a bladed weapon, it required skill to use. As was the case with swords, if the angle of the blade was slightly off, it would not cut very well, and could easily break. The *yari*, on the other hand, was a simple but revolutionary weapon. It started to become widespread usage from around the middle of the fourteenth century and records indicate that in the period stretching from 1467-1600, it accounted for somewhere around 80% of inflicted casualties in close quarter fighting. This far exceeded damage inflicted by swords which were rarely used after 1467.[10] It was still used by warrior monks (*sohei*) but would later on become a weapon studied primarily by women of warrior families as a "hidden" martial art.

4. Naginata in the Tokugawa Period

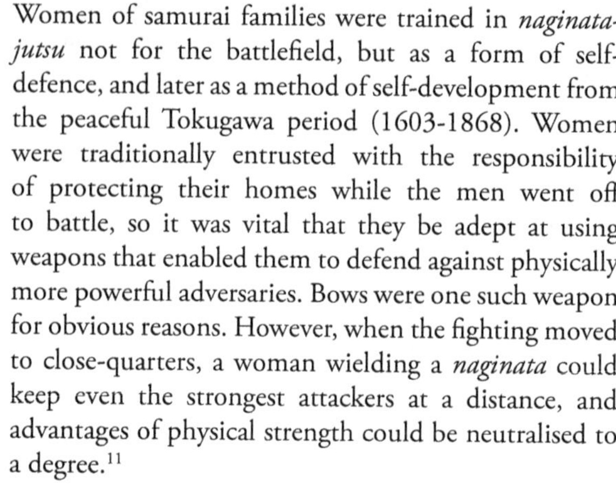

Women of samurai families were trained in *naginata-jutsu* not for the battlefield, but as a form of self-defence, and later as a method of self-development from the peaceful Tokugawa period (1603-1868). Women were traditionally entrusted with the responsibility of protecting their homes while the men went off to battle, so it was vital that they be adept at using weapons that enabled them to defend against physically more powerful adversaries. Bows were one such weapon for obvious reasons. However, when the fighting moved to close-quarters, a woman wielding a *naginata* could keep even the strongest attackers at a distance, and advantages of physical strength could be neutralised to a degree.[11]

During the Tokugawa period, the *naginata* became considerably shorter in length. Shafts were very ornate and often decorated with mother-of-pearl or gold leaf inlays making them look more like accessories than weapons. They became an essential item in the dowry of women of warrior families, often passed on from mother to daughter as family heirlooms.

As with the other martial arts during the Tokugawa period, the bulk of *naginata-jutsu* training centred on the repetition of *kata*. This period provided neither wars nor battles for warriors to test their skills. Having lost the arena of actual combat, martial artists concentrated on perfecting the forms, and new, untested techniques that were developed became increasingly ostentatious.

Women in kimono engaged in naginata training during the Tokugawa period.

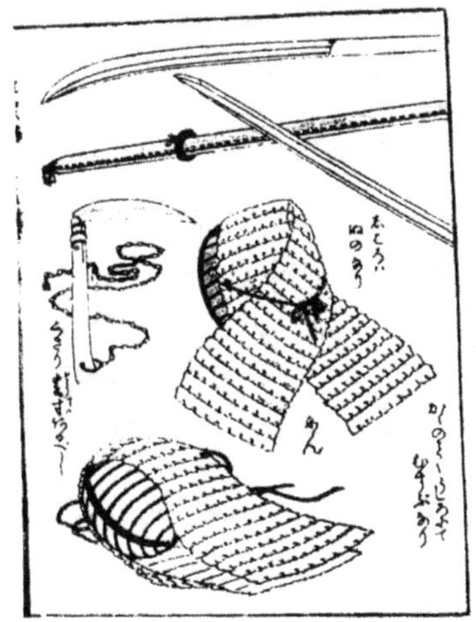
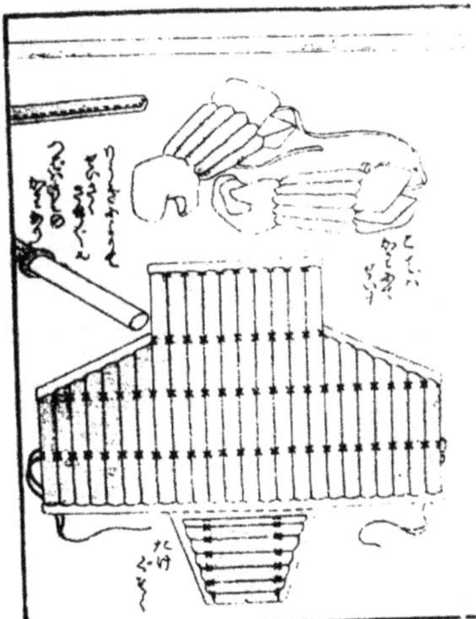

Naginata, shinai, bokuto, kusarigama, and bogu in "Hokusai manga" (1817).

This trend was held in contempt by purists who described such methods as *kaho kenpo* ("flower-style swordplay"). In order to remedy the situation, new training methods were experimented with that promoted spontaneity and full contact striking rather than the choreographed movements of *kata*. For this purpose, bamboo swords and practice *yari* along with training armour (*bogu*) not much different to the protective equipment used in Naginata and kendo today appeared during the seventeenth and eighteenth centuries. The armour was gradually improved as were new training methods that made use of it. These innovations enabled full-contact strikes without the concern of training partners killing or maiming each other.

The famous military and Confucian scholar, Yamaga Soko (1622–85), recorded some interesting observations concerning the utilisation of protective equipment in *kenjutsu*.

> With regards to the benefits of the system of training in *kenjutsu* with a *shinai*...adepts used to attach armour, with an iron protective mask, and engage in rigorous mock-combat to their heart's content [without the worry of injury]. [12]

Not all schools, however, were keen to adopt these revolutionary new training methods. In 1663, Kamiya Denshin Yoriharu, headmaster of the Jikishin-ryu, wrote to Osawa Tomoemon concerning the use of protective equipment.

Chiyo no tomozuru.

> In trainings conducted by other schools, leather armour is worn accompanied by various paraphernalia including face masks. In the Jikishin-ryu, however, we do not intend to use such equipment...

Ironically, later on it was Naganuma Shirōzaemon Kunisato of the Jikishin Kage-ryū who improved on previous simplistic equipment designs and led the way from the early eighteenth century. In 1682, a collection of illustrations sketched by Hishikawa Moronobu titled *Chiyo no tomozuru* depicts two young warriors wielding safety-tipped *yari* (spear) engaged in a contest with another young warrior equipped with *men* (face-mask), *do-tare* (body armour), and what is probably a wooden *naginata.*[13] Judging by the illustration, it appears that *naginata-jutsu* was practised in the same manner as *kenjutsu* and *sojutsu.* Nevertheless, unlike most of the other martial arts I have been unable to locate records of samurai who specialised only in the *naginata* during this period. Obviously, the techniques of *naginata-jutsu* were still studied, but it seems that for the most part they were learned in order to know how to counter the *naginata*, not so much to utilise it as the primary weapon. *Kenjutsu* was by far the most prominent martial art, whereas *naginata-jutsu* was typically a secondary skill.

A survey of the martial art *ryuha* of the Tokugawa period uncovers virtually none that specialised solely in the art of the *naginata*. For example, *Honcho bugei shoden* (1717), a comprehensive almanac of martial art *ryuha* contains chapters pertaining to *kenjutsu*, *shorei* (etiquette), *shajutsu* (archery), *bajutsu* (horsemanship), *tojutsu* (sword), *sojutsu* (spear), *hojutsu* (gunnery), *kogusoku* (grappling with and without weapons), and *jujutsu* (grappling), but nothing dedicated to *naginata-jutsu*. Again, another reference book published in 1844, *Shinsen bujutsu ryuso-roku*, only mentions *naginata-jutsu* techniques included in Anazawa-ryu, Sen'i-ryu and Masaki-ryu, but they are found under the *sojutsu* heading. The well-known martial tradition Tendo-ryu (one of the main surviving classical schools of Naginata today) is also mentioned, but in the *kenjutsu* section, and no allusion is made to its *naginata* techniques.[14]

Synthesised martial traditions such as Shinto-ryu (Anazawa-ryu), Nen-ryu, Araki-ryu, Yoshin-ryu and have *naginata* techniques included in their curricula, but are generally for the sake of *kenjutsu* training rather than for the *naginata* itself, and thus are not given much attention by the chroniclers. Schools that added *naginata-jutsu* to their repertoire toward the end of the Tokugawa period (Bakumatsu) and in the Meiji period in the early and mid-nineteenth century were not included in these texts.[15]

5. Naginata in the Meiji Period

Depiction of the Shinpuren Rebellion of 1876 in Kumamoto prefecture where warrior rebels fought against the government westernisation policies. Note the warrior wielding a naginata as he fights government troops.

During the turbulent Bakumatsu era and start of the Meiji period, the *naginata* were rarely, but not totally unseen in battle. Although not always the case, the Soke (headmaster) of *ryuha* that did have *naginata-jutsu* continued training in the techniques, not so much for combat application, but to keep that part of the tradition alive. Still, when duty called, as it did with the string of insurgencies and conflicts that characterised Japan's journey to modernity, a razor blade on a long shaft was always an option.

The arrival of Commodore Perry's 'Black Ships' in Japanese waters in 1853 was a wake up call for Japan. It was a case of modernise the country's military, or fall prey to Western powers already snooping around Japan's shores. After centuries of self-imposed isolation (*sakoku*), Japan found itself outdated, outgunned, and out of its depth compared to Western nations. Although seclusion from the rest of the world had given the Japanese martial arts time to develop into fascinating martial antiques, rich in ritualistic symbolism and spiritualism, they were no match for the devastating firepower that had been developed in the West. Following the Meiji Restoration (1868) and the dismantling of the shogunate and the feudal system, the new imperial government set about rebuilding the nation by drawing on the latest technology and ideas the West had to offer.

This meant that traditional Japanese martial arts such as *kenjustu* fell into decline due to a lack of perceived practical application. Guns, cannons, and a new conscript army were the order of the day if Japan was to catch up with the rest of the world. The era abounded with catch phrases such as *wakon-yosai* (Japanese spirit, Western technology) and *fukoku-kyohei* (rich country, strong military) as the government strove to educate the masses, arm the nation, and match the West in terms of a new modern civil society.

Naginata-jutsu, along with the other martial arts, was considered symbolic of the now outdated feudal hierarchy, and was thus relegated to the realm of archaic nonsense with no practical use to the newly emerging modern society. With the dissolution of feudal domains and domain schools in 1871, martial arts were no longer included as part of the educational curriculum, which was redesigned on Western models to educate all citizens of the nation.

With class distinctions dismantled, former samurai rapidly lost all of their special privileges. The final nail in the coffin was the edict denying them the right to wear the item considered the symbol of their very souls, the *katana*.[16] Apart from politically proactive samurai who occupied positions of authority in the organs of Japan's new government, a fair few found themselves without status, employment, or income. Not having any specific trade or business skills, some were reduced to utter destitution.

Amidst of this social upheaval, those hit particularly hard were the *bujutsu* instructors formerly in the employ of the shogunate or domains, or those who managed their own private dojos in the cities. With no stipends any more, and no students in their dojos, many subsisted from one day to the next not knowing where their next meal would come from as *bujutsu* was no longer in vogue.

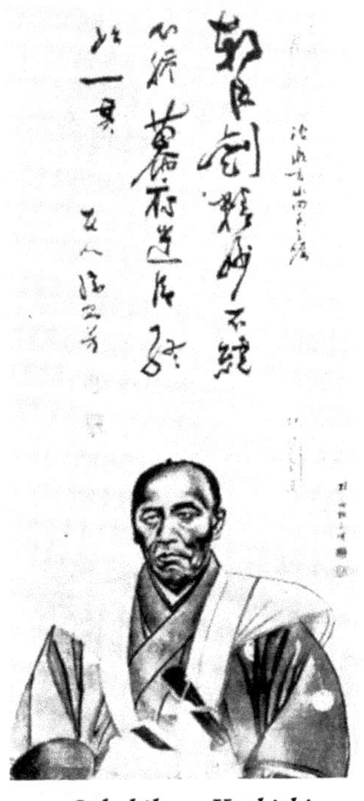

Sakakibara Kenkichi.

Like *kenjutsu, naginata-jutsu* struggled to survive this period. Their saviour appeared in the most unlikely guise. The martial arts shows called *gekken kogyo* (*gekiken* or *gekken* was another term for *kenjutsu,* and *kogyo* means entertainment). The demonstration matches were initiated by Sakakibara Kenkichi—a former instructor at the shogunate's military academy (Kobusho) and master of the Jikishin Kage-ryu—as a way to revive *bujutsu* and provide unemployed martial arts experts with income in the 1870s and 1880s. The majority of fighters were swordsmen, but there were also a small number of women who fought with *naginata.*

Until this time, public demonstrations of *bujutsu* were unheard of, but with the rise of *gekken kogyo,* fee-paying members of the public were encouraged to come and enjoy the spectacle. Furthermore, the fact that challengers from the public were also welcomed to compete if they were brave enough was an about turn from the typically exclusive world of *kenjutsu*. The initiative was destined to transform *bujutsu* into something not for a select few, but for anybody who was interested, and later for all Japanese through the school system.

Gekken kogyo was a hit with the newspapers of the day once word got out that the authorities had given permission to hold such events. The initial coverage by the press served to spread the word far and wide. The interest held by the general public was clearly evident in the first ever *gekken kogyo* demonstration on April 26, 1873 where people were turned away at the gate as the venue was already packed beyond capacity. There was an interesting article printed in a journal titled *Nihon oyobi Nihonjin* (Japan and the Japanese, September 1917) quoting one of the original fighters in the event.

> The arena soon filled up so that there was standing room only. The wooden doors were closed and no more spectators were admitted.

> Still, they tried to gain entry by any means possible. This was a cause for great confusion, so it was decided to make the venue bigger by 5-*ken* (approximately 10 metres) each way for the next day. Early the next morning, there was a great commotion as it was decided that the venue was to be enlarged. This, it was thought, would certainly solve the problem of overcrowding. Keen spectators gathered in front of the arena in droves well before the starting time, so on the second day as well, we were forced to turn people away at the gates…

Compared to sumo, where even people unversed in the subtleties of the techniques can easily recognise the victor and the vanquished, *gekken* matches left most spectators bewildered. It was the novelty factor rather than the actual competition that seemed to hold the most appeal, in the same way as pro-wrestling today. Another problem was the commercial inexperience of the proprietors. Too many troupes were formed after Sakakibara's early successes, and the public started to lose interest.

Gekiken kogyo scene. The layout of the venue was based on popular sumo events.

To critics, it was lamentable to see once proud samurai selling their souls and martial skills for a pocket full of coins. Also, in the name of entertainment and keeping the punters coming, the shows started introducing theatrical techniques and bizarre sound effects. This was seen as detracting from the true spirit of *bujutsu*. The shows were deemed to be an almost sinful abomination by traditionalists. Notwithstanding, the historical importance of the *gekken kogyo* cannot be denied, and in many ways it is thanks to this chapter in history that we still have Naginata today. The *gekken kogyo* provided a narrow footbridge connecting feudal society with modern society. It was a precarious crossing, and many martial traditions died out along the way, but it was enough to keep some interest in traditional *bujutsu* alive long enough for new possibilities to be explored.

The shows became recruitment grounds for the newly formed police force. What Japan needed during the volatile times that followed the Satsuma Rebellion[17] was effective police constables. *Gekken kogyo* venues became the target of scouts who went in search of likely candidates to teach *kenjutsu* at the police. Famous fencers were well aware of the opportunities that awaited them, and the *crème de la crème* found stable careers.

This was a great turn of fortune for some swordsmen, but it essentially spelled the end of *gekken kogyo*. As the stars of the shows found gainful employment in the police, the troupes became depleted, and so too did interest among the general public. Apart from a few companies such as that headed by Satake Kanryusai who travelled the provinces taking his show to the people, all the other companies fizzled, thus signifying the end of an era.

Gekken kogyo was in many ways instrumental in the formation of the kendo and Naginata practised today in terms of rules and refereeing. As a professional sport it was far from successful, but as a predecessor and catalyst for the future prosperity of sports budo that is now enjoyed by people around the world, *gekken kogyo*'s significance cannot be overstated.[18]

6. Naginata and Education

In addition to the newly emerging Meiji police force which decided that *kenjustu* would be a good way to keep its officers in top physical condition, one of the important possibilities yet to be explored was the potential for traditional martial arts as an educational tool. The road to make *bujutsu* accepted as a part of the school curriculum was long and complicated. In the 1870s, there were a number of government officials and educators who voiced their concerns about totally westernising the education system, and at least wanted to retain certain aspects of 'Japaneseness' in the curriculum. This was especially the case with physical education, which was centred heavily on Western callisthenics. Advocates for keeping things Japanese suggested that the physical education curriculum could include the traditional *bujutsu* arts. Then again, there were many who were cautious about utilising the martial arts for such purposes.

The Ministry of Education conducted several official surveys to investigate the potential benefits and dangers of teaching *bujutsu* in schools. Of particular note was the 1883 survey conducted by the MOE backed National Gymnastics

Institute (Taiso Denshujo), and then the 1896 investigation carried out by the School Health Advisory Board (Gakko Eisei Komonkai). They focused on the potential of *kenjutsu* and *jujutsu*, but the findings directly influenced Naginata's fate as it was considered to be the girl's alternative to *kenjutsu*. The NGI's findings regarding *kenjutsu* and *jujutsu* (for boys) were submitted to the MOE in October 1884 after reaching the following conclusions:

Benefits

1. An effective means of enhancing physical development.
2. Develops stamina.
3. Rouses the spirit and boosts morale.
4. Expurgates spinelessness and replaces it with vigour.
5. Arms the exponent with techniques for self-defence in times of danger.

Disadvantages

1. May cause unbalanced physical development.
2. Always an imminent danger present in training.
3. Difficult to determine the appropriate degree of exercise, especially as physically strong boys must train together with weaker individuals.
4. Could encourage violent behaviour due to the rousing of the spirit.
5. Exhilarates the will to fight, which could manifest into an attitude of winning at all costs.
6. There is a danger of encouraging a warped sense of competitiveness to the extent that boys could even resort to dishonest tactics.
7. Difficult to sustain unified instructional methodology for large numbers of students.
8. Requires a large area to conduct training.
9. Even though *jujutsu* requires only a *keiko-gi* (training wear) *kenjutsu* requires armour and other special equipment, which would be expensive and difficult to keep hygienic.

On the one hand, it was recognised that *bujutsu* could be beneficial in complementing the knowledge-oriented school system with its emphasis on spiritual development. On the other, it was deemed to run counter to the medical or physiological benefits expected from physical education activities. It was thought to be detrimental to balanced physical development, encourage violence, foster antagonistic competition, dangerous, to be difficult to find a common medium between styles to coach, expensive, and unhygienic.

It should be noted here that the founder of Kodokan Judo in 1882, Kano Jigoro, was fiendishly proactive in the quest to get budo education into schools. He continually developed judo to suit the parameters laid out by the MOE to make it safe, rational, and educational in terms of moral, intellectual and physical development. I believe that he chose to use white uniforms in judo, not so much because of ancient traditions associating white with purity (as is often stated), but simply to meet the MOE's requirements for hygiene. It is very easy to see when a white judo *gi* has not been washed for a while! Needless to say, Kano's innovations were instrumental in budo's eventual induction into the education system.

With weapon martial arts, however, ticking the MOE's criteria box was no simple task. Traditionally, *bujutsu* had been taught one on one, and knowledge passed on from teacher to students on an individual basis. This was impossible in the modern educational environment. There had to be a revolutionary new way to address this particular issue. The first concerted effort to do this for weapon martial arts resulted in the creation of *bujutsu* callisthenics (*bujutsu-taiso*). In 1894 and 1895, during and after the Sino-Japanese war, a handful of educators attempted to develop a style of gymnastics utilising martial techniques. The idea soon caught on, and before long a number of schools throughout Japan allowed students to participate in newly developed calisthenic exercises using *bokuto* or *naginata*.

One of the chief innovators was Ozawa Unosuke. He stated that the purpose of developing *bujutsu* callisthenics was not only as a tool for education, but also to "nurture a nation of people with physiques by no means inferior to the people of Western nations". He also outlined the many problems faced by the current system of gymnastics such as the difficulty in procuring equipment and suitable facilities which could be overcome by introducing *bujutsu* into the system. As a curricular activity, he proposed the *bujutsu*-derived exercises would be an effective means of nurturing physical adeptness, and as an extra-curricular activity it would be an enjoyable form of recreational exercise or games that encourage discipline and overall physical wellbeing.

Ozawa had two types of *bujutsu* exercise in mind. They were "*bujutsu* games"(*bujutsu-yugi*) and "*bujutsu* callisthenics" (*bujutsu-taiso*). In the former he developed *naginata-yugi*, *bojutsu-yugi* (staff), *kenjutsu-yugi*, and *shageki-yugi* (shooting). The latter contained *naginata-jutsu*, *bojutsu*, *kenjutsu*, *sojutsu* (spear), and *kaiken-jutsu* (dagger). These were further categorised into two types of "*bujutsu kata taiso*" based on set forms, and "*bujutsu shiai taiso*" where match play was the focus. He wrote textbooks such as *Budo kairyo kyoju bujutsu taiso-ron* (1896), *Bujutsu taiso-ho* (1897), and *Kaisei naginata taiso-ho* (vols. 1 & 2 1906). With the growing international popularity of the "scientific" gymnastic approach pioneered by the Swede Per Henrik Ling, Ozawa introduced a revised version of his *bujutsu* callisthenics in a new publication *Kenjutsu kata taiso* (1911). Again, in 1918 he published *Taiiku-ryu kenjutsu naginata-jutsu*. In these books we can see a significant change in the techniques utilised, and the inclusion of more pair work, warm-ups, and even breathing techniques.[20]

Ozawa Unosuke posing with a naginata on a hot summer day

Apart from Ozawa, there were others also experimenting with an indigenous system of gymnastic exercises based on *bujutsu*. Of particular note was Nakajima Kenzo who had studied the Jikishin Kage-ryu martial tradition in his childhood. He also wrote some books on the subject such as *Naginata taiso-ho* (1909) and *Bokken oyobi naginata taiso-ho* (1918). It is unknown whether or not Ozawa and Nakajima ever collaborated; however, the efforts of both men saw their initiatives spread throughout the nation with seminars being held in various localities and greeted with considerable enthusiasm.

There were also staunch critics who vehemently opposed the systems. Reasons for opposition varied, but the most common criticisms were that the techniques utilised were unrealistic and ineffective, paying little attention to correct flight or cutting direction of the blade, and that there was too much ostentatious movement. Many could not see the difference between *bujutsu* callisthenics and baton twirling, another form of popular exercise at the time. Also, with the introduction of more scientific innovations in gymnastics, especially from Sweden, naysayers failed to see the point of doing exercise routines with sticks.

Books written solely as *bujutsu* textbooks (as opposed to callisthenics) appeared from around 1904–05, but were clearly influenced by the callisthenics style and methodology. Despite the criticisms, *bujutsu* callisthenics did prove that the martial arts could be practised or taught in groups quite easily, and without the need for expensive equipment, contrary to previous belief. From this standpoint, it is fair to say that it had a profound effect on the subsequent development of martial arts pedagogy overall.

After decades of heated debate over what should be taught in the school PE curriculum, the Ministry of Education eventually issued the "Syllabus of School Gymnastics" (*Gakko taiso kyoju yomoku*) in 1913. This syllabus prescribed the Lingian approach to gymnastics, as was the trend in Great Britain, America, and Scandinavia. This was supplemented with military drill and games (*yugi*), and each school was supposed to devise its own curriculum in accordance with the guidelines set out by the MOE. The new guidelines spelled the end of the "*bujutsu* callisthenics" initiatives as *bujutsu* itself was now accepted.

Martial artists began avoiding association with *bujutsu* callisthenics, preferring instead to describe their pedagogical approach as "group teaching methodology". It is interesting to note the influence Western gymnastics exerted on the development of *bujutsu* callisthenics, and then on this group teaching methodology. When one takes into consideration the modern rhetoric asserting that modern budo is "traditional Japanese culture", it begs the question of what exactly is tradition? Tradition, as we can see in the context of modern budo, is continually being invented.

Undoubtedly the formation of the Dai-Nippon Butokukai (Greater Japan Society of Martial Virtue) in 1895 was a major turning point in popularising the martial arts in schools and the community. By this stage, Japan had forged ahead in its quest to modernise, and was embarking on expansionist activities with a nationalistic fervour to match any other colonialist power of the day. The Sino-Japanese war (1894–1895) saw a surge of nationalism in Japan which in turn led to increased interest in *bujutsu*.

The year 1895 marked the 1100th year of Kyoto becoming the capital of Japan. At that time, Emperor Kanmu is said to have constructed the Butokuden (Hall of Martial Virtue) to promote martial spirit and encourage the warriors to further develop their military prowess. Thus, in commemoration of this, and riding a growing wave of nationalism, the Butokukai was

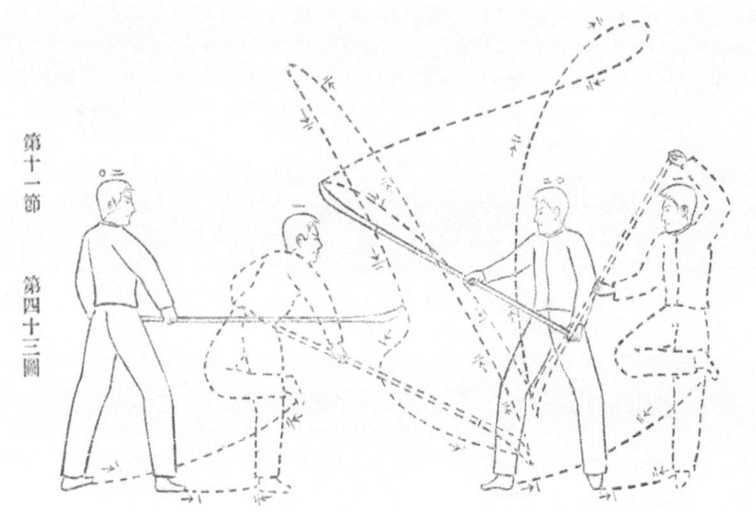

An illustration from Ozawa Unosuke's "Naginata taiso-ho" (1903).

Ozawa Unosuke and his students in "Taiiku-teki Naginata-mai" (1904).

established in Kyoto, authorised by the Ministry of Education and endorsed of the Meiji Emperor. Its goals were to promote and standardise the many martial disciplines found scattered throughout Japan. In 1899, the Butokuden was built near the grounds of the newly constructed Heian Jingu Shrine in Kyoto.

The Butokuden in 1899.

In 1902, the Butokukai created an awards system to acknowledge individuals who had made contributions for the promotion of traditional *bujutsu*. In 1905, a division was established to train specialist *bujutsu* instructors. The curriculum was refined, and in 1911, the School of Martial Virtue (Butoku Gakko) was formed. This became known as the Bujutsu Vocational (Bujutsu Senmon Gakko) in 1912, and then the Budo Vocational School in 1919 when the term *bu-justu* was officially replaced with *bu-do* to emphasise the "martial *way*", or educational aspects of the martial arts. From then on, the terms *gekken* and *kenjutsu* were replaced with kendo. Naginata was also called Naginata-do by some instructors, but it was not widespread.[21]

Thus, the Butokukai was instrumental in the promotion of budo through rewarding prominent individuals, training teachers, and holding special events and tournaments. The Budo Vocational School (or *Busen* as it became known) together with the Tokyo Higher Normal School (Tokyo Koto Shihan

Gakko) led the way in producing young instructors to teach martial arts to children in schools nationwide. In 1904, the Butokukai formed a division to promote Naginata nationally as a martial art primarily for women.

Irrespective of initial reservations to elevate Naginata and other martial arts to the status of mandatory subjects, some schools did encourage their students to learn Naginata. For example, Hoshino Shinnosuke, a well-known advocate of *bujutsu* education for girls, started teaching Naginata forms from the Hokushin Itto-ryu and Yagyu-ryu traditions at Tokyo Meiji Girls' School from as early as 1889. In 1897, Ozawa Unosuke taught Naginata to senior students at the Tokyo Aijitsu Primary School where he promoted his hybrid exercises utilising techniques from various *ryuha*.

Other notable examples include Mitamura Akinori, the 14th Soke of the Tendo-ryu tradition, who began instruction at Doshisha Girls' School in Kyoto in 1899. In 1901, Yazawa Isako introduced Buko-ryu Naginata into the Physical Education Department of Nihon Women's University. In 1908, Sonobe Hideo, the 15th Soke of Jikishin Kage-ryu *naginata-jutsu* commenced instruction at Himeji Normal College. Also, starting in 1911 Arai Tsuta taught techniques that she developed in the Kyoshin-ryu at Nara Women's Normal College for 20 years.[23] It was these pioneers who demonstrated the value of teaching Naginata at schools as physical education. This aided in Naginata's eventual inclusion into the school curriculum, but it was a long process.

Arai Tsuta and her students at Nara Women's Normal College during winter training (kan-geiko).

In 1910, five sports were cited by the MOE as being suitable extracurricular subjects for girls in normal schools. *Naginata-jutsu* was included, along with ice-skating, swimming, tennis, and archery. In the "School Gymnastics Curriculum Teaching Syllabus Outline" for middle schools released by the MOE in 1913, *naginata-jutsu* was included as one of the exercises acceptable for girls as an extracurricular subject in higher and middle schools, along with *jūjutsu* and *kenjutsu* for boys.[22]

Education in the 1930s and 1940s became increasingly nationalistic. Budo was considered an effective means of facilitating militaristic indoctrination, and preparing Japanese youth to fight to the death for their country. Naginata, along with the other martial arts, was used to advance these goals. It became an elective subject for girls undertaking tertiary education at higher schools in 1936 (along with kyudo). Further reforms to the education system in 1942 saw girls in primary schools receive compulsory Naginata training. The Butokukai had already created a teacher's training course in the Budo Vocational College in 1934 in which Mitamura Kunihiko, Mitamura Chiyo, and Nishigaki Kin taught Tendo-ryu techniques. Similarly, a rival training college called the Shutokukan was formed in 1936 by Sonobe Hideo of the Jikishin Kage-ryu. These two schools were responsible for training the bulk of Naginata teachers until the end of the war, but there was no unified national style like that which had been developed for kendo.

Sonobe Hideo teaching a class of girls in 1941.

7. Naginata and Militarism

Busen Naginata students practising Tendo-ryu kata in the Butokuden (1939).

With the decision to include Naginata as an elective subject in 1936, a survey was conducted by the MOE to ascertain the number of schools in the nation which already offered Naginata classes. Evidently, there had been a steady increase during the 1930s; in 1933 there were no more than 21 schools offering Naginata, but by 1937 the number had grown to 149. As we can see in the table on the following page, Jikishin Kage-ryu had the largest number of instructors in schools, followed by Tendo-ryu. Documents suggest a certain amount of rivalry between the two traditions, which some say still survives to an extent today. More importantly, there was clearly an acute shortage of instructors overall.

The only two Hanshi (awarded by the Butokukai) at the time of the survey were Sonobe Hideo (Jikishin Kage-ryu), and Mitamura Chiyo (Tendo-ryu). Considering Naginata was now an elective subject in schools, the number of qualified instructors was very scant indeed. It would have been impossible to elevate Naginata to the status of compulsory subject. There was an urgent need to nurture instructors if Naginata was to be the government's budo-of-choice for girls to meet the exigencies of war.

Survey of the State of Naginata in Middle Schools[24]

Survey Topic	Results
Schools that offer Naginata as an elective subject	127
Number of students studying Naginata as an elective subject	32,660
Schools that offer Naginata as an extra-curricular activity	149
Number of students studying Naginata as an extra-curricular activity	22,364
Instructor qualifications and numbers	Menkyo (traditional licence): 7 Hanshi: 2 Kyoshi: 10 Renshi: 13 6th *dan*: 1 5th *dan*: 2 4th *dan*: 1 3rd *dan*: 3 2nd *dan*: 1 1st *dan*: 3 1st *kyu*: 2 Other: 117
Instructor *ryuha* affiliation and numbers	Jikishin Kage-ryu: 141 Tendo-ryu: 80 Kyoshin-ryu: 17 Butokukai-ryu: 6 Jozan-ryu: 2 Other: 20
Positions held within the school by the Naginata instructor in other subjects	Kyoron (Full-time teacher): 191 Jo-kyoron (Assistant teacher): 1 Shokutaku (Part-time teacher): 12 Other: 6
Teachers who only instruct Naginata	Kyoron: 11 Shokutaku: 52 Other: 12
Graduation qualifications of Naginata instructors	University: 3 Higher specialist school: 168 Middle school: 33 Elementary school: 8 Other: 35

The Budo Vocational School and the Shutokukan both published detailed textbooks on so-called "school Naginata-do" (*Gakko naginata-do*). For example, to promote Tendo-ryu centric school Naginata, books such as *Dai-Nihon naginata-do kyohan* (1940), and *Joshi budo Tendo-ryu naginata-jutsu kaisetsu* (1940) were published. Representative books from Jikishin Kage-ryu included *Gakko Naginata-do* (1936), *Kokumin gakko naginata seigi* (1941), *Joshi budo naginata no tsukaikata* (1942).[25]

Teaching Naginata basics at a school for girls.
(Sonobe Shigehachi "Gakko Naginata-do" 1936)

The bulk of Naginata training revolved around repetitive *kata* practice. As its popularity increased, so too did the desire to engage in more competitive activities. Kendo had always been competitive, and although it was generally considered "un-ladylike" to engage in matches, some instructors saw the thrill of competition as a good way to keep students interested.

A light wooden *naginata* was developed for matches in which the blade was covered with a protective leather covering to soften the impact. Eventually this was replaced with a bamboo blade attached to the end of a wooden shaft. This prototype resembled the type of *naginata* which are used today, except nowadays the blade is secured with white plastic tape rather than twine and glue.

Influenced greatly by kendo rules, Naginata also introduced match regulations which stipulated what constituted a valid strike and foul play. The techniques and conventions gradually moved away from those of the traditional *ryuha*. In fact, it was through the development of this competitive element that we start to see *naginata* versus *naginata*. This is standard today, but in the prewar period most matches were conducted against kendo practitioners. Predictably, any move away from "traditional" Naginata met with significant opposition.

By 1942, the government had banned participation in most Western sports, and more emphasis was placed on budo. In March, 1942, physical education classes now centred on kendo, kyudo, judo, Naginata (for girls), and marksmanship. Government motivations for budo's role in the war are succinctly summed up in the following passage in a 1943 guideline for budo instructors in normal schools:

1. We must encourage [our students] to master our nation's unique martial arts, and train healthy, vigorous minds and bodies.
2. As well as nourishing a disposition to hone a martial spirit, esteem propriety, and value modesty, we must encourage an aggressive spirit and a confidence in certain victory.
3. We must inculcate a spirit of self-sacrifice and train an actual fighting mentality.[27]

During the war years, several Naginata instructors worked with the Butokukai and MOE to create "Standard Naginata Forms" (*seitei kata*) that transcended *ryuha* affiliation.[26] A totally new set of *kata* utilising *naginata* versus *naginata* was to be formulated—an initiative that was considered to be more conducive to effective teaching and propagation of Naginata *en masse*. As a traditionalist, Mitamura Chiyo was the staunchest opponent to the new *kata* on the basis that it was "irrational". Her open resistance to the government-backed plan caused quite a commotion. Chiyo and her husband Kunihiko retired from their positions at the Butokukai and the Budo Vocation College after years of dedicated service as a result. A replacement, Yoshimura Seki, was hurriedly summoned from Hiroshima.

This squabble came to a head just before the outbreak of the Pacific War, just as expectations for budo education were peaking. A leader in the development of Naginata at this time was Sakakida Yaeko—a former student at the Budo Vocational School under Mitamura Chiyo. She was renowned for her feisty competitiveness, and was considered to be somewhat of a nonconformist. Nevertheless, her skill and dedication to the promotion of Naginata was second-to-none. Her biggest gripe with the state of Naginata was the difficulty in teaching large groups of students at once and that they also had to learn sword usage in the *kata*.

Sakakida Yaeko.

She and others like her were keen to develop a unified method of Naginata that only used the *naginata*. There is a fascinating interview published in *Kendo Nihon* in 1982 which outlines her life and contributions to Naginata. The following excerpt explains a vital step in the development of modern Naginata in her words.[28]

> Although it was an improvement from an educational perspective I was still not satisfied. With kendo, anybody with a *shinai* (bamboo sword) is able to travel wherever they want and enjoy training with others. In Naginata, all we could do was '*ichi, ni, san, ieiii*!' and thrust at air. I couldn't stop wondering if there wasn't a way for *naginata* to fight against *naginata*...
>
> What I learned through teaching Naginata in schools was that "*ichi, ni, san, ieiii*!" was not enough to keep students interested. When you tell students to thrust, if they don't have anything solid to thrust at it's difficult for them to learn the principles behind the techniques if all they do is *kata*. It is even more pointless if *kata* isn't practised in pairs, which was often the case with group teaching. To top that off, I had to teach how to use the sword as well. There were a number of prominent teachers who opposed introducing full contact training [akin to kendo], but the students loved it. They were able to realise the purpose of the *kata* they had been taught.
>
> Another problem was that students would be taught Jikishin Kage-ryu at primary school and then Tendo-ryu at higher school, because Tendo-ryu was taught by the Butokukai at this level. The students would get confused, and it was also frustrating for the instructors. Faced with these problems, I became even more determined to do something about the status quo. I had no intention of negating the value of the old styles (*koryu*), but from my experience teaching, I could see a necessity to create unified Naginata forms that were not directly linked to Jikishin Kage-ryu or Tendo-ryu. Furthermore, I thought that these new forms should be conducted with two *naginata*. The Butokukai were also thinking along the same lines. They invited instructors from Tendo-ryu and Jikishin Kage-ryu to cooperate and create a new set of "Butokukai Naginata Kata". However, I had different ideas for utilising *naginata* against *naginata*, and independently presented them to the Ministry of Education. In 1942, I received a message from Ishii Michinori, Section Chief of the Physical Education Department in the MOE. He informed me that he was coming to Kyoto and wanted to meet…
>
> After telling him my thoughts, I was subsequently contacted a month later and informed that I would be given the official title of "MOE Physical Education Researcher", and was asked to come up with a new Naginata program for schools… To make a new Naginata curriculum, I visited teachers from many different *ryuha*. I talked at length with each

> of them, and watched them demonstrate their techniques. I initially envisaged taking the strong points from each *ryuha*, and combining them all to make a completely new style. However, the merits of each *ryuha* were not always compatible, which meant that it was an impossible task. In the end, all I could do was learn as much as I could about the various *ryuha* and then come up with something completely from scratch. In fact, I even had to forget all the Tendo-ryu techniques that I had so painstakingly learned over many years.
>
> I finally came up with a rough draft. It was by no means complete, but I was asked to present my findings. I'll never forget it. On the sixth floor of the MOE building, there were officers from the MOE and various other education related organisations. Even representatives from the armed forces were present at the meeting… They were gathered there to listen to what I had to say. It was in 1943, about the time when the War Office was starting to get rather desperate… There was a fellow named Onitsuka from the army, a colonel I think. He spoke. "What's the story with Naginata these days. Wouldn't it be better to teach girls how to fight with a bamboo spear?" I exploded when I heard him say that! I felt the blood surging through my veins, and snapped back at this colonel Onitsuka. "I beg your pardon!" I heard afterwards that I even thumped the desk and had a frightful scowl on my face. "Are you saying that we should make Naginata training and spear training the same?! I will have you know that Naginata is authorised by the MOE for girls' education, and it's not meant to be taught as a way to kill people! If it gets to the stage where Naginata has to go to war, then Japan is already beyond help!"
>
> There was a deathly silence in the room, but nothing could stop me now. Even if it was only for one hour per week, I wanted my style of new Naginata as an official part of the school curriculum. I declared rather pompously "I want to teach students a wonderful style of Naginata that will last well into the future." After making quite a scene that left everybody in stunned silence, Mr. Ogasawara said, "Okay then, and we'll leave it there for today…"

Sakakida did continue her research, and was assisted by influential individuals in politics and the budo world such as the Minister of State and legendary kendo master, Sasamori Junzo. Her efforts resulted in the official unveiling of the "Monbusho Seitei Kata".

> After all the hard work, at last Naginata was introduced into the primary school curriculum for year-five girls, and in budo classes in normal schools. The MOE authorised the new forms, the first to pit *naginata* versus *naginata*. From there, it was matter of teaching them nationwide. As I traipsed all over the country to hold seminars from Kyushu to Tohoku, Japan lost the war. Then there was a long period where we could train no more…

The newly devised form of Naginata was essentially shelved, and would not see the light of day for another ten years.

8. Postwar "New Naginata"

Sakakida Yaeko (right) demonstrating the MOE Seitei Kata.

Between 1945 and 1952, the US occupying forces led by General Douglas A. MacArthur, enacted widespread reforms to purge Japan of any militaristic influences. The occupation came to an end with the signing of the San Francisco Peace Treaty in 1952. The objective of the newly founded "Fundamental Law of Education" in the educational reforms was "the development of people healthy in spirit and body, who are filled with an independent spirit, respect the value of individuals, and who love truth and justice." The "School Education Law" of 1947 was promulgated next, and a new school system was established. The Butokukai was dissolved after the war, and budo was excluded from the education system because it afforded "military or quasi-military training" and "provides for the perpetuation of militarism or a martial spirit in Japan."[29] The practise of budo was also prohibited in the community.

Depending on the budo, the blanket ban lasted for around five years. Judo was reinstated relatively quickly because it was already established internationally before the war. Kendo and Naginata were reintroduced into schools in the 1950s, albeit as a modern sport in a form conducive to promoting "new democratic values". Following the lead of kendo, a research committee of eight people was formed in 1954 to investigate potential forms of Naginata to teach in schools.

The core members of this committee to establish so-called "school Naginata" (*gakko-naginata*) were Konishi Shizuko, Shirai Kanji, Sakakida Yaeko, Sonobe Hidehachi, Tokunaga Chiyoko (all holding the title of Naginata Kyoshi at the time), Tsuyama Katsuko, Jinbo Masako, and Yagida Tsuruko (all regional education supervisors). There were also advisors from local boards of education: Nakakaichi Katsuhisa (Kyoto), Iwano Jiro (Osaka), Hori Kohei (Hyogo), and Inoue Masataka (Osaka). Also, Ministry of Education Physical Education Section Chief Nishida, Nippon Sport Science University President Kurimoto Yoshihiko, and Osaka Physical Education Chief Hamada also attended meetings to discuss the possibilities for school Naginata.

While these meetings were being convened, there was also a movement to launch the All Japan Naginata Federation. Another committee was formed to this end, and was based at Konishi Shin'uemon's Shubukan Dojo in Itami city, Hyogo prefecture. Former marchioness Yamanouchi Teiko became the first chairwoman of the All Japan Naginata Federation inaugurated on May 4, 1955, at the Butokuden in Kyoto. In 1960, Yamanouchi took voluntary retirement, and Vice Chairwoman Konishi Shizuko took her place. The fruits of 19 meetings by the research committee was a new style of Naginata which was very distinct from *ryuha* Naginata. They had created a new sport version of Naginata with an entirely new corpus of techniques and training methodology which was designed to be taught to girls.[30]

In 1959, the proposal was ratified by the MOE, and the introduction of Naginata into junior high schools and above as an extra-curricular club activity was officially sanctioned. Traditional *ryuha* affiliations were transcended with a hybrid sport version of Naginata. It was initially called school Naginata, but was later changed to "new Naginata" (*atarashii naginata*) in a concerted break away from any militaristic era connotations. It was a fresh start, so to speak, but in actuality the wartime innovations of Sakakida Yaeko and her colleagues formed the basis. To quote Sakakida again:

> It was in May of 1953 when they the first postwar Kyoto Taikai for kendo was held. After that tournament, Sonobe Hideo, Mitamura Chiyo, Nishigaki Kin, Sonobe Hidehachi, Tokunaga Chiyoko

Officials from the Mombusho and the AJNF when Naginata was admitted into the education system in 1959.

> and some other Naginata instructors met in the sub-dojo of the Butokuden. We discussed creating a federation and popularising Naginata once again. We also talked about creating new Naginata forms for teaching in schools. When the topic of formulating new *kata* came up, somebody said, "Hey Sakakida, what about those *seitei kata* you made for the MOE? Could we use those as a base to come up with something?" To be honest, I was a bit hesitant to take on the responsibility. I had all manner of insults and slander thrown at me when I tried to disseminate the forms during the war, and really didn't want to go through that again. Then, Sonobe Hideo tapped me on the shoulder. "The cold hard truth is we, the old guard, really died in the war. You've got the experience and the youth, so shut up and do it." I decided to do as she said. So, using the Monbusho Seitai Kata to start things off, I solicited opinions from numerous teachers, and eventually created what is now known as *atarashii naginata*… It was quite revolutionary. The forms were not referred to as *kata*, but called Shikake-Oji (attack-counterattack), and consisted of eight predetermined patterns which featured an array of techniques. Even the equipment was changed, and the *naginata* blade was modified by joining two slats of bamboo. This meant that Naginata practitioners could go anywhere in the country and compete or train with others, just like kendo. This was "new Naginata"…

Her book, "New Naginata: Instructional Handbook" (*Atarashii naginata: shido no tebiki*), co-authored with Tsuyama Katsuko, became the standard textbook for many years.[31] The MOE advised the new AJNF that they should promote Naginata using the phonetic *hiragana* characters rather than Chinese characters (*kanji*). The glyph used to write naginata was not included in the "list of kanji for general use" (Toyo kanji) circulated by the MOE in reforms carried out in 1946 to simplify the written language.

Sakakida Yaeko's book.

This was not the only reason. According to my former Naginata teacher, the late Tokunaga Chiyoko, who was directly involved in negotiating with the MOE for the reinstatement of Naginata in the 1950s, the ministry was ever wary of perceived militaristic connotations associated with the *kanji*, especially as it included the character for "*katana*". The MOE also directed the federation not to use the suffix "*-do*" (Way) to circumvent any correlation with wartime moral education and soften its image. Thus, the characters "な(*na*)- ぎ (*gi*)-な (*na*)-た (*ta*)" are used to this day, although *kanji* are still used for the traditional styles such as Tendo-ryu and Jikishin Kage-ryu, and so on.

In April 1966, the MOE revised its policies pertaining to the teaching of budo in schools, and issued a directive stating that kyudo, wrestling, and Naginata were allowed to be taught in high school clubs. The following year in 1967, Naginata instruction was permitted in physical education classes subject to there being a qualified teacher. The AJNF changed its legal status to a foundation in 1968. Consequently, Naginata started to flourish in schools, and in the community (although never to the extent of kendo or judo), which prompted the AJNF to develop a set of *kata* and also official guidelines for the concept and instruction of Naginata. (See Chapter 2).

Nowadays, most Naginata practitioners train primarily in 'new' Naginata, although there are a number who train in both the new form and a traditional style as well. Naginata is reportedly practised by over 65,000 people in Japan. The vast majority of participants are women, although there has been a marked increase in the number of men in recent years. The annual All Japan Mens' Naginata Championships commenced from 2002 as testament to the number of men becoming involved. The World Naginata Championships are held every four years, and the International Naginata Federation now has over 14 fully affiliated countries. More countries are in the process of becoming affiliated as Naginata continues to grow, slowly but surely.

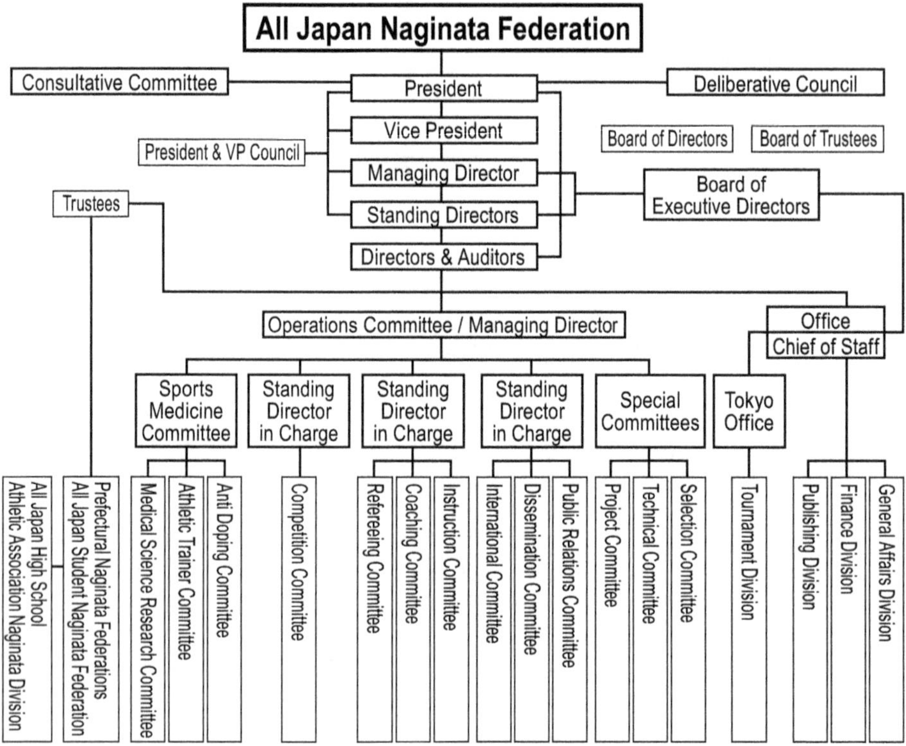

(2010 numbers)

Chapter 1: The History of Naginata

Year	Event
1946	Budo participation prohibited
1952	Budo reinstated
1955	Inauguration of the All Japan Naginata Federation
1956	1st All Japan Naginata Championship (held by the All Japan Kendo Federation for the first three times)
1962	1st All Japan Student Naginata Championship
1967	Permission granted to teach Naginata in PE classes at high school level
1968	The AJNF recognised as a nonprofit foundation
1971	1st National Engi Tournament
1973	*Dan* rades above 5-dan abolished US Naginata Federation becomes affiliated with the AJNF
1975	Creation of the AJNF Kata (5 forms)
1977	Two more forms added to AJNF Kata (7 in total). Name changed to All Japan Kata (Zen Nihon no Kata)
1978	AJNF became affiliated with the Japan Amateur Sports Association
1981	Promulgation of "The Concept of Naginata" & "The Principles of Instruction"
1982	First appearance at the National Sports Meet held in Shimane
1983	Accepted as an official event at the National Sports Meet in Gunma
1988	Formation of the All Japan Student Naginata Federation
1990	Inauguration of the International Naginata Federation (INF)
1992	Affiliation to the All Japan High School Athletic Federation
1993	1st All Japan Junior High Naginata Championship Tournament
1995	1st World Naginata Championship (Tokyo)
1996	All Japan Naginata Championship becomes an Emperor's Cup event
1999	2nd World Naginata Championship (Paris)
2001	1st All Japan Men's Naginata Championships
2003	3rd World Naginata Championship (San Jose)
2007	4th World Naginata Championship (Brussels)
2011	5th World Naginata Championship (Himeji)
2015	6th World Naginata Championship (Montreal)

Part 2: Two Pioneers[32]

There are many individuals who influenced the development of *naginata-jutsu* into the modern budo art practised widely today, both in the prewar and postwar periods. In the following section I will introduce two well-known masters, Mitamura Chiyo and Sonobe Hideo, as they represent the two core traditional lines of Naginata from which the AJNF is made up today—Tendo-ryu and Jikishin Kage-ryu. Of course, there are other important classical *ryuha* affiliations in the AJNF such as Toda-ha Buko-ryu; numerically speaking, however, these two *ryuha* are by far the most predominant.

1. Mitamura Chiyo (1885–1966)

Fifteenth Headmaster of Tendo-ryu Naginata-jutsu

Mitamura Akinori.

Mitamura Akinori (1850–1931) was born December 4, 1847. From the age of 10, he studied Tendo-ryu Heiho under Shimogawara Soke, the twelfth headmaster and chief *bujutsu* instructor for the Kameoka domain. The curriculum included *kenjutsu*, *naginata-jutsu*, and the *kusarigama*. He also studied *kyujutsu*, *bajutsu*, *sojutsu*, and *hojutsu* (gunnery), and was a highly regarded student of all of them.

When the country's feudal domains and class distinctions were dismantled following the Meiji Restoration, some former samurai were able to eke out a living by turning to farming, some became school teachers, and others ventured to start up companies and try their hand at commerce. With little enthusiasm for the now "outdated" martial arts, *bujutsu* instructors had a particularly hard time with few tangible skills to thrive in an era of modernisation.

In May, 1885, a group of 94 volunteers in Kameoka, Kyoto prefecture, formed an association they called Seitokusha to counter the effects of unbridled Westernisation, which they saw as bringing about the demise of traditional Japanese culture and ideals. They promoted all manner of traditional arts and activities including special imperial study groups, Japanese literature

Some Seitokusha members.

appreciation meetings, martial arts training, tea ceremony, flower arranging, and even silk production. The Seitokusha taught members the martial arts of *kyujutsu* (archery), *bajutsu* (horse riding), *kenjutsu*, *naginata-jutsu*, *kusarigama* (sickle and chain), *sojutsu* (pike), *jujutsu*. Akinori was tasked with the responsibility of instructing *naginata-jutsu* and the *kusarigama*.

In 1889, the Seitokusha constructed a dojo called the Enshukan. The opening was quite a lively affair, with a host of matches conducted by leading swordsmen of the day. Until then, all *bujutsu* lessons were conducted in the respective instructors' houses. Akinori's classes were no exception. He laid straw mats down on the earthen floor, and trained himself and his students with much enthusiasm. In fact, many of the locals joked that "he trained so much he didn't have time to sit down and eat".

The new dojo was a gamble, and was only allowed to open its doors after 6:00pm so as not to hinder peoples' work ethic with pointless divertissements. Akinori busied himself during the day with various chores and odd jobs to keep his family fed. He studied the "art of photography" and even opened a studio, but soon found that most Japanese at the time were suspicious of photographs; they believed it drained them of their souls. Before long, he was forced to close his business.

All the while, he continued to teach at the Enshukan. In 1890, he was invited by Prince Yamashina-no-Miya to give a demonstration of Tendo-ryu at the

Mitamura Chiyo.

Kanshuji temple in Kyoto. The following year, he was made the new headmaster of the tradition. It was about this time that a young girl of seven joined the dojo. Her name was Naito Chiyo. Chiyo, a relative of Akinori, was born on April 18, 1885, into a former samurai family. As a child she enjoyed watching *bujutsu* training, and would spend hours at the Enshukan observing the lessons. As soon as she started formal lessons, it was apparent that she was gifted, and Akinori held high hopes for her.

In due course, the number of Tendo-ryu students increased, and Akinori was often called upon to give demonstrations. On one occasion in 1894, Chiyo accompanied him to a demonstration in front of members of the imperial family. The performance met with high acclaim. It was probably about this time that Akinori decided to train Chiyo as heir to the tradition. In 1895, he officially adopted her into his line of the family.

That same year, the Dai-Nippon Butokukai was launched in Kyoto. On December 25, 1895, a martial art festival—the 1st Butokusai, precursor to the annual Kyoto Taikai—was conducted at the newly constructed Heian Shrine. This was followed by another large commemorative demonstration event for the martial arts held over three days at the Expo Hall in Kyoto. Chiyo demonstrated there with Akinori, and they were asked back each year after that.

In October, 1898, the Meiji Emperor requested to see *bujutsu* matches. On October 24, a venue was prepared at the Sanjusangendo temple in Kyoto, and a series of contests was conducted for his benefit. According to records, in attendance at this particular gathering were 14 *kyujutsu*, 10 *jujutsu*, 28 *kenjutsu* and 3 *naginata-jutsu* practitioners (Akinori, Chiyo, and Nagasawa Kiyo). The first time Chiyo ever participated in a match against a swordsman was in May, 1902, at the 7th Butokusai. She was 18 years old at the time, and ended up losing the match to a swordsman from Toyama. Nevertheless, onlookers were so impressed by her showing, Butokukai officials decided to award her a certificate and a commemorative *tanto* (dagger).

In 1903, the Enshukan became the official Kameoka branch of the Butokukai. The following year, the Butokukai created a Naginata division, and Mitamura Akinori was appointed as the teacher in charge. He relocated his family to Kyoto city to be closer to the Butokukai headquarters. Five students including Chiyo were inducted into the Butokukai's new teacher's training school as full-time students. From 1906, Chiyo began assisting Akinori with his teaching at the school. She gained quite a reputation for her refined technique. Mitamura Akinori died at age 83 on January 1, 1931. He had spent his life promoting Tendo-ryu. Chiyo succeeded him as the head of the tradition becoming the fifteenth Soke.

Another Naginata practitioner becoming quite famous was her contemporary, Sonobe Hideo. Sonobe had honed her skills in the famous *gekken kogyo* martial arts shows that were held around the country at various venues to entertain the public. In many ways, Chiyo and Hideo were very different in their approaches to Naginata. Hideo had a fiery temperament and learned her skills in a competitive environment; whereas, Chiyo's formal training was *kata* based, and her movement was more subdued and deliberate. After training, people would comment on how clean the soles of her feet were. She would reply, "My feet are always elevated about one sheet of paper off the floor..."

When the Butokukai created a Naginata program in the Budo Vocational College (Busen) on June 8, 1934, Chiyo was appointed professor in charge of the course. She selected some techniques from the extensive Tendo-ryu curriculum and created a syllabus for training new instructors to go forth and propagate the art. She was married to Kunihiko, also a student of Akinori and a well known *kenjutsu* expert.

As we have seen, in March, 1941, the Butokukai decided to develop a unified set of Naginata Kata for teaching basics in schools, but Chiyo objected strongly. Instead of going along with the plan, she quit her position in the Butokukai and formed her own school called the Tendojuku, specialising in teaching Tendo-ryu to trainee teachers. She kept this school going until the end of the war.

Mitamura Kunihiko.

Mitamura Chiyo teaching Busen students in the Butokuden.

After the war the Butokukai was dissolved, and martial arts were prohibited for several years. It was not until 1955 that Naginata was revived with the launching of the All Japan Naginata Federation. The federation set about creating a number of new techniques and practice routines to revive the art in schools and the community. Mitamura Chiyo served as the federation's executive advisor until her death in 1966, aged 81. Her influence in the development of modern Naginata is immeasurable, and many of Japan's top Naginata masters are direct students of her, and her husband Kunihiko. Her daughter, Mitamura Takeko, became the sixteenth Soke of the Tendo-ryu tradition, but she passed away in 2010. Kimura Yasuko is the seventeenth, and current, Soke of Tendo-ryu.

Mitamura Chiyo.

Chiyo (right) demonstrating with Nishigaki Kin.

Busen Naginata students and teachers.

Kimura Yasuko's accession to the Sokeship of Tendo-ryu in 2013.

2. Sonobe Hideo (1870–1963)
Fifteenth Soke of Jikishin Kage-ryu Naginata-do

On March 18, 1870, a baby girl was born into the family of Kusaka Yosaburo. Yosaburo "the horse-minder" was the third son of Matsumae Tetsunosuke, a retainer of Date Sodo of the Sendai domain. Yosaburo was adopted into the Kusaka family through marriage to Kiji. They already had two boys and five girls, so this latest addition was named Tarita ("Enough") by her grandmother. Another daughter was named Aya (Mistake)!

The year after Tarita was born, feudal domains were disbanded and replaced with the prefectural system. The Kusakas moved to a small village called Kaminome in Miyagi prefecture, and turned their hand to agriculture to make a living. Despite his loss of status due to the great social and political reforms of the time, Yosaburo found it difficult to treat horses as farming animals. To him, horses were as noble as the samurai they were trained to carry into battle. Although now 'relegated' to farming the land, the horses he kept in his stable were for riding, not pulling ploughs.

Like her father, the young Tarita had a passion for horses, and was often seen galloping bareback through the village. When she turned 16, she had a fortuitous meeting with Satake Kanryusai. Kanryusai, a samurai from Echizen, was a student of Sakakibara Kenkichi's in the Jikishin Kage-ryu. Sakakibara Kenkichi is now known for his efforts to popularise traditional martial arts in an era of decline. He did this by organising martial art extravaganzas in which swordsmen competed in matches in front of paying spectators (*gekken kogyo*). Kanryusai was one of the original participants, and later formed his own company. He and his wife, Shigeo, a skilled exponent in *kenjutsu* and *naginata-jutsu,* brought their show to the town of Furukawa. The sound of a conch and the beating of drums signalled the arrival of the troupe, and excited locals and would-be challengers rushed to the venue.

Tarita had heard about the shows and was determined to go and see. She walked over the mountain path to Furukawa and witnessed a sight that stirred her like nothing else had before. She asked her father if she could join the company and learn the martial arts. Of course, he said no. Not one to give up so easily, she crept out of the house in the middle of the night and made the journey back to Furukawa where Kanryusai was staying. Her older sister, Oyoki, followed her and tried convince her to come home. Kanryusai agreed to accept her as a student as long as she had a letter of permission from her father. It was Oyoki who finally managed to persuade Yosaburo on Tarita's behalf. "Women should be allowed to make a name for themselves in the martial arts, too. At least it's a living." When Yosaburo finally conceded, grandmother Oyoshi took her *naginata* from its resting place on the wall, and gave it to her as a farewell present. Kusaka Tarita entered the tutelage of Satake Kanryusai on April 7, 1886. She was destined to become known as Sonobe Hideo, the fifteenth Soke of Jikishin Kage-ryu *naginata-jutsu*.

Kanryusai was a stern man. He told Tarita "Training is going to be hard girl. Shigeo and I are going to take you to hell and back, but you will become a fine martial artist. Don't falter!" Her training commenced that day, but the *gekken* show had to keep moving to survive. There were about 40 members in Kanryusai's troupe who travelled from one locality to the next to entertain the masses, and make a living out of the thing they knew best. There were a number of married couples with children, and also single swordsmen trying to make ends meet. Tarita was kept busy with chores for her new family. Whenever she had a break, the Satakes would teach her *kata* and techniques.

Not much is known about Shigeo except she had studied Jikishin Kage-ryu from the age six under the auspices of Kurihara Bo in Edo. Although she was a ferocious fighter, she treated Tarita with great compassion. Tarita responded to her kindness by doing the best she could to improve. She would get up early in the morning and secretly do 500 practice cuts, followed by another 500 before she went to sleep in the evening.

In October 1888, Satake Kanryusai's company set up in Kajikazawa after performing in Kofu (Yamanashi prefecture). Two-and-a-half years had passed since Tarita joined the Satake troupe. She had competed in some of the matches, but only as an extension of her training. Shigeo taught Tarita many things about the spirit of the martial arts. "Tarita, the *naginata* is not just a stick that you swing around with your hands. You have to move it with your '*ki*'. Try and imagine that you are cutting an enemy on the opposite riverbank. You must learn the importance of *ki*." On the other hand, the only advice that Kanryusai ever offered was "Learning *bujutsu* is learning how to die." Apart from that gem of wisdom, he seemed almost indifferent to her training. This was of some concern to Tarita.

Determined to succeed, she decided to go and pray at one of the temples in the region. After the day's matches had finished, she asked Shigeo if she could go to a famous Nichiren temple in the mountains overlooking Kajikazawa.

Sonobe Hideo.

She arrived at the Kuonji temple in the early hours. She entered the temple gates and ascended the steep stone steps. After reaching the top, she walked past the great temple halls and noticed a giant cedar tree. Letting loose with a shrill *kiai* she proceeded to pound the old cedar with her *naginata*. Before long, she had become so frenzied in her attacking that she had no sense of where she was, or what she was doing. She continued on and on, screaming and cutting, oblivious to the time that was passing. When she had finally exhausted all of her reserves of energy and gave that old cedar a sound whipping, she fixed her stance and stood calmly to finish in perfect tranquillity.

Sonobe Shigehachi- Hideo's successor as Soke of Jikishin Kage-ryu.

Suddenly, a voice thundered down from the belfry. "Well done girl!" It was Satake Kanryusai. He had followed her up to the temple, and remained hidden as he watched her furious self-imposed training session. "I hereby licence you in Jikishin Kage-ryu *naginata-jutsu*. From this day forth, you shall be known as Hideo."

Satake Kanryusai's company continued to travel the country conducting shows for the general public. Kusaka Hideo fought swordsmen from all of the provinces they ventured into, and maintained an exemplary record without loss. Kanryusai and Shigeo officially

Sonobe Hideo on the right.

Hideo demonstrating with Shigehachi.

designated Hideo as the fifteenth Soke of the tradition on May 29, 1896.

The last time that Kusaka Hideo participated in a *gekken* contest was in January, 1897. Not long afterwards, she married Sonobe Masanori, a dojo owner from Kobe and a student of Chokuyushin-ryu. Together they managed the dojo and continued to teach the martial arts. Hideo also made many appearances in tournaments and demonstrations sponsored by the Dai-Nippon Butokukai. She had numerous memorable matches against well-known swordsmen, and nearly always prevailed.

Probably the most famous of her matches was against Watanabe Noboru in May, 1899. Watanabe, of Shinto Munen-ryu, was a high ranking official in the Meiji government and a celebrated swordsman. Hideo was far from perturbed by his fame, and set about systematically dismantling Watanabe. The hiding he received at the end of Hideo's *naginata* was so resounding, that he was forced to concede before the match reached its inevitable conclusion.

In May 1918, she moved to Tokyo to take up teaching positions at some girls' schools culminating in the formation of Shutokukan Naginata Teacher Training College (Shutokukan Naginata Kyoin Yoseijo) where she concentrated her efforts on nurturing instructors. Apart from one defeat at the hands of Hotta Shajiro, a student of Watanabe Noboru, she won every other match in her long career. She died September 29, 1963, aged 93.

Endnotes

[1] Chronicle of the reigns of the imperial court; also called *Shikanki* and *Geki-nikki* compiled 934-1153. The first reference to the *naginata* was made in the 1146th entry.
[2] Futaki Ken'ichi (ed.), *Budo*. See the section on "Naginata" by Inoue Aya, pp. 202-03.
[3] Ellis Amdur, "The Development and History of the Naginata", *Journal of Asian Martial Arts*, Volume. 4. No. 1, 1995. pp. 33-49
[4] Roald M. Knutsen, *Japanese Polearms*, p. 32
[5] I referred to Helen Craig McCullough's translation, *The Tale of the Heike.*
[6] I confirmed that the original term used was *naginata* by referring to the text reproduced in *Heike monogatari,* annotated by Kajihara Masaaki and Yamashita Hiroaki, pp. 239-241.
[7] McCullough, p. 153.
[8] See, for example, I. Bottomly and A.P. Hopson, *Arms and Armour of the Bushi: The History of Weaponry in Ancient Japan* p. 49; Gregory Irvine, *The Japanese Sword: the Soul of the Bushi*, pp. 36-38; Clive Sinclaire, *Bushi: The Weapons & Spirit of the Japanese Warrior*, p. 45.

[9] See Thomas Conlan's *State of War: The Violent Order of Fourteenth Century Japan* and Suzuki Masaya's *Katana to kubi-tori: Sengoku kassen isetsu*, pp. 78-80 for interesting analysis of medieval warfare based on records of battle casualties.
[10] See Karl Friday's "Off the Warpath: Military Science & Budo in the Evolution of *Ryuha Bugei*" in Bennett (ed.), *Budo Perspectives*, pp. 249-265.
[11] Ellis Amdur, "Women Warriors of Japan", http://www.koryu.com/library/wwj1.html
[12] Yamaga Soko, "Tetsuwa" in Hirose Yutaka (ed.), *Yamaga Soko zenshu shiso-hen* Volume 11.
[13] For a detailed analysis of the history of the development of *bogu* in English, see Nakamura Tamio's "The History of *Bogu*", (translated by Alex Bennett) in *Kendo World* Volume 1, No. 1, pp. 3-12.
[14] Nakamura Tamio, "*Kindai naginata shoshi*" in *Kindai Naginata meicho senshu* Volume 8. p. 7.
[15] Ibid.
[16] The *Haitorei* of March, 1876.
[17] This was the last major armed uprising against the new Meiji government and its reforms, and was carried out by former samurai of the Satsuma domain (now Kagoshima prefecture) under the leadership of Saigo Takamori. The rebellion lasted from January 29 to September 24, 1877.
[18] No major study of the *gekken kogyo* has been made in English. For further information regarding this important episode in budo history, refer to Ishigaki Yasuzo's *Gekkenkai shimatsu*.
[19] Nakamura Tamio, *Kendo jiten*, p. 176.
[20] Nakamura, "*Kindai naginata shoshi*", p. 12.
[21] In 1919, Nishikubo Hiromichi, the newly appointed principal of the Butokukai's Budo Vocational College (Busen) changed the prefix *-jutsu* to *-do* thus making *bujutsu* into *budo*. Henceforth, *kenjutsu* became *kendo*, *kyujutsu* became *kyudo* and so on, to stress the character building attributes of the martial arts as opposed to the combative or competitive aspects.
[22] *Zenkoku shihan gakko-cho kaigi-yoko*, Monbusho Futsu Gakumukyoku, 1911.
[23] Inoue Aya, Op. Cit.
[24] Taken from the report "*Zenkoku chuto-gakko ni okeru kyudo naginata ni kansuru chosa*", Monbudaijin Kanbo Taiiku-ka, 1937.
[25] Nakamura Tamio, "Kindai naginata shoshi", p. 17.
[26] In March 1942, the Butokukai was transformed into a government controlled national organ encompassing of all the budo arts to meet the exigencies of the war effort. There were five sections for kendo, judo, kyudo, jukendo (bayonet), and marksmanship. Naginata was included under the auspices of kendo.
[27] Translation quoted from G. C. Hurst's *Armed Martial Arts of Japan*, p. 165. (Originally from S. Nakabayashi's *Kendo-shi*, p. 106).
[28] The following excerpts are from an interview with Sakakida Yaeko published in the *Kendo Nihon Monthly*, June and July, 1982.
[29] *Political Reorientation of Japan, September 1945 to September 1948*; Report. Contributors: Supreme Commander for the Allied Powers. Government Section,

Publisher: U.S. Govt. Print. Off., Washington DC, 1949.

[30] See *Budo hokan* 1975. pp. 261-63.

[31] Sakakida Yaeko, Tsuyama Katsuko, *Atarashii Naginata: Shido no tebiki*, 1960.

[32] Some of the following information was verified through conversations with Mitamura Takeko, former Soke of the Tendo-ryu, and Sonobe Masami current Soke of the Jikishin Kage-ryu.

CHAPTER 2
FORM AND THEORY

Benkei and Yoshitsune on the Gojo bridge.

Part 1: Naginata Concepts

1. Why Naginata?

Naginata kata from the Katori Shinto-ryu.

Why study Naginata? What can be gained by training in a martial art that has no obvious self-defence applications? These are valid questions for practitioners of Naginata, and indeed other budo disciplines. The physical and mental benefits gleaned from training in any sport is obvious. The educational potential of budo is widely acclaimed in Japan, but there is an all-too-common misconception that just training is enough for it to be an effective means for "self-cultivation". The practitioner does not become a "good person" by virtue of merely turning up at the dojo. Conscientious and continual effort is needed to comprehend the many, often nebulous principles that provide the philosophical basis for budo.

When trying to work out what these principles actually are, a good place to start is the official "Budo Charter". I was a member of the English translation revision committee convened by the Nippon Budokan in 2004, so took the liberty of including the entire text. It provides a reference point for the Naginata practitioner to reassess what budo ideals are, or at least, what they are meant to be. The all Japan Naginata Federation is a signatory of the "Budo Charter". The "Official Concept of Naginata" promulgated by the AJNF in 1977 is also reproduced after the "Budo Charter".

昭和六十二年四月二十三日制定

武道憲章

平成十六年九月十六日改訂

武道憲章英文

平成十六年九月十六日制定

こども武道憲章

日本武道協議会

The Budō Charter
(Budō Kenshō)

Budō, the Japanese martial ways, have their origins in the age-old martial spirit of Japan. Through centuries of historical and social change, these forms of traditional culture evolved from combat techniques (*jutsu*) into ways of self-development (*dō*).

Seeking the perfect unity of mind and technique, *budō* has been refined and cultivated into ways of physical training and spiritual development. The study of *budō* encourages courteous behaviour, advances technical proficiency, strengthens the body, and perfects the mind. Modern Japanese have inherited traditional values through *budō* which continue to play a significant role in the formation of the Japanese personality, serving as sources of boundless energy and rejuvenation. As such, *budō* has attracted strong interest internationally, and is studied around the world.

However, a recent trend towards infatuation just with technical ability compounded by an excessive concern with winning is a severe threat to the essence of *budō*. To prevent any possible misrepresentation, practitioners of *budō* must continually engage in self-examination and endeavour to perfect and preserve this traditional culture.

It is with this hope that we, the member organisations of the Japanese Budō Association, established *The Budō Charter* in order to uphold the fundamental principles of *budō*.

ARTICLE 1: OBJECTIVE OF BUDŌ
Through physical and mental training in the Japanese martial ways, *budō* exponents seek to build their character, enhance their sense of judgement, and become disciplined individuals capable of making contributions to society at large.

ARTICLE 2: KEIKO (Training)
When training in *budō*, practitioners must always act with respect and courtesy, adhere to the prescribed fundamentals of the art, and resist the temptation to pursue mere technical skill rather than strive towards the perfect unity of mind, body, and technique.

ARTICLE 3: SHIAI (Competition)
Whether competing in a match or doing set forms (*Kata*), exponents must externalise the spirit underlying *budō*. They must do their best at all times, winning with modesty, accepting defeat gracefully, and constantly exhibiting self-control.

ARTICLE 4: DŌJŌ (Training Hall)
The *dōjō* is a special place for training the mind and body. In the *dōjō*, *budō* practitioners must maintain discipline, and show proper courtesies and respect. The *dōjō* should be a quiet, clean, safe, and solemn environment.

ARTICLE 5: TEACHING
Teachers of *budō* should always encourage others to also strive to better themselves and diligently train their minds and bodies, while continuing to further their understanding of the technical principles of *budō*. Teachers should not allow focus to be put on winning or losing in competition, or on technical ability alone. Above all, teachers have a responsibility to set an example as role models.

ARTICLE 6: PROMOTING BUDŌ
Persons promoting *budō* must maintain an open-minded and international perspective as they uphold traditional values. They should make efforts to contribute to research and teaching, and do their utmost to advance *budō* in every way.

Member Organisations of the Japanese Budo Association: All Japan Judo Federation; All Japan Kendo Federation; All Nippon Kyudo Federation; Japan Sumo Federation; Japan Karatedo Federation; Aikikai Foundation; Shorinji Kempo Federation; All Japan Naginata Federation; All Japan Jukendo Federation; Nippon Budokan Foundation

Established on 23 April, 1987 by the Japanese Budō Association (Nippon Budō Kyōgikai). English translation revised 16 September, 2004.

The Concept of Naginata

The concept of Naginata is to foster people harmonious in body and mind through training in its techniques.

The Principles of Instruction

Through correct Naginata instruction, practitioners are encouraged to hone their technical skills, polish their minds, cultivate vitality, and develop physical strength. Practitioners will also be taught to preserve aspects of traditional Japanese culture embodied within the art of Naginata, maintain discipline, show courtesy and respect to others, act honourably, and strive to become a useful member of society promoting peace and prosperity among all peoples.

Naginata is frequently touted as a "way" (*michi* or *do*) of lifetime development. The radicals that make up the glyph for "*do*" (道) convey the idea of travelling a road while peering in various directions. Thus, "the character for *michi* can be interpreted as representing the path that one travels or pioneers during their lifetime."[1] This is the ideal, but its application depends on each individual practitioner. As I mentioned in Chapter 1, although "*-do*" was attached as a suffix to Naginata before and during the Second World War to emphasise the spiritual and traditional aspects, it was removed by a Ministry of Education directive when Naginata was resurrected in the postwar period. Most of the other budo disciplines retain the suffix (kendo, judo, karatedo etc.) but it is supposedly inferred in the case of Naginata.

The potential for physical and mental development through the study of Naginata is undeniable, but what is it that makes Naginata a vehicle for personal cultivation?

2. The Mechanics and Mentality of Engagement

Naginata has little practical application in this day and age in the true combat sense. After all, who carries *naginata* around now? Nevertheless, Naginata is a vestige of samurai culture, and is premised on an exchange of techniques that simulate the cutting or thrusting of vital points in an opponent to decide victory or defeat. Despite the absence of danger of death or injury, the actual process and mechanics for engagement remain theoretically similar. It is this process that is the quintessence of Naginata, and indeed the other budo disciplines. In simple terms, the process is as follows:

> 1. Two protagonists face off in the on-guard position (*kamae*) → 2. Mutual probing of defences and application of physical and psychological pressure (*seme-ai*) → 3. Detection of openings and weaknesses, and selection of suitable techniques → 4. Execution of a valid strike (*yuko-datotsu*) with conviction and a coalescence of spirit, *naginata*, and body → 5. Maintaining physical and psychological composure and alertness after the attack (*zanshin*).

Emphasis is placed on valid strikes born of "a unity of spirit, weapon and body (*ki-ken-tai-itchi*)". From a technical standpoint, a valid cut requires that the practitioner wields the blade with the correct cutting trajectory; which in turn is directly related to the manner in which the *naginata* is gripped (*tenouchi*) in the fighting position (*kamae*).

In addition, vital elements to a successful strike include good posture, smooth technique initiation, and accurate striking angle path (*hasuji*)—all deriving from correct *kamae*. The ability to strike with abandon (*sutemi*) is also requisite. This comes form the unity of mind, spirit and technique (*shin-ki-ryoku-itchi*), and enables an immediate strike in response to any opening that is revealed during the probing stage. Moreover, *zanshin*, or psychological composure following the strike, is concomitant with *sutemi*.[2]

Seme (the act of probing or forcing openings) can be explained with the teaching "*san-sappo*" (killing the spirit, sword, and *waza* of the opponent). In essence, *seme* is the process of searching for a way to break the deadlock of *kamae*, putting oneself in an advantageous position to capitalise on opportunities to execute valid attacks.

To defeat one's opponent, one must first have to prevail in the *seme* stage before striking. This means that one must be creative and proactive in seeking or forcing openings rather than deploying random attacks and relying on chance. *Seme* is not just passively watching for an opponent's shortcomings, but needs to be a vigorous, progressive process of actually creating chances by pressuring the opponent. Needless to say, one's opponent is trying to do the same thing.

An opening may be visible when the opponent becomes physically unbalanced, or it may be formless, such as sensed psychological weakness. As Oya Minoru observes,

> External form and internal psyche are opposite sides of the same coin: external form will influence the psyche and, conversely, one's psychological state will be manifest in outward appearance. If the opponent's *kamae* is steadfast and strong with no openings, then executing an attack will be futile. First, the opponent's *kamae* must be broken or unsettled thereby creating an opening for attack. The opponent 'must be beaten before being struck.'[4]

The main factors for breaking the deadlock and setting yourself up to execute a valid strike—the main objective of *seme*—are: 1. Taking the initiative with a strong spirit (*ki*); 2. Dominating the centre; 3. Controlling distance (*maai*). Taking the initiative is to control the opponent in the phase prior to striking and "achieving *ki* superiority". *Ki* is a difficult term to define, but is considered a central component in Naginata and other *budo* arts. The All Japan Kendo Federation defines *ki* as:

> The basic energy which exists in all matter that is born, develops, and dies. In human beings, it is the source of the kinetic energy responsible for perception, sensation, and instinct. In kendo (also applicable to Naginata), it refers to the environment surrounding one's self and one's opponent, and it is the basic energy making the functioning of one's body and mind full and harmonious.[6]

There are many related terms such as "*ki-atari*" (showing an intention to attack in order to observe the reaction); "*ki-gamae*" (total alertness and preparedness to attack at an instant); "*ki-haku*" (the strength of spirit to face any situation); "*ai-ki*" (having one's *ki* in sync with the opponent), and so on. The rather complex notion of "*shin-ki-ryoku-itchi*" was described by the famous prewar kendo master, Takano Sasaburo, in his classic book *Kendo*:

> *Shin-ki-ryoku-itchi* is the mental action induced from the senses of looking and listening, and the resulting immediate manifestation and application of a technique...When these three elements are in perfect synchronisation, then the opponent's weaknesses or openings can be taken advantage of, and victory obtained...Victory or defeat is not decided through random manoeuvring, but by promptly taking control of the opportunity as it manifests.[7]

The mind initiates and is calm like water. Sparked by the mind's initiation, *ki* is the energy that puts one's will in motion like wind. Will, fuelled by *ki*, leads to the execution of *waza* which are like waves. In other words *shin-ki-ryoku-itchi* is "wind blowing over a body of water creating waves"; or, 1. Initiation→2. Mobilisation (of the will)→3. Execution. When this sequence is completed instantaneously and in unison, it leads to a valid strike.[8]

3. Striking Opportunities & Waza

Techniques are executed in accordance with the opponent's movements and reactions that arise through *seme*. Not only is manipulation of the *naginata* in the attack important, so too is the psychological workings of the process. Timing and intent can be defined by the concept of "*sen*", of which there are three kinds: 1. "*Sensen-no-sen*" refers to having the keen insight to quickly sense the opponent's start, and then taking the initiative and striking first. This is the most important *sen*, as it completely stymies the opponent's moves. 2. "*Sen*" refers to the situation in which the opponent perceives an opening and initiates attack, but you nip it in the bud and strike before their attack is successful. 3 "*Go-no-sen*" refers to the timing in which the opponent has made a full attack but you are able to destroy their initiative by parrying and counter-attacking when their *waza* is coming to completion.

When you take the initiative and probe the opponent, they will be prompted into attacking first. Respond with *oji-waza* (counter-techniques). Although *oji-waza* are referred to as counter-attack techniques, they are actually initiated by coaxing the opponent into striking. In order to do this, psychological readiness and control must be maintained throughout the encounter. The following striking opportunities are based on the various stages occurring during a bout:[9]

1. Striking when opponent is immobile
Control your opponent to the point where they cannot strike, retreat, or move at all, and then strike.

↓

2. Striking when opponent shows signs of moving
Sense when your opponent is about to strike, and then strike.

↓

3. Striking when opponent is moving to attack
The opponent's *ki* begins to take physical form in the movement of the *naginata* tip and hands. Strike as the technique starts to form.

The techniques hitherto are considered superior by virtue of being the result of openings created by applying mental pressure being applied on the opponent. These techniques are described as "striking the heart (*kokoro*) with the heart",[10] "striking essence (*iro*) with essence",[11] or "striking scent (*nioi*) with scent".[12] The opponent's intentions to attack are revealed in changes in the eyes, facial expression, and also a change in the *kamae*. These techniques are regarded as superior.

↓

4. Striking at the start of the opponent's technique
The opponent's *ki* manifests in the form of slight movement. Strike at the unbalanced point just as the opponent begins technique execution. The opponent will start to lean forward, or lower slightly from the knees.

↓

5. Striking the middle stage of the opponent's technique
Strike as the opponent's technique is in mid-flight, taking advantage of their unbalanced posture. This is where the opponent's movements start to take the shape of a technique and must be cut down before it manifests fully.[13]

↓

6. Striking when the opponent's technique is nearing completion
Strike at the point that the opponent's psychological, physical and technical impetus is just reaching full extension.

↓

7. After the opponent's attack has been completed
Strike when the opponent has completed the technique and they are stretched out.[14]

These striking opportunities are sometimes simplified as the "three unforgivable chances": The start of a technique; when the technique has been blocked; when the technique has reached its conclusion. The AJNF defines striking opportunities as:

1. Just as the opponent is about to launch into an attack (*debana*).
2. When the opponent is moving back from a tussle at *seriai*.
3. When the opponent has completed an attack, and is temporarily physically and mentally spent.
4. When the opponent freezes and is unable to react.
5. When the opponent is changing *kamae* (*mochikae*).
6. When the opponent is breathing in deeply.
7. When the opponent succumbs to the "four sicknesses" (*shikai* – surprise, fear, doubt, and confusion), or *kogishin* (hesitation or doubt).
8. *Kyojitsu* (hole and full). In other words, bringing oneself into the *jitsu* (full or replete) state showing no weakness, thereby forcing the opponent into the *kyo* state where they will reveal openings (holes) in their *kamae*. Strike when they are in a state of *kyo*, but be careful

when they are showing great concentration and no weakness in the *jitsu* state.

As soon as you see an opening (*suki*) in the opponent's mind, *kamae*, or movement, you must be ready and able to attack instantaneously without needing to mull it over. There is no time for "ready-set-go", just "ready-go". This state of constant readiness is referred to as *kan*. The chance to win the match can vanish in an instant, and *suki* are few and far between in a strong opponent. *Kan* is the ability to read ahead and to preempt the situation.

4. The Characteristics of Naginata

Category				Content
Theory	Naginata Outline			History, characteristics, training methodology, facilities and equipment, regulations
Technical Aspects	*Kihon* (Basics)	*Shizentai* (Posture)		Posture when standing and holding the *naginata*
		Reiho (Etiquette)		*Ritsurei (standing bow); zarei (sitting bow)*
		Kamae (Stances)		*Chudan-no-kamae; gedan; hasso; waki-gamae; jodan*
		Tai-sabaki (Footwork)		*Okuri-ashi; ayumi-ashi; hiraki-ashi; fumikae-ashi; tsugi-ashi*
		Datotsu	*Datotsu-bui*	*Shomen; soku-men; sune; do; kote; tsuki* (throat)
			Striking	*Furiage* (lift up straight); *mochikae* (change grip); *furikaeshi* (overhead twirl)
			Thrusting	*Chokutotsu* (straight thrust); *kuridashi* (extended thrust)
		Uke-kata (Blocking)		*Ha-bu* (with the blade); *e-bu* (with the shaft)
		Furi-kata (Swinging)		*Joge-buri* (vertical); *yoko-buri* (horizontal); *naname-buri* (diagonal-up, down); *furikaeshi*
		Uchikaeshi		Continuous striking moving forwards and backwards; grip; distance
	Waza (Techniques)	*Shikake-waza*	*Harai*	Knock the opponent's *naginata* from the left or right (*omote-ura*) with the *ha-bu or e-bu*
			Fumikomi	Striking with *hiraki-ashi* or *okuri-ashi*
			Debana	Striking just as your opponent is about to
			Nidan	Two continuous strikes
			Sandan	Three continuous strikes
		Oji-waza	*Uke*	Block with the *e-bu* or the *ha-bu*
			Nuki	Avoid opponent's strike then follow up with your own attack
			Ukenagashi	Move out of the way of opponent's attack as you parry and slide their *naginata* off with the *ha-bu*
			Uchiotoshi	Knock opponent's *naginata* down with the *ha-bu* or *e-bu*
			Makiotoshi	Use the curve of the *ha-bu (sori)* to flick the opponent's *naginata* down
		Oyo	Shikake-Oji Kata	Performing set forms *(kata)* or techniques in pairs; *kiai; ma-ai; zanshin*
	Competition (*Kyogi*)			1. Shiai-kyogi- Individuals event; Teams event 2. Engi-kyogi- Designated forms; Free forms

The table defines the technical and theoretical components of Naginata.

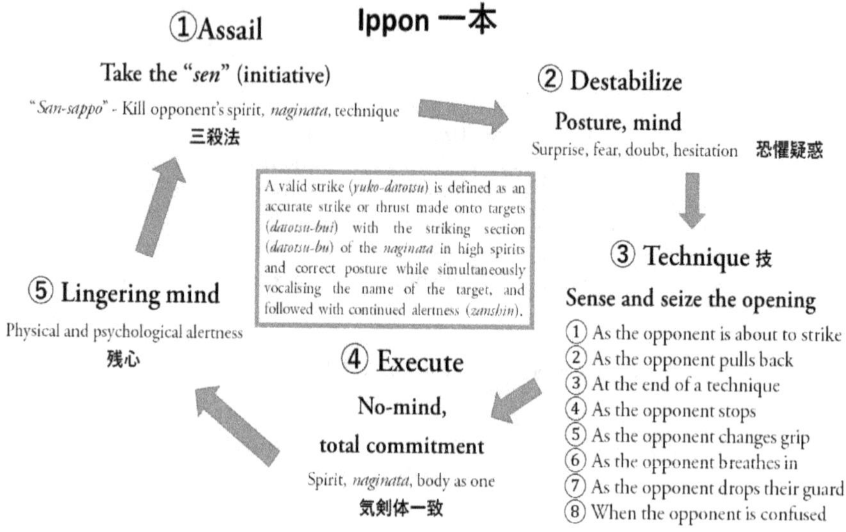

By gaining a keen understanding of this curriculum through training, the practitioner theoretically learns the following:

1. Etiquette and good manners are emphasised in Naginata, and become second nature so that even outside the dojo appropriate courtesies are always shown to others.
2. Naginata techniques are employed using both sides of the body. There are many subtle movements utilised to manipulate the *naginata* such as *mochikae* (changing grip or *kamae*), *kuridashi* (pushing the *naginata* out to extend distance) and *kurikomi* (pulling the *naginata* in), and so on. Learning to wield the *naginata* in a relaxed and nimble fashion develops coordination.
3. The practitioner learns to manoeuvre in all directions: backward and forward, pivoting on the spot. Learning to adjust speed and power instantaneously and rationally while employing various techniques enhances flexibility, balance, power, and reflexes.
4. Practising Naginata fosters physical stamina and intuition.
5. Naginata is a physical pursuit which can be adapted for all ages, and can be practised throughout one's lifetime.

The physical benefits of Naginata are relatively easy to discern. As with diligent participation in any form of physical exercise, one will quickly notice a boost in energy and vitality. In addition, as perfection in form is stressed in Naginata, long-time practitioners will naturally develop a straight posture, graceful movement, coordination, muscular strength and flexibility.

The mental or spiritual benefits are more difficult to gauge. The emphasis placed on etiquette (*rei*) encourages the practitioner to treat others courteously. The cooperation of training partners and opponents is crucial for individual improvement. Gratitude and humility are expressed through rituals of bowing, speech and demeanour. Also, the quest to master the techniques requires patience, resilience, determination, discipline, concentration, powers of analysis and insight. Even if not blessed with such attributes from the outset, the practitioner will develop in these areas as their proficiency in Naginata improves. Moreover, the rigours of training, and constant yelling (*kiai*) and attacking in a controlled environment (dojo) is a particularly effective way of relieving stress!

How does one become mentally stronger through practising Naginata? Of course, this depends entirely on the effort and intentions of the individual. Through facing off against a determined opponent, the practitioner is faced with many difficulties to overcome; the greatest being not so much the strength or skill of the opponent, but more one's own weaknesses. To be more precise, personal development through Naginata is related to overcoming what are referred to as the *shikai* (four sicknesses of the heart or mind—surprise, fear, doubt, and confusion.)

When any of these weaknesses are present, openings will result, and defeat is inevitable. For example, when faced with an opponent who is particularly large, has a strong presence, or is renowned for their skill, this could incite fear. If they attempt something unexpected such as a flashy technique, you may find yourself becoming a little surprised. Your opponent may try to entice you into making an attack against your will by leaving a target open for attack. This may cause doubt as you wonder whether it is safe to make an attack. Similarly you may be momentarily confused as to the best course of action or which technique to employ. This confused mental state resulting in hesitation is referred to as *kogishin.*

These are just some examples of what happens in a bout with an opponent who is trying to defeat you. To take control of the encounter, one must be able to suppress fears and doubts, and make instantaneous judgements attacking with confidence and conviction. Inability to suppress negative emotions will result in hesitation, and annihilation. After all, it only takes a fraction of a second for a strike to be made, or a point to be scored. Even the slightest hesitation can be disastrous.

Overcoming personal weaknesses is no easy task when faced with an opponent. That is why it is often said that in order to defeat one's opponent, first one must defeat the self. In other words, one must develop the strength to control one's emotions. In this sense, one's opponent in a match or training is a valuable collaborator whose cooperation affords opportunities to face one's fears front-on. One cannot, should not, simply give up. There is no recourse to run away. This can be extremely frustrating at first, but consciously tackling your weaknesses in this way is how Naginata can serve as a vehicle for continual development in mind and body.

Personal Cultivation

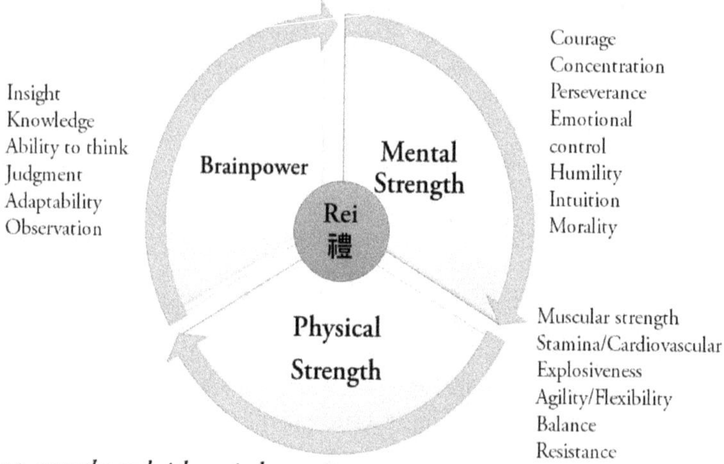

Insight
Knowledge
Ability to think
Judgment
Adaptability
Observation

Brainpower

Mental Strength

Courage
Concentration
Perseverance
Emotional control
Humility
Intuition
Morality

Rei
禮

Physical Strength

Muscular strength
Stamina/Cardiovascular
Explosiveness
Agility/Flexibility
Balance
Resistance

Rei=Respect, empathy and richness in humanity

Thus, one's opponent should always be respected for their assistance. If one successfully strikes the opponent, it is not a time to rejoice, but a time to reflect on what was done correctly, and what could be improved. Likewise, a successful strike made against you is a perfect opportunity to reassess. Hence, opponents should be afforded the utmost respect and gratitude, for without them progress is impossible. As one becomes more proficient, one will become more aware of the fact that failure is more often than not a problem stemming from the "four sicknesses" or some other personal deficiency, rather than something awesome in your opponent. The encounter should be a mutual learning experience.

An important point to note here is that interaction is based on trust and observance of the rules of engagement. Although both practitioners are vying to strike each other, it is considered weak or cowardly to gain victory through trickery or underhanded means. Of course, learning to develop strategy is an important part of one's overall development, but at the same time it is considered virtuous to fight fairly and squarely. You can win sometimes by fooling your opponent, but essentially that is taking the easy route, and only fooling yourself. Having said that, one must be prepared to tackle any kind of opponent. Everybody has their idiosyncrasies, but strive to match them by doing Naginata as correctly and as honestly as possible.

As your understanding deepens, you will develop strength of mind and an integrity which will serve you well, not only in the dojo, but in all aspects of your life. You will become confident, and be able to remain calm in adversity. At least, that is the ideal.

Kigurai **(Presence)**

After years of training, the practitioner will develop a dignified demeanour and graceful deportment. One will naturally learn to discern between right and wrong, good and bad, and overcome concerns for winning and losing. The experienced practitioner will have an indomitable air of confidence, and radiate an aura of vitality. These attributes are cultivated through continued training with the aims of developing not only physical technique, but strength of mind, and a refined sense of morality. Collectively, all of these qualities are referred to as *kigurai*, and a person who embodies *kigurai* has gravitas—not a fearful presence, but a respectful, assured one.

Heijoshin **(Placid state of mind)**

Heijoshin refers to a state of mind in which one is calm, collected, and unperturbed. It is the fundamental, unfettered mind. When confronted with something frightening or out of the ordinary, one must be able to "keep calm and carry on". People will often become confused or lose confidence when challenged with something they are not used to. Remaining unfazed in such circumstances is referred to as having *heijoshin*. Developing the confidence to deal with any kind of adversity without becoming emotional is crucial to survival.

Fudoshin **(Immovable mind)**

Fudoshin is similar in meaning to *heijoshin*. It is a state of mind which is not moved or distracted by anyone, or anything. It is a steadfastness of mind which enables apposite responses to changing conditions. In other words, it is referring to the mental strength which enables *heijoshin*.

Zanshin (Lingering mind)

Zanshin, "lingering mind", refers to the physical and mental posture in which one remains alert and ready to respond after having making a strike. This is accomplished by moving to a safe distance after the strike (usually in *chudan*) and being ready for a possible counterattack. Even if the attack was decisive and the referees have put their flags up, one's must always be vigilant. In the days of mortal combat, this mindset had obvious advantages, but even in the modern sport version of Naginata it is regarded as an essential part of what constitutes a valid attack. Dropping your guard immediately after making a successful strike may result in the point being nullified by the referees. Maintaining mental and physical alertness at all times enhances your power of concentration and overall perception.

"Shingitai" = *Coalescence of min, technique and body*

This diagram shows the connection *mushin* and *zanshin*. *Mushin* is the Zen concept of "no-mind". In this context, the protagonist faces her opponent with a clear mind, devoid of superfluous thoughts or desires, and then attacks with total physical and psychological commitment (*sutemi*). *Zanshin* is not a performance, but is the by-product of the first two components in the attack. Although there are various level of *zanshin*, it is one of the important lessons one can learn in Naginata and apply to everything you do in daily life. Simply put at its most basic level, *zanshin* is to never be complacent. Even crossing the road requires *zanshin*. You take you life in your hands without it.

A valid men strike is scored in a Naginata shiai-kyogi match.

Students of the IBU Naginata club.

Part 2: Competition and Forms

1. Shiai

Shiai or participation in matches is an effective way to gauge the results of your efforts in training, and uncover new things that require attention. One should be well-prepared for *shiai*, realising that it is an important opportunity to test your true ability. Of course, nobody enters a competition with the intention of losing. We all want to win, and not having that attitude would be disrespectful to opponents. How one wins, however, and with what kind of demeanour is very important.

Again, the term "correct" is of the essence here. One of the characteristics of Naginata is the competitor is expected to fight cleanly, and as closely to the rules as possible. This is the ideal in any sport, but there is always leeway given and athletes are rarely criticised if they take play to the edge, as long as they do not cross the line and break the rules. In Naginata, however, employing questionable tactics for the sake of winning is seen as an indication of one's character. One should compete ferociously and with all the skill one can muster, but without resorting to trickery, and always maintaining respect for the opponent and referees.

It is the individual's prerogative to do Naginata purely as a competitive sport with no other objectives than winning tournaments. However, in what is considered to be ideal Naginata, *shiai* is not the sole objective *per se*, but an important part of the process for self-perfection. *Shiai* should be contested tp the best of one's ability, but won with modesty, and lost with grace. There is much to be learned from victory and defeat as long as one keeps an open mind. Attitudes demonstrated before, during and after a *shiai* are a good indication of the practitioners understanding of the higher principles of Naginata.

There are two different kinds of competition in Naginata. The first type of contest is called "*engi-kyogi*". Teams of two compete against each other by performing set forms or techniques. There are two variations: one is a competition in which a set number, usually three, of the Shikake-Oji sequences (see Chapter 3) are performed in pairs. The attacker is called *shikake*, and the defender or counter-attacker is *oji*. The bamboo and oak *naginata* used for *bogu* training and *shiai* is used in Shikake-Oji. (There are eight Shikake-Oji sequences in total, and they are performed as a competition event, in promotion examinations, and as an integral part of training for all levels as one of the most basic and important forms of training.)

The other variation of *engi-kyogi* is the All Japan Naginata Federation Kata. *Kata* (sequences of choreographed movements) utilise a wooden *naginata*, similar in function to the *bokuto* (wooden sword) employed in kendo. The set of *kata* consists of seven forms, and includes some extremely sophisticated techniques. (Due to the intricacy of the forms, and the danger in using a solid wooden *naginata*, in principle *kata* are only practised from the rank of 3-dan and above.)

The second type of contest is "*shiai-kyogi*". It is similar to kendo in that *bogu* is utilised, and the aim is to outscore the opponent. The first to get two points within the designated time limit is the winner (*sanbon-shobu*). There are also three referees (*shinpan*) and they use calls and red and white flags similar to those used in kendo.

Technically speaking, Naginata is in many respects similar in nature to kendo. Apart from the longer weapon involved, the basic armour (*bogu*) is the same as that used in kendo (with the addition of *sune-ate* to protect the shins, and split-finger *kote*), and so too are the criteria required for scoring a valid point in matches. The main differences lie in the left and right sided *kamae* used in Naginata, and the resulting ambidextrous techniques. There are many similarities to kendo in what defines a valid strike, also. According to the All Japan Naginata Federation's "Naginata Match Regulations" (Article 22), a valid strike is defined as follows:

> A valid strike (*yuko-datotsu*) is defined as an accurate strike or thrust made onto targets (*datotsu-bui*) with the striking section (*datotsu-bu*) of the naginata in high spirits and correct posture while simultaneously vocalising the name of the target, and followed with continued alertness (*zanshin*).

The targets in Naginata are also similar to those in kendo with the addition of the *sune*, or shins. Also, more emphasis is placed on striking *sokumen* (*yoko-men* in kendo), and *mochikae* (changing the stance or side on which one holds the *naginata*) to attack from *hasso* or another *kamae*. Actually, the *kamae* in Naginata are identical to those found in kendo. The difference being that whereas *chudan* is the mainstay for what is considered orthodox kendo, Naginata practitioners are encouraged to use as many *kamae* and techniques as possible, even though *chudan* is considered the fundamental stance. This has significant weight when a *shiai* result is has to be decided by referees' decision (*hantei*), as is often the case when the score is even at the end of time.

Target Areas	*Part of the Naginata*
Men	*Monouchi* (15~20cm from the *kissaki*).
Sokumen	25° ~30° either side of the *men's* centreline.
Kote	*Monouchi* (15~20cm from the *kissaki*).
Do	*Monouchi* (15~20cm from the *kissaki*).
Sune	When striking with the *ha-bu* (blade), strike with the *monouchi.* When striking with the *e-bu,* strike with the spot about 20cm from the *ishizuki.*
Inko (Throat)	*Kissaki.*

Note: ***Tsuki*** **is prohibited up to high school level, and** ***tsuki*** **with the** ***ishizuki*** **has been outlawed in** ***shiai*** **as it is considered dangerous.**

One obvious difference, however, is what happens after a cut has been made. Kendo practitioners are encouraged to keep the momentum going forward and cut through after making a strike. In Naginata, the *naginata* and body are pulled back after striking. In fact, one of the common mistakes that kendoka who take up Naginata make is to keep running through after striking, and to have the body facing forward instead of to the side. Similarly, many people who move to kendo from Naginata often find themselves being remonstrated for pulling back after striking with a *shinai* (bamboo sword). The difference in striking styles stems from the different length of the weapons.

Another difference between kendo and Naginata is that one rarely sees body clashing (*taiatari*) in Naginata. When Naginata practitioners clash and come into close-quarters (*seriai*), they will usually attempt to strike *hiki-waza* (particularly *sune*) while moving back, but will be called to separate (*wakare*) if they stay in the tussle too long. Stamping as the strike is made (*fumikomi-ashi*) is not as pronounced in Naginata as it is in kendo. Also, loud vocalisations to intimidate the opponent are not encouraged (apart from at the instant of contact), but the opposite is true in kendo.

As is the case with kendo, three referees (*shinpan*) adjudicate matches in order to obtain impartial and accurate decisions. Three *shinpan* observing from various angles diminishes the possibility of misjudgment. A referee must have confidence in their own decisions. If two of the three referees agree on a point, it will be called as such. In case there is some confusion, it is possible to suspend the match and convene a consultation in the middle of the court (*gogi*). If judgements are flawed or biased, this will discourage competitors and spectators, and portray a mistaken image of Naginata. The immense burden of responsibility of referees for the propagation of Naginata cannot be overstated, and even one wrong decision can have far-reaching effects on the practitioner's enthusiasm for Naginata.

Apart from judging which strikes are valid or not, the referee also has the added responsibility of penalising competitors for foul play. Although foul play by competitors should be avoided, anything can happen during the course of a match. Illegal acts include insulting the opponent or referees, stepping out of bounds, striking *men* with the *e-bu* (shaft), holding onto the opponent's *naginata* or wedging it between any part of the body, intentionally hitting around the ear area or any area not protected by *bogu*, or other dangerous behaviour, excessive pushing, stopping for no reason, equipment falling off, and so on. Two penalties (*hansoku*) constitute one point for the opponent. In the most serious cases of violent or blatantly disrespectful conduct, the offender may be disqualified from the match altogether, and two points automatically awarded to the opponent. This would be the equivalent of a red-card, and is one of the most shameful things that could happen in Naginata. The consequences would be far more serious than, say, a one match suspension. Fight hard, but play by the rules.

2. Shikake-Oji

Shikake-Oji is practised not only as a way to perfect Naginata techniques from the beginner level up, but is also an important match event, and an integral segment of any examination. Shikake-Oji is a set of eight different predetermined technical sequences using a *naginata* with a wooden shaft and bamboo blade. "Shikake" is the initiator, and "Oji" is the "counterattacker". The point of Shikake-Oji is to teach the basic *waza*, and also cultivate the flexibility to adapt to any situation. One learns correct etiquette, *kamae*, body movement, grip (*tenouchi*), distance (*maai*), breathing, striking chances, *zanshin*, principles of attack and defence, proper posture, strong spirit (*kiai*), and so on. Shikake-Oji is how beginners are initiated, and high ranking practitioners stay polished in every aspect of the art.

Apart from various *waza*, all of the Naginata *kamae* are utilised in the sequences as well. These are *chudan-no-kamae, gedan-no-kamae, wakigamae, jodan-no-kamae*, and *hasso-no-kamae*. All Naginata techniques and *kamae* can be executed from either the left or right side of the body. Shikake-Oji encourages the ability to use techniques from either side. In *engi-kyogi* competition, two pairs (with red or white ribbons tied around the waist) march to the start line. At the command, they bow and complete the designated forms. Even though there are eight Shikake-Oji forms altogether, usually only three are performed in competition. When the pairs have finished, they march off the court, and then the head referee blows a whistle to which all five referees (as opposed to three in *shiai-kyogi*) instantaneously raise their red or white flag to indicate their judgment for the superior pair. The judges are looking at the following:

An engi-kyogi match.

- **Attitude**
  Clothing: Worn neatly.
  Posture: Natural, unforced posture.
  Etiquette: Etiquette must be conducted naturally and with sincerity.
- **Accuracy**
  Furiage (lifting *naginata* overhead), *mochikae* (changing *kamae*), *furikaeshi* (large circular *waza* where the *naginata* is spun overhead), *kuridashi* and *kurikomi* (sliding the *naginata* in or out to adjust the distance), body movement and the handling of the *naginata* should be accurate, and in perfect unison.
- ***Datotsu* (Strike)**

Posture: Body movement and positioning should be adequate.
Maai: Striking and receiving at the correct distance.
Hand positioning: Accurately striking the target with the hands holding the correct area of the shaft.
Tenouchi: The direction of the blade (*hasuji*) must be precise.
Kiai: Loud and clear voice.
Eyes: Always focussed on the other person. Eye-contact.
Zanshin: Unrelenting *zanshin* following the execution of a technique.

- **Evidence of Training**

Harmony between Shikake and Oji; balance of *waza*.
Breathing: Breathing should be controlled and in sync.

Shikake-Oji matches usually occur before *shiai-kyogi*, and are hotly contested. Emphasis is placed on beauty in form in Naginata, and Shikake-Oji epitomises this. Competitors even see to small details like whether their hair is tied back and tidy, and is similar in style to their partner. Timing of entry into the court, departure, bows, *kamae*, and so on are all immaculately performed and pairs practise relentlessly with each other to get their synchronisation exactly right.

3. Kata

Two students at the IBU practise Naginata Kata.

Kata has always been an important method for passing on knowledge and techniques in Japanese martial art schools throughout history. Great warriors of the Warring States period and early Tokugawa period devised *kata* in order to convey the wisdom they had amassed through the experience of combat. *Kata* are choreographed sequences of movements which contain the very essence of the school. The student seeks to embody the *kata* teachings of the master, following their instructions to the letter. Through constant and arduous repetition of *kata,* the techniques gradually become a natural part of the adept's movement.[15]

In the modern education environment, this methodology of rote memorisation where the teacher's word is absolute could be perceived as counterproductive to developing problem-solving skills and initiative. There is, however, a fundamental teaching in budo known as *shu-ha-ri* (守破離) which defines the traditional process of learning. The first stage of *shu* refers to the act of learning the techniques (through *kata*), becoming proficient enough to apply them in any situation (*ha*), and finally the enlightened stage of breaking away and moving freely in one's own style (*ri*). This is a lifelong process in which individuality is the ultimate objective. I sometimes equate this process (admittedly rather simplistically) with a university education: undergraduate degree (*shu*), masters degree (*ha*), and finally a Ph.D. (*ri*).

Although the Zen-Nihon Naginata Kata follow the same tradition, they were actually developed quite recently, in 1977. What was the process and motivation for their creation? As we have seen, a new sportified version of Naginata was designed in the postwar era. As its popularity increased, many experts began to lament that the true principles of the art were being compromised with unorthodox techniques or tricks to score points. To counter this trend the AJNF devised the "Concept of Naginata Committee" along with the "Kata Development Committee" in 1973. The stated purpose was to clarify the underpinning philosophical and technical principles to prevent the erosion of Naginata's essence while also keeping it relevant with the times.

With regard to the creation of new *kata*, the aim was to incorporate as many facets of traditional schools as possible which would serve to enhance comprehension of the more sophisticated technical and mental aspects difficult to teach just through Shikake-Oji. This, it was hoped, would ensure the survival of true Naginata for future generations.

Instructors from many traditional schools scattered around Japan gathered, discussed, researched, and devised a set of seven *naginata* versus *naginata kata* which embodied all the subtleties of technique, roundness of spirit, and beauty of form to be mastered by advanced practitioners. Characteristics such as the *kamae* and key components of each school represented were recorded on film and assessed by the committee. The *kata* took five years to complete, and the finished product is a fusion of various traditional styles.

The wooden *naginata* used in *kata* is considerably more detailed in its shape than the standard training *naginata*. In order to perform the *kata* properly requires knowledge and skill in utilising the refined curves and corners (*mune* and *shinogi* etc.) on the sculptured wooden blade. Due to the subtlety of the techniques, and the inherent danger involved in using a wooden *naginata*, the Zen-Nihon Naginata Kata (the name was changed from Zen Nihon Naginata Renmei Kata in 2002) is only taught to practitioners 3-dan and upwards. They are included in promotion examinations from 4-dan, and also contested at tournaments such as the All Japan Championships.

Kata matches are conducted much in the same way as the Shikake-Oji contests. Two teams of two enter the court, perform the designated three forms, and five referees raise their red or white flags as the competitors leave the court to decide the victorious pair. The referees look for resonating *kiai*, accuracy of technique, timing, synchronisation, and proof of an understanding of the principles (*riai*) that underlie the *kata*. Aspects such as tidy appearance, simultaneous movement when entering and leaving the court, and protocols of etiquette are also carefully assessed. It is the minor details that decide the winner when all else is even. Everything has to be perfectly timed right up to the very end.

Any mistakes in *kata* appear more obvious than they would in Shikake-Oji, requiring complete mastery of all the *kihon* basics to be able to perform them properly. As the techniques make full use of the curvature in the blade (*sori*) and side of the blade (*shinogi*) in execution, and contain many techniques which would be impossible to do properly with a *shiai naginata*.

4. Ishu-jiai

As we have seen, prewar Naginata mainly consisted of *kata* utilising a *naginata* versus the sword. *Kata* with *naginata* versus *naginata* was virtually unheard of, and whenever a Naginata practitioner donned armour and engaged in a match, it was often against a kendoka, something referred to as *ishu-jiai*. *Ishu-*

Pre-war photo of Naginata versus Kendo (1939).

jiai in which women took on sword-wielding men were a popular spectacle in public demonstration matches during the Meiji period.

Following the formation of the Dai-Nippon Butokukai in 1895, a high-profile annual tournament also featured Naginata experts against swordsmen, and onlookers were delighted when the woman defeated her foe. Although a loss was considered a source of great embarrassment to the male fencers, it was seen as some as being unavoidable due to the "advantage of length". Some, however, thought that this was merely an excuse.

In special festival-like tournaments such as the famous Kyoto Taikai held in May every year at the Butokuden in Kyoto, spectators are still able to witness the odd *ishu-jiai.* Also, at official Naginata tournaments, often a five-man team of local kendoka are pitted against a team of Naginata exponents for a demonstration match to liven up the day's proceedings. The Naginata team usually ends up victorious. The crowd is not only pleased to see women defeating men despite the obvious physical disadvantages, but also to see hapless kendoka hopping comically around the court, desperately trying to avoid unfamiliar attacks to the shins, and the phenomenal extended reach in thrusts to the throat, and strikes to the *men.*

What is it about the *naginata* that makes it so effective? First, one of the main

An ishu-jiai at the prestigious Kyoto Taikai (1989).

reasons for *naginata*'s success against kendo is the element of surprise. The Naginata competitor is not required to make any changes in fighting style against kendo. All of the target areas are the same, and the fighting distance (*maai*) is easily altered. Kendo practitioners, on the other hand, are only used to making attacks to the upper-body (*men, kote, do, tsuki*) and are totally unfamiliar with the shins (*sune*) as a valid target. Normally, an attack to the lower-body would result in penalisation in kendo, and so techniques for protecting the lower body are unheard of. Also, kendoka are unaccustomed to such variation in *maai*. The *shinai* is gripped in one place, and is not slid forwards or backwards through the hands to alter distance as it is in Naginata (*kuridashi and kurikomi*). Thus, the kendoka must overcome many unfamiliar movements to engage in a match against Naginata. The main differences and advantages of the *naginata* compared to a *shinai* are as follows:

1. The *naginata* is long, so is advantageous from further away.
2. The *naginata* utilises *kurikomi* and *kuridashi* movements in which the length of the *naginata* can be adjusted to alter the distance for engagement.
3. In Naginata, *kamae* and attacks can be executed from both the left and right sides. This makes it difficult for the kendoka to read the direction of the attack.
4. Both ends of the *naginata* can be used to make strikes to *sune*. Until

recently it was also permissible to thrust to the throat (*tsuki*) with the *ishizuki*, but this is now prohibited in Naginata matches. However, it has not yet been officially outlawed in *ishu-jiai*.

5. *Sune* strikes to the inside and outside of the shins are common in Naginata, and can be executed from close in, or far away.

Assuming the kendoka has had experience fighting against Naginata, there are a number of techniques that can be effectively used against the *naginata*. When the kendoka takes on Naginata in a match, the norm is to assume a lower *chudan* or *gedan-no-kamae* to guard against attacks to *sune*. This tends to leave the upper body open for *men* or *tsuki* attacks. As long as the kendoka moves forward rather than back, suitable pressure can be applied and Naginata attacks can be more successfully stifled. From extremely close-quarters, *hiki-waza* is usually very effective against Naginata, as are *kaeshi-waza* or *nuki-waza* when moving in. Ultimately, both weapons have their advantages and disadvantages. Once the element of surprise is removed, the match is usually decided by the better fighter. Although relegated to an attraction rather than an officially contested event, *ishu-jiai* offer both Naginata and kendo exponents a wealth of valuable experience and insights into crucial factors in both arts such as *maai*, striking opportunities, *seme*, footwork and movement, etc.

The author (right) blocks sune while moving in to make an attack. Despite appearances, the author's leg has not been cut off.

Performance of Rhythm Naginata at the IBU.

5. Rhythm Naginata

Although not so common, one more division of Naginata sometimes demonstrated at tournaments is Rhythm Naginata. In this event, teams of Naginata practitioners complete a routine of techniques in time with music. Participants are encouraged to develop a unique choreography with music and a theme of their choice. It is still fairly rare, and the only time you are likely to see it is at the World Naginata Championships, where it is staged as a public demonstration and judged for a special prize by visiting VIPs. It has been performed on occasion at major tournaments in Japan, usually by student clubs. There are no stipulated rules *per se*, and much is left up to the artistic sensibilities of the performers. Guidelines for Rhythm Naginata at the World Naginata Championship are as follows:

1. Each country may enter one team of two or more performers.
2. Performing time shall not exceed five minutes including entering and leaving.
3. The performance shall be accompanied by music of any kind.
4. The court size is 15 meters by 15 meters.

Budo traditionalists tend to scoff Rhythm Naginata as being little more than a modern dance performance, and of little intrinsic value to the serious martial artist. This is not exactly true, as the practitioner gets the chance to apply various techniques in different situations. For the performance to be successful, team work, breathing synchronicity, timing, distancing, and of course, sense of rhythm are of the essence. These are all attributes that are refined through preparation and performance of Rhythm Naginata. Another overlooked feature is that the practitioners are encouraged to use their imagination to create what is essentially their own *kata*. This can be very stimulating for practitioners who are used to repeating the same *kata* in the course of their usual training.

It may come as a surprise to many that Rhythm Naginata is not actually that new. In fact, in *Kyoiku jiron* (a journal dedicated to education) there is an interesting report about martial arts training in 1912.

> There I saw a dance by girls holding naginata. They swirled their naginata around while reciting poems (waka). Their poetry renditions left a lot to be desired, but the fact that they were using naginata while doing so made it an extremely interesting activity indeed. (March 25)

I have never seen Rhythm Naginata performed to poetry, but the Belgian team's performance to the theme of the Pink Panther at the 2nd World Championships in Paris (1999) was curious to say the least. In a nutshell, Rhythm Naginata is a kind of budo version of synchronised swimming!

Part 3: Examinations and Qualifications

Grading examinations are an integral part of Naginata. They provide goals and yardsticks for the practitioners, and much-needed revenue for the federations. Naginata has grades ranging from 8-kyu through to 1-kyu, 1-dan through to 5-dan, and then the *shogo* titles of *Renshi*, *Kyoshi* and *Hanshi*. In Japan, examinations up to 4-dan are conducted by the respective local federations, and 5-dan and above are national examinations held twice a year at the AJNF headquarters in Itami city, and in Tokyo (from 2014).

1. Dan Grades

The requirements for examinations are as follows:

1-dan (Shodan)	Candidates must be able to demonstrate a good command of the basic techniques and be able to engage in sparring
Basics	*Joge-buri*, *datotsu* (striking *men*, *sokumen*, *sune*, *do*)
Waza	Shikake-Oji up to *gohon-me* (number 5)
With *bogu*	Depends on federation
Shido-ho	Not necessary to demonstrate teaching beginners
Written test	Necessary
Age	13 and above
Prerequisite	Must have *ikkyu*

2-dan (Nidan)	Candidates must be able to recognise valid striking opportunities and make powerful attacks
Basics	*Happo-buri*, *datotsu* (*men*, *sokumen*, *sune*, *do*, *kote*)
Waza	Shikake-Oji up to *hachihon*-me (number 8)
With *bogu*	*Uchikaeshi*, *kakari-geiko* (attack practise), *gokaku-geiko* (sparring)
Shido-ho	not necessary to demonstrate teaching beginners
Written test	Necessary
Age	16 and above
Prerequisite	Must have had *shodan* for over 1 year

3-dan (Sandan)	Candidates must have a firm command of all techniques, and be capable of instructing beginners
Basics	*Happo-buri, datotsu* (all target areas)
Waza	Shikake-Oji up to *hachihon-me* (No. 8)
With *bogu*	*Uchikaeshi, hikitate-geiko* (instructional sparring), *shiai*
Shido-ho	Necessary

Written test	Necessary
Age	19 and above
Prerequisite	Must have had *nidan* for over 2 years

4-dan (Yondan)	Candidates must be able to execute all techniques at a high level, and be capable of refereeing matches.
Basics	*Happo-buri, datotsu* (all target areas)
Waza	Shikake-Oji up to *hachihon-me* (No. 8) Naginata Federation Kata up to *gohon-me* (No. 5)
With *bogu*	*Uchikaeshi, hikitate-geiko* (instructional sparring), *shiai*, refereeing
Shido-ho	Necessary
Written test	Necessary
Age	22 and above
Prerequisite	Must have had *sandan* for over 3 years

5-dan (Godan)	Candidates must have a solid understanding of the principles of Naginata, and be of good character
Basics	*Happo-buri, datotsu* (all target areas)
Waza	Shikake-Oji up to *hachihon-me* Naginata Federation Kata up to *nanahon-me* (No. 7)
With *bogu*	*Uchikaeshi, hikitate-geiko* (instructional sparring), *shiai*, refereeing
Shido-ho	Necessary
Written test	Necessary
Age	25 and above
Prerequisite	Must have had *yondan* for over 3 years

2. Shogo

Shogo are titles issued after *godan*. Whereas the focus of *dan* grades is mainly concerned with the level of technical mastery, *shogo* are awarded according to technical mastery, understanding of the deeper philosophical principles of Naginata, personal characteristics, and also contributions made to promoting and teaching Naginata.

Criteria:

- *Renshi*: 28 years and above, and have held *godan* for over 3 years.
- *Kyoshi*: 35 years and above, and have held *Renshi* for over 7 years.
- *Hanshi*: 55 years and above, and have held *Kyoshi* for over 20 years.

Each candidate is recommended by their federation, and they are subjected to rigorous testing. Needless to say, *Hanshi*, being the highest rank in Naginata, is the most difficult to pass. There are examples of people who have been awarded the title posthumously, or as honorary gesture for services rendered on behalf of Naginata even though the recipient may not actually be a practitioner.

3. Shinpan Qualifications

Official referees are divided into three classifications:

- Class-1 (*Isshu*)
- Class-2 (*Nishu*)
- Class-3 (*Sanshu*)

Class-1 Referees must hold the title of All Japan Naginata Federation *Kyoshi* or above, and be deemed to "possess a suitable level of technical competence." Class-2 Referees must hold the grade of 5-dan or above, and Class-3 Referees must be 3-dan or above. Applicants for the examinations for Official Referee authorisation must be registered members of the All Japan Naginata Federation (or the International Naginata Federation).

The AJNF will only recognise Class 1~3 Referees if they have been recommended by their organisation of membership, have completed the necessary hours of seminar time, and have passed the final examination. In principle, all referees at competitions held by the AJNF and affiliated organisations should be officially recognised referees, and wear their patches to prove their status. For more information about the role of *shinpan* and the technicalities of refereeing please refer to Appendices 1–3 at the back of this volume.

Part 4: The Equipment

1. The Naginata

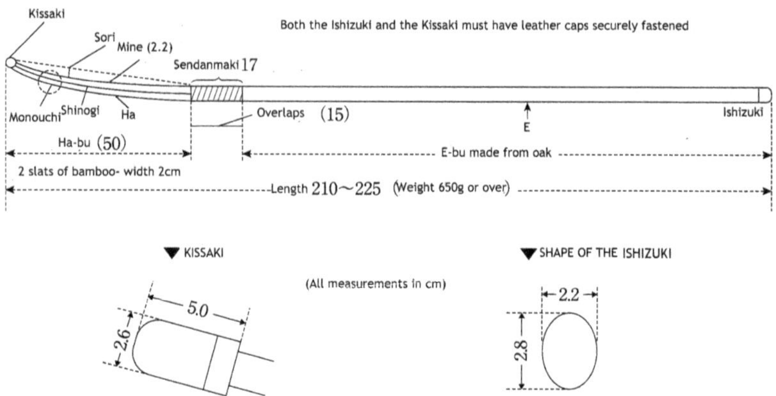

- Total length 2.10m-2.25m.
- Weight 650g+.
- The blade (*ha-bu*) consists of 2 slats of bamboo (2cm x 50cm) placed together. There is a hole at the tip (*kissaki*) where a leather cap is tied into place with a nylon thread (*tsuru*), and secured with tape.
- The two *monouchi* are situated 15-20cm from the *kissaki*, and 20-25cm from the *ishizuki*.
- The joint of the shaft (*e-bu*) and the blade (*ha-bu*) is 15cm and is secured by winding white plastic tape to form what is called the *sendan-maki*.
- The shaft is made from white oak, is oval and slightly thicker at the *ishizuki* end. A leather cap is attached to the *ishizuki*.

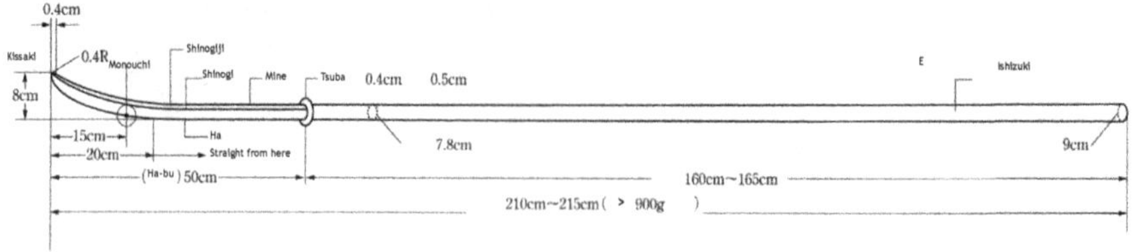

Kata Naginata

Benkei's Pointers

Always check your equipment before training.

1. Make sure that the leather caps on the *kissaki* and the *ishizuki* have not become loose.
2. Check that the bamboo blade is not splintered.
3. Check that the shaft is not warped or split.
4. Make sure that you name is clearly marked near the *ishizuki* end. All *naginata* may not be the same, but they sure look it!

2. Carrying, Passing, and Receiving

When receiving or passing a *naginata*, hold the centre of the shaft with the blade at the top and *ishizuki* at the bottom. Pass the *naginata* with the blade facing toward you on a slight angle to the right. The receiver takes the *naginata* with the left hand in the centre of the passer's hands, with the right hand closest to the *ishizuki*.

3. Training Gear

Naginata training gear consists of the *keiko-gi* (jacket), *obi* (sash), and *hakama* (split-skirt). It is also permissible to wear a normal exercise clothes. It is important that training wear is the correct size so as not to impair movement, and it must be clean. The state of your training wear is said to reflect your attitude to training. Don't wear jewellery, accessories, or socks.

a) *Keiko-gi*

Length

Should be longer than the bottom of the slits at the sides of the *hakama*.

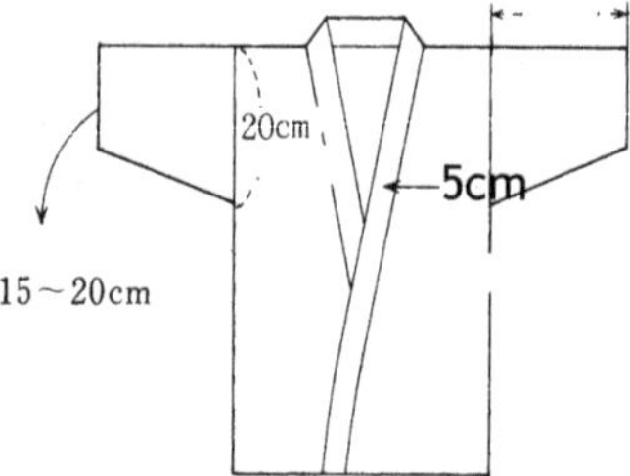

Sleeves

Should be about 15-20cm. Elastic may be inserted to prevent the *naginata* from entering the sleeve.

Arm length

Should reach the elbow.

Collar

The width of the collar should be approximately 5cm.

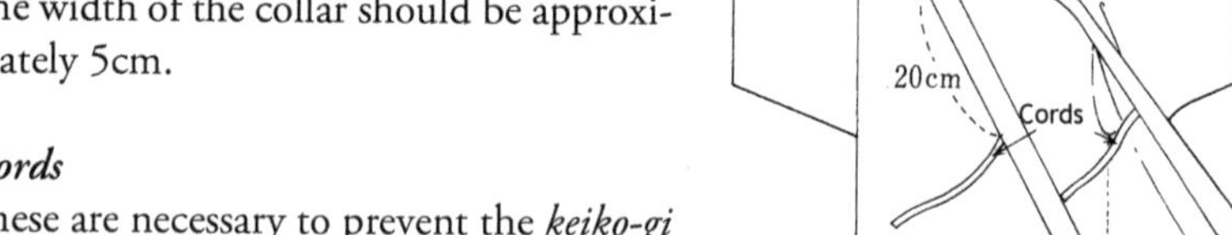

Cords

These are necessary to prevent the *keiko-gi* from opening. They should be fastened to allow tying from under the collar with the left lapel coming over the right. (See diagram.)

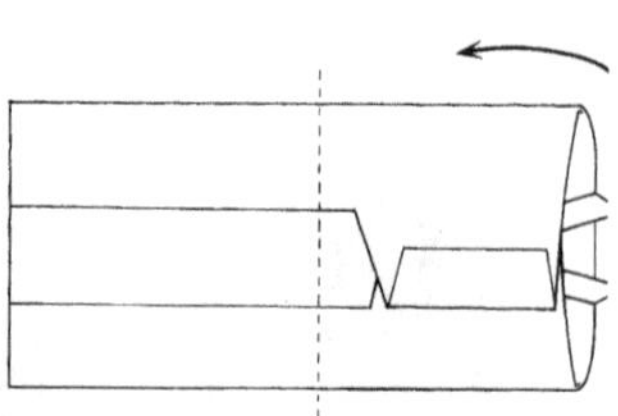

Wearing the keiko-gi

Make sure that the cords are tightly fastened, that the collar is straight, and that there are no wrinkles in the back.

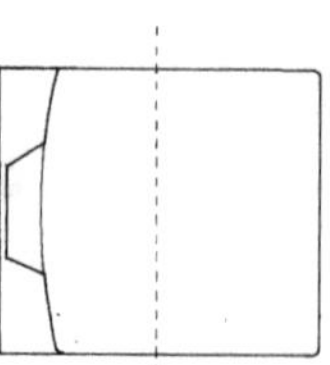

Folding the keiko-gi

It should be folded neatly after use, as shown in the diagrams, and washed regularly. Note that the *keiko-gi* should be made from white cotton. Cotton is preferable over synthetic materials for its sweat absorbing qualities.

b) *Obi* (sash)

The *obi* is made from the same material as the *keiko-gi*. It is 30cm in width but then folded to make the width 10cm. The *obi* should be long enough to wrap around your waist twice, and then tied in a bow at the back. When folding the *obi*, remove any wrinkles, and fold it over eight times keeping it flat.

c) *Hakama*

The *hakama* is a kind of split-skirt made from navy blue or black cotton or synthetic material.

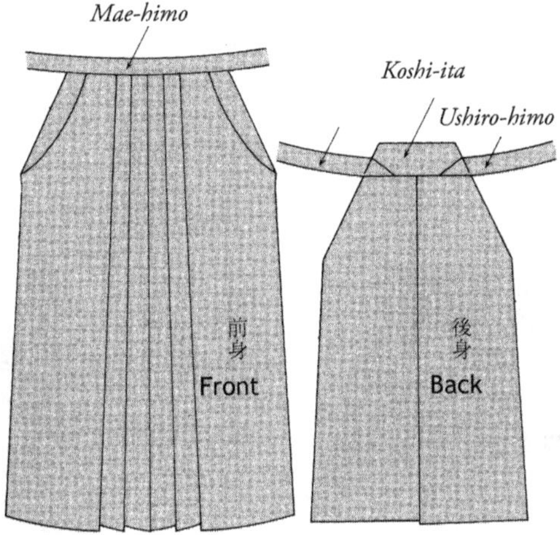

Putting the Hakama on

The *hakama* should be worn at waist height with the back-board (*koshi-ita*) fitting snugly into the small of the back.

Method 1

1. Taking the top-front of the *hakama*, step into it left foot first. Bring it up just above the *obi*.
2. Pass the two *mae-himo* around the back, cross right over left, and bring them round to cross over at the front ①.
3. Twist the *mae-himo* held in the left hand upward as in ①, and pass once again around the back. Tie in a bow at the back ②.
4. Take hold of the *koshi-ita* and insert the plastic tag inside the *hakama*

from above into the *mae-himo* at the back. Bring the *ushiro-himo* (back straps) around to cross over at the front. The right *himo* should be on top as you thread the left *himo* underneath all the other straps. Then tie in a knot at the front, tucking the remainder into each side of the *hakama* ③.

①

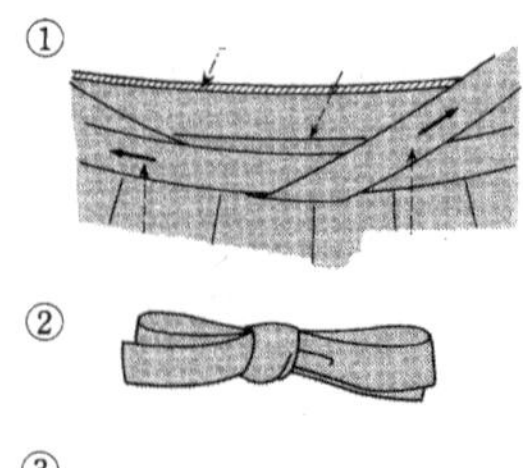

②

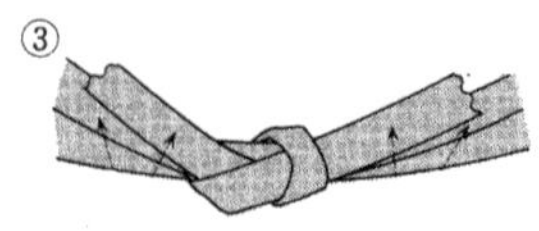

③

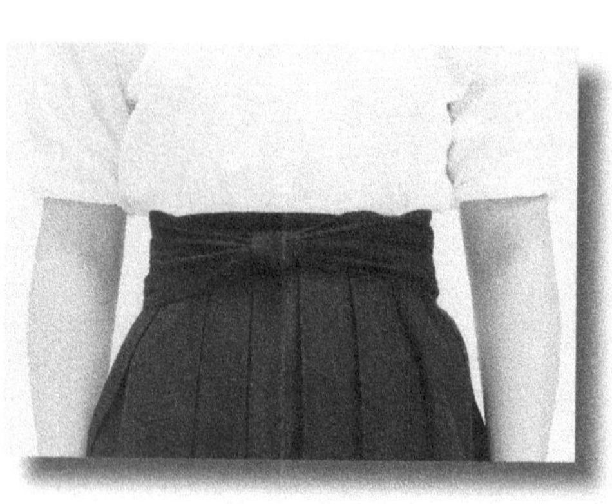

Method 2

1. Taking the top-front of the *hakama*, step into it left foot first. Then, placing the *koshi-ita*'s plastic spatula into the knot of the *obi*, bring the *ushiro-himo* around to the front and secure temporarily.
2. Take the *mae-himo*, wrap them around to the back and cross them over on the *koshi-ita* seam. Bring the *himo* to the front again, cross them over 2cm from the top, and then wind them back around and through the slits at the side of the *hakama* to tie inside at the back, just under the *obi* knot.

3. Then untie the *ushiro-himo* temporarily fastened at the front. Tie in a knot in the front, and make a cross as shown in diagrams①-③ below.

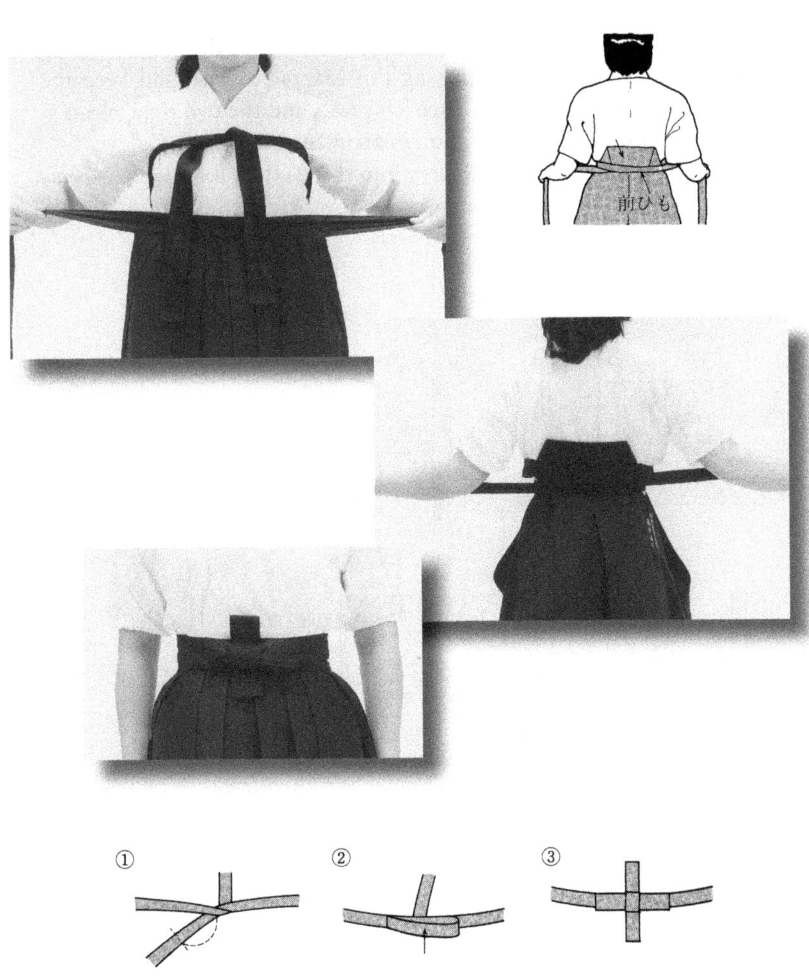

Folding the Hakama

1. Place your hand inside the *hakama* and move the crotch seam to the right.
2. Lay the *hakama* face down on the floor with the right centre seam aligned on top of the left centre seam. Smooth out any creases and align the hems.
3. Turn the *hakama* over, taking care not to ruffle the back. Pressing down on the hem while flipping the *hakama* over should keep the back in shape. Arrange the three left pleats and the two right pleats.
4. Fold both sides inward approximately 10cm.
5. Fold the length of the *hakama* into three. Then fold the *mae-himo* (long straps) into quarters and cross over. Fold the *ushiro-himo* as shown in the diagram below.

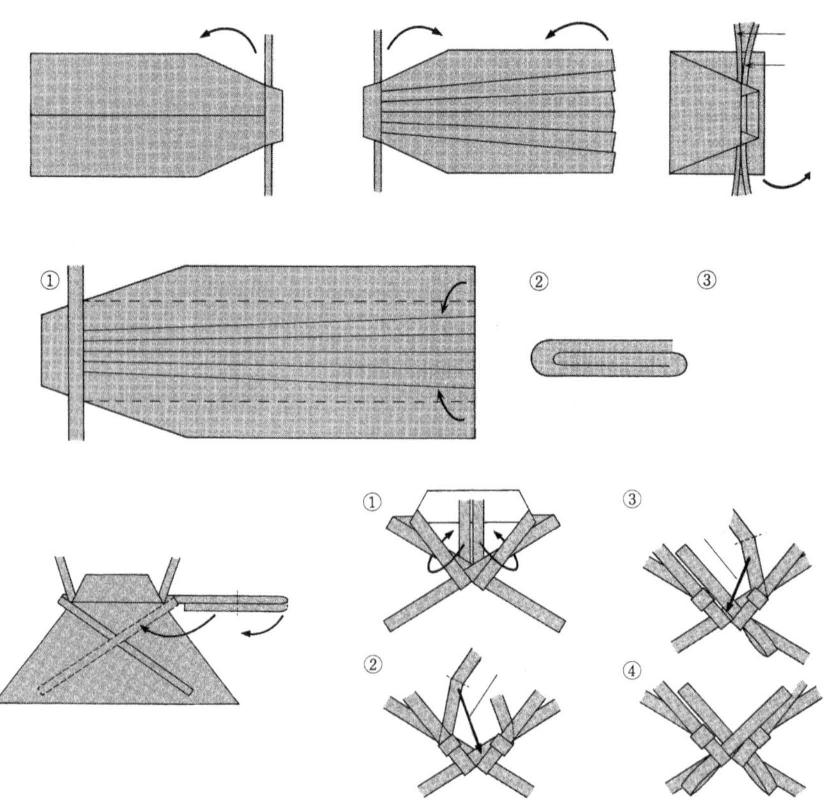

Benkei's Pointers

Hakama are loose trousers tied at the waist with a cord and worn over a *kimono* as part of formal or ceremonial Japanese-style dress by women and men. The *hakama* has undergone a variety of changes in style over the centuries: the legs were widened, pleats were added at the waist, and they were bound at the ankles with a cord threaded through the hem. The type of *hakama* used in Naginata now came into vogue during the late seventeenth century, and was designed for horse riding.

The five pleats in the *hakama* represent the five Confucian virtues:

Jin: Benevolence
Gi: Honour or justice
Rei: Courtesy and etiquette
Chi: Wisdom, intelligence
Shin: Sincerity

The symbolism of the pleats should be kept in mind while folding. Also, the one line in the back of the *hakama* represents the virtue of sincerity and single-minded resolve.

4. Bogu

The armour used in Naginata is collectively called *bogu*. It is designed to protect all the designated target areas (*datotsu-bui*), without impeding movement. It is important to choose *bogu* which is the right size. Also, make sure that it is kept in good order. Mend or replace bits which show signs of deterioration, and place it out to dry after use.

Men

The cords (*men-himo*) are attached to leather straps which are fastened to the fourth or fifth bar from the bottom of the face-grill (*men-gane*). It is also possible to attach the *men* cords at the top of the *men*. Note that the shoulder protectors (*men-dare*) are not as long as they often are on a *men* used for kendo.

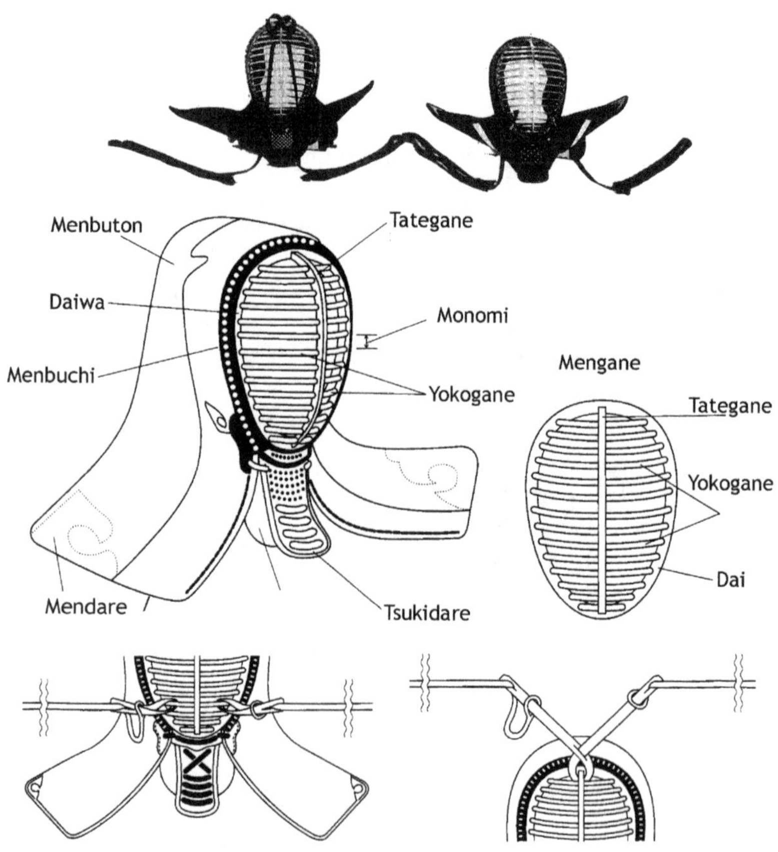

Do

The *do* is made from bamboo and lacquer, or from fibreglass. The trimmings are usually made of leather. It is important to use a *do* which is suited to your body size.

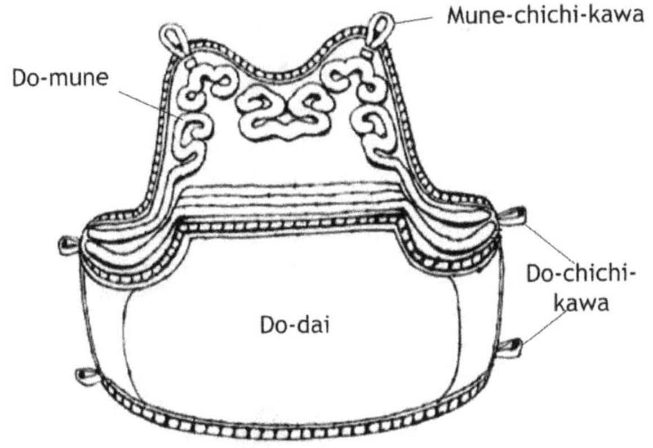

Tare

The *tare* has three large protective panels in the front. The middle panel is where the *zekken* or name pouch is attached. The *tare* straps are usually 6-7cm in width.

Kote

The *kote* are designed with a split finger and thumb in order to allow *mochi-kae*. Thus, it is preferable to use these special Naginata *kote* rather than the type used in kendo.

Sune-ate

The *sune-ate* have 5-7 black bamboo slats 2cm in width attached to protect the shins. Some *sune-ate* also have knee and ankle protectors. The cords should be long enough to wrap around twice.

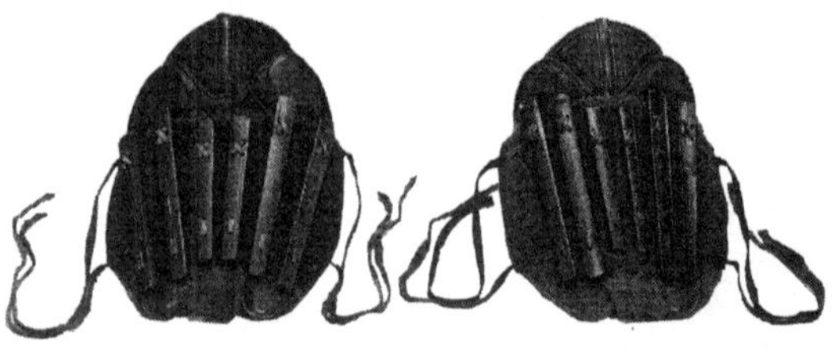

Chapter 2: Form and Theory

Endnotes

[1] Oya Minoru "Central Issues in the Instruction of Kendo: With Focus on the Interconnectedness of Waza and Mind", in A. Bennett (ed.), *Budo Perspectives*, pp. 203-19.
[2] Ibid., p. 204.
[3] Ibid., p. 205.
[4] Ibid., p. 206.
[5] Ibid.
[6] All Japan Kendo Federation *Japanese-English Dictionary of Kendo.*
[7] Takano Sasaburo, *Kendo*, pp. 190-92.
[8] Oya, p. 216.
[9] Ibid., p. 210.
[10] Kinoshita Hisanori, *Kenpo shigoku shoden*, pp. 154-55.
[11] Ibid.
[12] Ibid.
[13] Ibid.
[14] Ibid.
[15] Nakabayashi Shinji, *Budo no susume*, pp. 162-67.

Chapter 3
Practical Drills Without a Partner

Part 1: Shizentai and Rei

Before learning techniques, it is important to understand the etiquette for training in Naginata. Correct posture must be maintained and appropriate courtesies observed at all times in the dojo. By adhering to protocols of courtesy during the course of training, the practitioner will learn to act in a courteous manner to others outside of the dojo, if they don't already do so. This is why form and courtesy are considered as central components to character development through the study of Naginata.

1. Shizentai

Holding the *naginata* upright is referred to as *shizentai*, or natural standing position. This should be a comfortable and stable stance from which bows are conducted at the beginning and end of a set of techniques, or a match.

1. Stand the *naginata* up straight with the *ishizuki* placed to the diagonal right front of the right foot.
2. The blade should be facing forward, the right wrist lightly touching the hip, and the left hand hanging down the left thigh with fingers closed.
3. Keep your back straight, shoulders relaxed, and chin in.
4. Look straight ahead, or into the eyes of your partner.

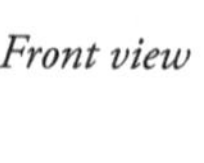

Front view

Side view

2. Rei

Rei (courtesy, etiquette, bow) is one of the most important concepts in Naginata. As with other budo arts, Naginata is said to "begin and end with *rei*". Simply put, *rei* is the sentiment of empathy, respect, and gratitude one holds toward training partners, other members of the dojo, and the training environment itself. Such feelings are expressed physically through ritualistic bowing, both from the seated position (*zarei*), and standing (*ritsurei*).

It is important to bow correctly and to express respect with sincerity, rather than merely going through the motions. Regardless of how technically skilled one may be, or successful one is in the arena of competition, arrogance, slovenly or rude behaviour, and inconsiderate actions toward opponents and other people in general is not in line with the Naginata ideal. The importance of strict observance of *rei* in both its physical expression and philosophical ideal cannot be overstated.

a) *Ritsurei* (Standing bow)

Ritsurei is performed from *shizentai* in two situations; to the *shomen* before and after a match or practice, and also to one's opponent. When performing *ritsurei* to the *shomen*, bend the upper body 30 degrees from the waist. When performing *ritsurei* to your partner, bend the upper body 15 degrees.

In either case, the *naginata* should remain perfectly stationary, but the left hand should slide down the left thigh as the bow is performed. A mutual bow should be done in unison, and eye-contact maintained at all times.

Note that the bow in the picture to the right is deeper than the one above. This is a bow to the *shomen*.

b) *Zarei* (Seated bow)

1. To sit down into *seiza* (formal seated position), draw the left foot back slightly and kneel down on the left knee. Then draw the right leg back and kneel on both knees.
2. Cross the tips of the big toes, bring the knees together (one fist apart for men), and keep the back straight.
3. One's posture should be upright, chin pulled in with the mouth lightly closed, and the gaze focussed straight ahead.
4. Both hands are placed on the upper thighs with the fingers together.
5. The *naginata* is placed parallel to the right side with the *ishizuki* 30cm in front of the knee. The blade is pointing behind and facing out.
6. To perform *zarei*, keep your back straight and bend forward from the hips as you place both hands on the floor simultaneously with the index fingers and thumbs touching to form a triangle. Stay in the prostrated position for approximately one breath, then rise up again to the kneeling position.
7. When standing up from *seiza*, stand the toes up first, pivot to the right and pick up the *naginata* with the right hand underneath and left hand on top.
8. Step out with the right foot bringing the left foot up next to it as you stand up. Place the *ishizuki* on the floor, hold onto the *naginata* with the right hand, and drop the left hand down onto the left thigh.

Whether sitting or standing you must always try to maintain a straight but relaxed posture. The picture to the right is a good example of *seiza*. This formal seated position is utilised when lining up to start or finish a training session, and when sitting and watching demonstrations by other practitioners. If possible, refrain from sitting cross-legged or sprawled out on the floor. The dojo is a formal area, and efforts must be made to look tidy. Notice also that the *naginata* is placed neatly to the side with the blade facing outwards at the back. All equipment should be placed neatly when not in use.

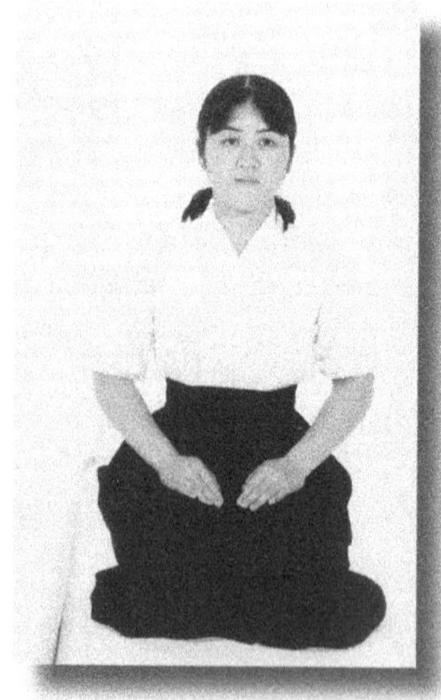

The photo to the right is a good example of *zarei*. The back is straight and the neck is not showing. The forefingers and thumbs form a neat triangle without being splayed out. The hands slide from the thighs to the floor and back up in unison.

This is an example of incorrect *zarei*. Note that the neck is showing, and the back is not straight.

Part 2: The Five Kamae

The *kamae* (fighting stances) have the two functions of defence and offence. The five *kamae* in Naginata are *chudan*, *gedan*, *hasso*, *waki*, and *jodan*. All the *kamae* have left and right variations, but it is standard practice to start with the left *kamae* (left foot forward).

1. Chudan-no-kamae

Chudan-no-kamae is considered the base for all of the different *kamae*, and is the most suitable for adapting to any situation.

a) From *shizentai* into *hidari-chudan* (left foot forward)

1. Standing in *shizentai*, place your left hand on top of the right hand.
2. Step out with the left foot to a distance approximate to shoulder width. The body should turn to face the right to take an oblique stance against your partner (*hanmi*).
3. The *kissaki* is pulled forward with the left hand as it slides through the right hand. The right hand ends up resting on the right thigh, with the distance from the back hand to the *ishizuki* the same length as the forearm.

Front view

Side view

b) From *shizentai* into *migi-chudan* (right foot forward)

Bring the left hand under the right, and then step out with the right foot using the right hand to slide the *naginata* through the left hand towards the *ishizuki*.

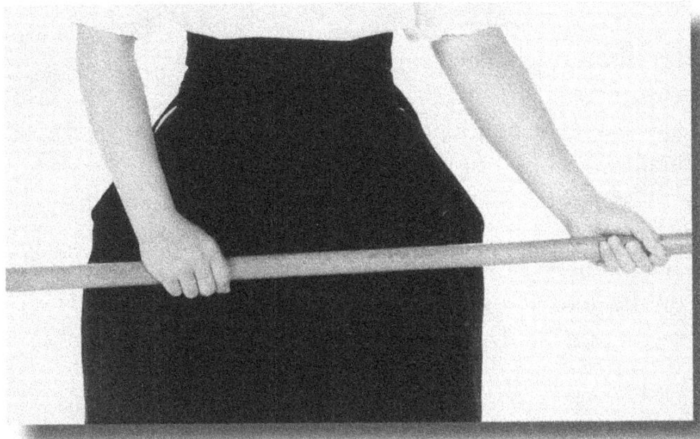

Correct grip for hidari-chudan

Incorrect grip

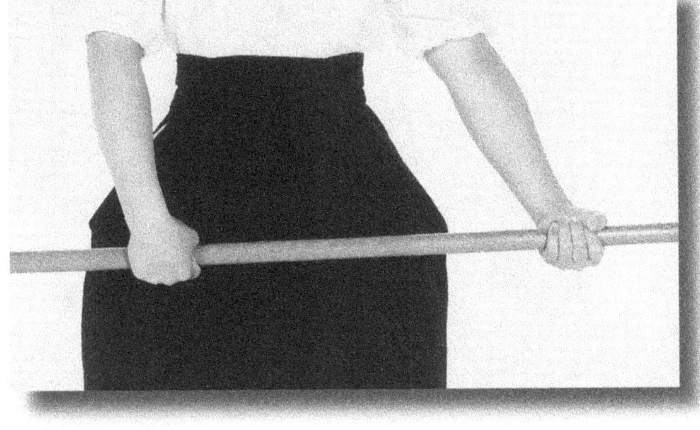

Feet are approximately shoulder-width apart

2. Gedan-no-kamae

Gedan is a defensive stance and is also used to apply pressure on the opponent's lower body. Like all of the *kamae*, *gedan* can be used on both sides. The following explanation is for the standard posture with the left foot forward (*hidari-gedan*).

1. From *chudan* twist the right hand anti-clockwise and turn the blade so that it faces up.
2. The right hand should be positioned by the right ear, and the elbow should sit naturally.
3. The left hand should slide slightly towards the *kissaki* and grip the shaft from underneath.
4. The *kissaki* should be in line with the centre of the body approximately 10cm off the floor.
5. The left elbow should lightly make contact with the body.

Correct grip for front hand

Incorrect grip

3. Hasso-no-kamae

Hasso is one of the more aggressive *kamae*. *Hasso* is frequently used on both the left and right sides. The following explanation is for *hasso* with the left foot forward (*hidari-hasso*).

1. From *chudan*, lift the *kissaki* up and swap the left hand over with the right at the centre of the body.
2. The right hand should be in line with the right ear, while the left hand slides down towards the *ishizuki*, leaving a forearm's length from the bottom hand to the *ishizuki*, and coming to rest on the hip. The elbow should not be protruding.
3. The *e-bu* should come across the chest and the *ishizuki* should remain on the body's side-on centreline. The blade (*ha-bu*) is facing forward.

Front

Side

4. Wakigamae

Wakigamae enables versatility in attack. The act of hiding the *naginata* from view serves to offer an element of surprise as the opponent will be unable to gauge the distance for attack easily. As one's own body is left open, however, it is not advisable to employ this stance too often during the course of a match. Both left and right sides are possible.

1. From *chudan*, lift the *kissaki* over and back as you swap grip (*mochikae*) at the centre of the body.
2. The *ishizuki* should be in the front guarding the centreline, the blade should be facing outwards, and the *naginata* should be level.
3. The distance between the hands should be the same as the distance between the feet (shoulder-width apart). Both arms should hang down naturally, and be relaxed.

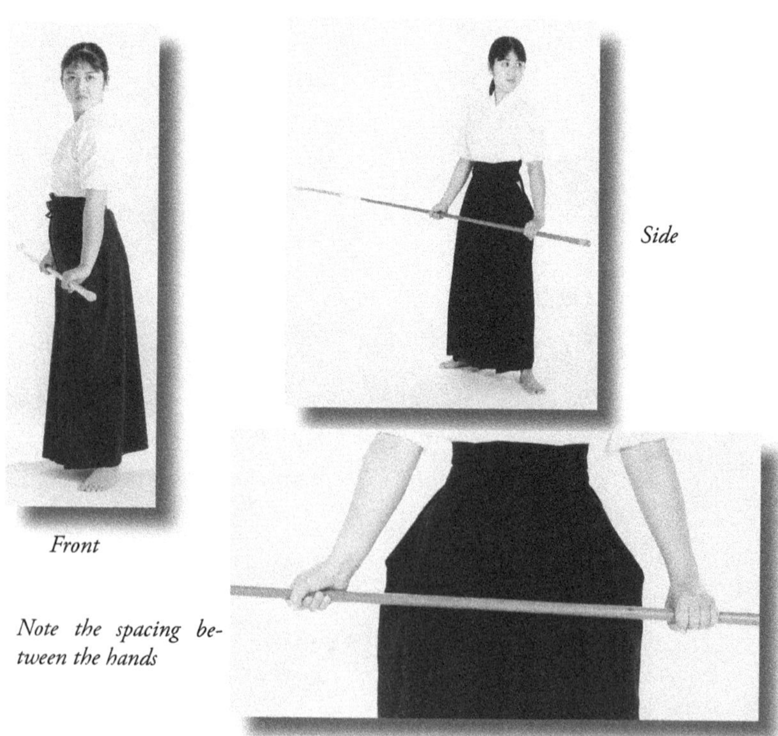

Side

Front

Note the spacing between the hands

5. Jodan-no-kamae

Jodan is where the *naginata* is held overhead, and is considered the most aggressive *kamae,* allowing immediate attack but little opportunity for defence. Due to the aggressive nature of this stance, it is difficult for the opponent to move in to make an attack. As the entire lower body is left open, a slip in concentration will quickly result in defeat. To utilise this stance effectively requires an advanced level of skill. *Jodan* can also be employed from both sides.

1. From *chudan*, *mochikae* in the centre of the body and lift the *kissaki* overhead.
2. The *ishizuki* should be at the front protecting the body's centreline, and the blade *(ha-bu)* should be facing up.
3. The *kissaki* at the rear should be slightly higher than the *ishizuki* at the front, leaving the length of the *naginata* on a slight incline.
4. The arms are spaced evenly apart; the front arm should not obstruct one's view in any way.

Front

Side

Part 3: Taisabaki (Footwork)

Taisabaki is the footwork used to attack and defend. This does not mean moving with the feet only. One must grasp the concept of moving in all directions from the hips, as this will make movement swifter and more stable. The power for striking also comes from the hips.

There is an old saying, "Don't strike with the hands, strike with the legs. Don't strike with the legs, strike with the hips. Don't strike with the hips strike with the heart." The important thing to remember is concentrate one's centre of balance, power, and movement in the hips. Aim to move silently, swiftly, and strongly, without any extraneous movement. This requires much practise.

All beginners and advanced practitioners alike must be drilled thoroughly in *taisabaki,* as this forms the foundation for technical development. The five kinds of footwork employed in Naginata are 1. *okuri-ashi*, 2. *ayumi-ashi*, 3. *hiraki-ashi*, 4. *fumikae-ashi*, and 5. *tsugi-ashi*. The feet should spaced at shoulder-width apart in all cases.

1. Okuri-ashi

Movement in any direction can be accomplished quickly and smoothly utilising *okuri-ashi*. It is also used when making an attack, and is the most common form of footwork in Naginata for both offensive and defensive movements.

1. When advancing, move from the front foot followed by the rear foot (see a).
2. When retreating, move from the rear foot followed by the front foot (see b).

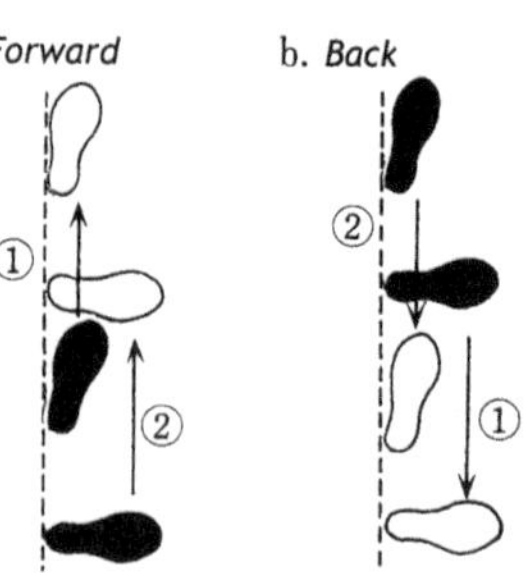

2. Ayumi-ashi

Ayumi-ashi is alternating the left and right feet just as in normal walking. It is useful for covering large distances quickly in attack and defence.

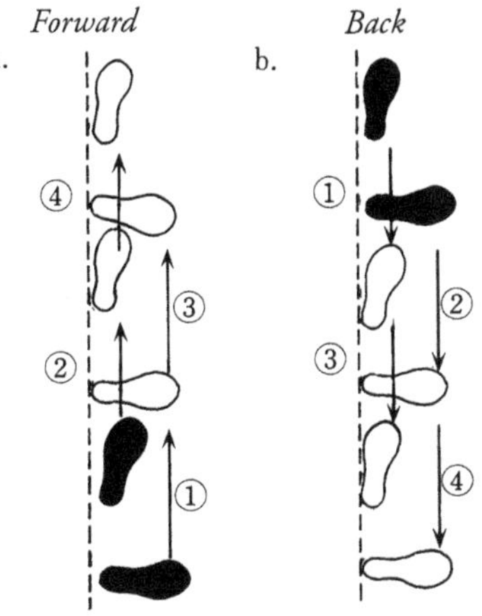

1. Alternate the feet as you would when walking while maintaining a slightly lowered but balanced posture.
2. When advancing, draw the back foot up first (a), and move from the front foot when retreating (b).

3. Hiraki-ashi

Hiraki-ashi is used for attacking the opponent from a diagonal or sideways, or when trying to dodge an attack. It is important to keep balanced and upright when employing *hiraki-ashi*.

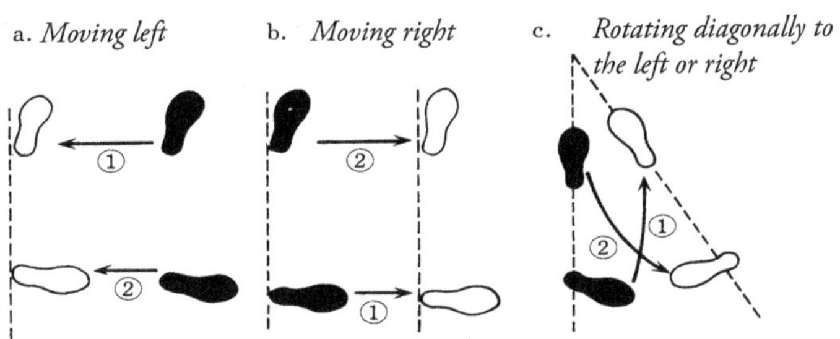

1. When employing *hiraki-ashi* to move to the left, lead from the left foot followed by the right (a).
2. Do the opposite when moving to the right (b).
3. When rotating diagonally to the left or right (c), step diagonally forward from the back foot, and pivot the body around to face the opposite direction.

4. Fumikae-ashi

This method of footwork is used for changing direction 180° on the spot during attack or defence.

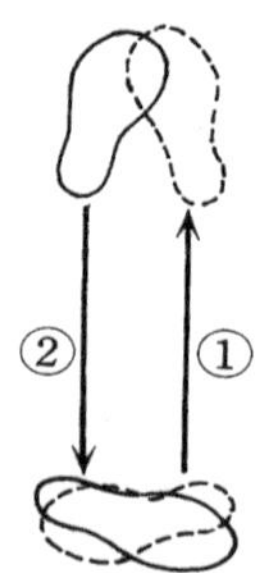

1. Bring the back foot up to the front foot, then immediately pull the front foot back to the rear. The opposite is also useful for dodging the opponent's attacks to the lower body.

5. Tsugi-ashi

Tsugi-ashi is mainly used when attempting to strike from further away. The back foot is pulled in close to the front foot, then the front foot immediately takes a big step forward. It can be used for advancing or retreating.

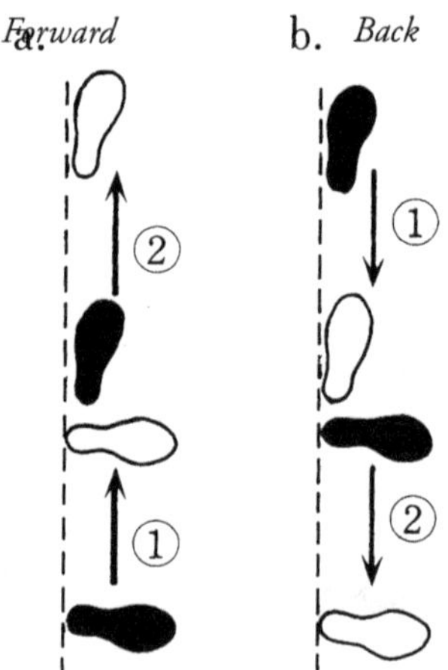

1. When advancing, bring your back foot up to your front foot, then immediately step out from the front foot.
2. When retreating, bring the front foot back level with the rear foot, then immediately take a large step back from the rear foot.

Benkei's Pointers

When instructing groups, first get students to assume *chudan* by giving the command "*chudan ni kamae.*" At the command of "*mae*" (advance) everybody should take one step forward with *okuri-ashi*. To retreat, say "*ato*". Note that the instructor moves the opposite way to their commands to create a mirror image with the students. Take the students through the different types of footwork by giving commands such as "*ayumi-ashi...mae*" (advance with *ayumi-ashi*), "*ayumi-ashi... ato*" (retreat with *ayumi-ashi*), "*hidari e hirake*" (*hiraki-ashi* to the left), "*migi e hirake*" (*hiraki-ashi* to the right), and so on. Also, practise moving in the various *kamae*. Another method of drilling *taisabaki* is for the instructor to move in a certain way and have the students follow without verbal instruction. For example, if the instructor was to move back with *ayumi-ashi* the students would be required to follow by moving forward with *ayumi-ashi*.

Another effective way to practise *taisabaki* is in pairs. Partners face each other in *chudan*. One person takes the lead and moves in various directions employing the various types of footwork, while the other follows as closely as possible making sure that they always maintain the correct distance (*maai*) with *monouchi* connected to *monouchi*. Eye-contact must always be maintained. Both students get used to moving in sync with their opponent and keeping at the correct striking distance.

Drills for *taisabaki* are usually conducted at the beginning of the training session. The importance of learning correct body movement cannot be overstated, and much time should be dedicated to giving students a firm grounding in this.

Part 4: Happo-buri (Practice Swings)

Happo-buri is the act of swinging the *naginata* vertically, diagonally, and horizontally. The point of *happo-buri* is to learn to cut correctly with the blade on various angles, master basic body movements and footwork for striking, correct grip, and how to wield the *naginata* smoothly. It is beneficial to practise *happo-buri* at the beginning of a training session and at the end as a cool-down exercise. *Happo-buri* is usually the first thing a beginner is taught, and is an essential part of training for all levels. *Joge-buri*, *naname-buri*, *yoko-buri*, *naname-buri-shita-kara*, and *furikaeshi* are performed respectively several times each.

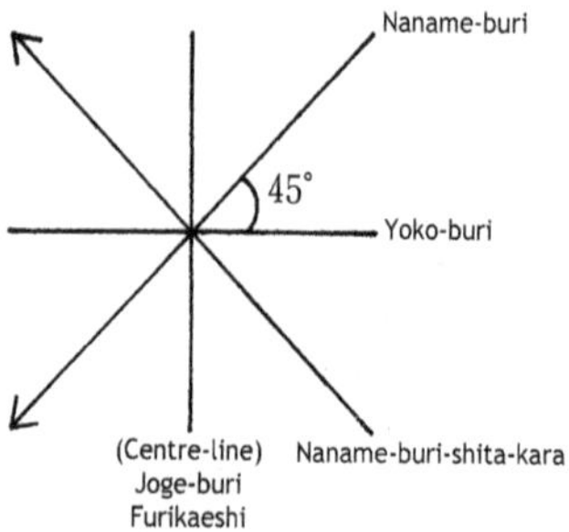

1. Joge-buri (Vertical Swing)

Starting from *chudan*, swing the *naginata* up and down in a vertical line down the centre of the body.

1. From *chudan*, bring the back foot up while lifting the *naginata* overhead, with the hips facing the front at the end of the upswing. (Photo 2).
2. Then pull the same foot back while bringing the *naginata* down in a large straight arc, turning the body to the side once again with the downswing. Keep a relaxed but firm grip on the *naginata* without opening the hands up. (Photo 3).
3. This up-down motion is repeated many times. The grip can be changed overhead and the other foot pulled back so that the swing comes down on the opposite side. As with all techniques in Naginata, it is preferable to be proficient at both the left and right sides.

1. From *chudan*,

2. Lift the *naginata* overhead while drawing the back foot level with the front foot.

3. Swing down in a large arc while pulling the back foot back again. Repeat 2 & 3 several times.

2. Naname-buri (Diagonal Swing)

From *chudan*, assume *hasso* and immediately swing down through the centre on a 45° angle. Using *hiraki-ashi* or *fumikae-ashi*, swing down alternately from the left and right. *Naname-buri-shita-kara* (*naname-buri* from below) is a diagonal swing going up instead of down, but still adheres to the same trajectory. To execute *naname-buri-shita-kara*, assume *wakigamae* and cut up alternately from the left and right sides through the centre on an angle of 45°, with *hiraki-ashi* or *fumikae-ashi*.

3. Yoko-buri (Horizontal Swing)

From *chudan*, assume *wakigamae* and swing around horizontally to the left and right alternately using *fumikae-ashi* or *hiraki-ashi*. The swing should be at *do* height, and the *naginata* level with the blade facing sideways. Left and right swings should be exactly the same. Note that *wakigamae* and the swing are at a slightly different height.

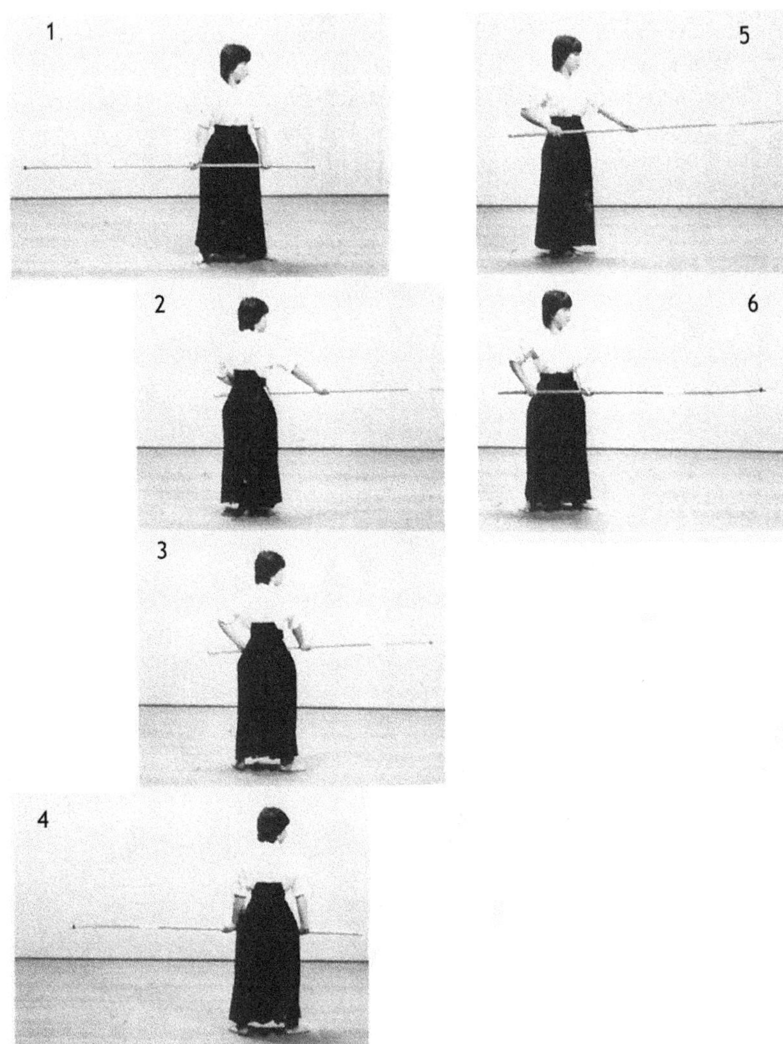

4. Furikaeshi (Windmill Swing)

This swing is representative of Naginata in that it is large and circular.

1. From *chudan*, draw the front foot back and face the hips to the front.
2. Drop the *kissaki* down the side and then back. Bring both hands to meet directly overhead.
3. *Mochikae* so that the left hand goes toward the *ishizuki* end while stepping out with the right foot, and turn the hips to the side as the *naginata* is brought down in a large straight arc. *Furikaeshi* is executed alternately on the left and right sides. Pull the left (front) foot in and step out with the right; pull right (front) foot in and step out with the left...

Part 5: Practice Strikes (-uchi)

All strikes must be to a designated target area (*datotsu-bui*), made with correct posture, in full spirits (*kiai*), and with the correct part (*monouchi*) of the *ha-bu* or *e-bu*. The name of the intended target must be called out on impact. After executing the strike, physical and mental alertness is maintained (*zanshin*) in order to make another strike if need be, or for protection against a counter-attack. These are things that must be kept in mind when practising strikes with or without a partner.

1. Datotsu-bui (Targets)

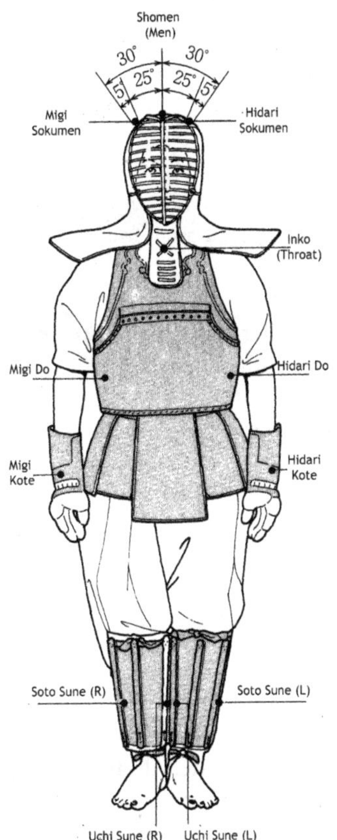

The *datotsu-bui* or stipulated target areas in Naginata are *men* (front, left, right); *do* (left, right); *sune* (left, right, both inner and outer); *kote* (left, right); *nodo* (*tsuki* to the throat). Basic methods for using the *naginata* include *furiage* (lifting the *naginata* overhead to strike); *mochikae* (swapping grip to enable attacking from the opposite side, or on a different angle); *furikaeshi* (spinning the *naginata* overhead); *kurikomi* (pulling the *naginata* in to shorten the length to strike from a closer distance); *kuridashi* (extending the *naginata* out to make attacks from a further away).

There are many variations depending on the situation, but in all cases the *monouchi* of the *ha-bu* or the *ishizuki* end must make contact with the target area to be counted as valid. (The *ishizuki* is only allowed for strikes to the *sune*. *Ishizuki-tsuki* to the throat is now prohibited.)

Benkei's Pointers

Furiage

This is the most basic movement when attempting to strike *men*, *kote*, or *sune*. From *chudan*, step forward from the back foot and lift the *naginata* overhead with the hips facing the front. Then step forward again with the other foot, and turn the body back to the side as the *naginata* is brought down for the strike.

Mochikae

A characteristic movement used for changing *kamae* to strike *men*, *do*, *kote*, and *sune*. From *chudan*, swap the position of the right hand with the left and assume *hasso*, *jodan*, or *wakigamae*.

Furikaeshi

Furikaeshi is used when attempting to strike *men*, *kote*, or *sune*. From *chudan*, the *naginata* is spun overhead in a large circular movement when launching into an attack.

Kurikomi

Shortening the length of the *naginata* is used after thrusting, when receiving or blocking, and for making an attack from close quarters.

Kuridashi

Kuridashi is extending the *naginata* out, making it longer to increase striking or thrusting range.

2. Striking

All strikes must be executed accurately, with correct posture, in full spirit, and with the body and *naginata* in perfect unison. Call out the name of the target in a loud, concentrated voice as the strike is made. Always look straight ahead, and not at the target you are striking. This is the same whether you are actually striking a training partner or practising solo.

Chapter 3: Practical Drills Without a Partner

a) *Furiage-men-uchi*

1. From *chudan*,
2. Draw the rear foot up while raising the *naginata* overhead with hips facing the front. Ensure that the little finger closest to the *ishizuki* does not stick out, and that the elbow is not fully extended.
3. Then, step through with the back foot as the *naginata* is brought down through the body's centre in a large straight arc to complete the strike. The body should be facing sideways at the conclusion of the strike. Shout "*men*" in a loud voice. The rear hand grips the *naginata* firmly, and finishes up positioned at the lower abdomen.

b) *Furikaeshi-men-uchi*

1. From *chudan*,
2. Draw the front foot back so that the hips are facing the front as the *kissaki* drops back and down to the side. Bring both hands together so that they meet and overlap directly above the head.
3. Swap grip so that the left hand goes toward the *ishizuki*. Simultaneously step out with the right foot, and turn the hips to the side as the *naginata* is brought down in a large straight arc. The bottom hand should end up lightly touching the area directly below the navel.

c) *Sokumen-uchi*

1. From *chudan*,
2. *Mochikae* into *hasso*.
3. Bring the rear foot through while pivoting on the front foot to strike *men*. (The body will be facing the opposite side to when the technique was initiated.) Shout "*men*" as the strike is executed. At the completion of the strike, the rear hand should be tucked snugly into the solar-plexus, and the front forearm should be in contact with the *e-bu*. As *sokumen* is a diagonal cut, the *ha-bu* should be angled diagonally down.

d) *Sune-uchi*

1. From *chudan*,
2. *Mochikae* into *hasso*.
3. Bring the rear foot through while pivoting on the front foot to strike *sune*. (The body will be facing the opposite side to when the technique was initiated.) Shout "*sune*" as the strike is made. The back hand should be tucked into the solar-plexus, and the front forearm should be in contact with the *e-bu*. The front knee should be slightly bent. Make sure that the feet are not too close together, and that the front knee does not come past the toes. The *ha-bu* faces diagonally down. Take care to actually strike *sune* with the cutting edge of the *ha-bu*, not the side.

e) *Furiage-sune-uchi*

1. From *chudan*,
2. Bring the rear foot to the front while lifting the *naginata* overhead and facing the hips to the front. Ensure that the little finger of the hand closest to the *ishizuki* is not protruding, and that the elbow is not fully extended.
3. Then bring the back foot through again as the *naginata* swings down to strike *sune*. The body should end up facing sideways again. The rear hand should grip the *naginata* firmly and be in contact with the lower abdomen area. Shout "*sune*" as the strike is made.

f) *E-zune-uchi*

1. From *chudan*,
2. Throw the *e-bu* (*kuridashi*) out while pivoting on the rear (or front) foot to strike with the *e-bu*. Bend both knees and maintain plenty of space between your feet and hands. Shout "*sune*" as the strike is made.

g) *Do-uchi*

1. From *chudan*,
2. *Mochikae* and assume *wakigamae*.
3. Step through from the rear foot while pivoting on the front, and strike *do*. The rear hand should rest firmly between the hip and navel. The *ha-bu* should be on a slight upward diagonal.

h) *Furiage-kote-uchi*

1. From *chudan*,
2. Draw the rear foot up to the front foot as the *naginata* is lifted overhead with the hips facing to the front. Ensure that the little finger closest to the *ishizuki* is not protruding, and that the elbow is not fully extended. The *ishizuki* be lifted no higher than chin height.
3. Step out with the front foot as the *naginata* is brought down to strike *kote*. The body should be facing sideways again. Shout "*kote*" as the strike is made. The *kissaki* should finish at a height slightly lower than *chudan*.

i) *Furikaeshi-kote-uchi*

1. From *chudan*,
2. Do the same as *furikaeshi-men*, but strike *kote* instead.

j) *Mochikae-kote-uchi*

1. From *chudan*,
2. *Mochikae* into *hasso*,
3. Draw your rear foot through while pivoting on the front foot, spin your body around and strike *kote*.

k) *Tsuki*

The thrust to the throat is a very powerful and frightening technique. If not executed correctly, it could easily result in injury to your opponent. Therefore, it is important to attempt this technique only when you are able to use the *naginata* skilfully. *Tsuki* is prohibited until high school in Japan, and *tsuki* to the throat with the *ishizuki* is no longer permissible. *Tsuki* can be executed directly (*chokutotsu*) from *chudan*, or by bringing the *naginata* in first (*kurikomi*).

Chokutotsu

1. From *chudan*,
2. Grip the *naginata* firmly with the rear hand and slide it forward from the back thigh to the lower abdomen area. The grip of the front hand should not be open, but light enough to allow the *naginata* to slide through. Stepping forward with *okuri-ashi* from the front foot while thrusting, turn the *ha-bu* outward and tighten grip on impact. Shout "*tsuki*". (Take care that the feet are not too close together.)

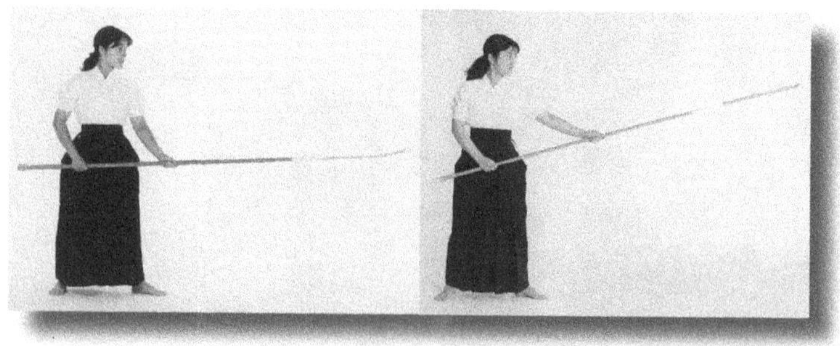

Kurikomi-tsuki

1. From *chudan*,
2. Pull the rear hand back so that it stops at shoulder height. Let the *naginata* slide back through the front hand (*kurikomi*) into *gedan*.
3. Then, stepping forward with *okuri-ashi*, thrust the *naginata* out by sliding it through the front hand until it hits the throat. Just as the *kissaki* makes contact, turn the *ha-bu* outward and tighten the grip. Shout "*tsuki*".
4. Note that this technique used to be done with the blade facing upward, but now the blade faces downward at all time.

Benkei's Pointers

Always shout the name of the target you are striking. When practising strikes by yourself, imagine the opponent is the same height as you, and strike accordingly. This will change when you have an actual partner to train with. Practise repeatedly until your *naginata*, body, and spirit (*kiai*) are all in unison. When doing *mochikae* before an attack, make sure that your body doesn't face the front as you change *kamae*. Regardless of how experienced you may be, always return to the basics (*kihon*) and check you are doing the most fundamental techniques correctly. Keep your posture straight, and make your techniques large and precise. That way it will be an easy step to make them your techniques smaller and faster but with correct form.

All of the *kihon* strikes outlined here can be practised alone or in groups. When instructing a group of students, the standard procedure at the beginning of training is to go over footwork first, followed by *happoburi* and then striking practice. The instructor stands at the front of the dojo, and the students all take *chudan* with *kissaki* pointed at the teacher who will then give commands to strike. For example, at the command of "*men wo* ***UTE!***" (strike *furiage-men*), the instructor will then drop the *kissaki* down as if to show an opening for *men*, and the students will strike *men* together. When the instructor lifts the *kissaki* back up, this is the signal to move back, ready for the next command. "*Men wo* ***ute!***" (strike *furiage-men*); "*sokumen wo* ***ute!***" (*mochikae* into *hasso* and strike *men*); "*sayu-men wo* ***ute!***" (*mochikae* into *hasso* and strike left then right *sokumen*); "*sune wo* ***ute!***" (*mochikae* into *hasso* and strike *sune*); "*furiage(te)-sune wo* ***ute***"; "*men-sune wo* ***ute!***" (strike *furiage-men*, then *mochikae* into *hasso* and strike *sune*); "*furikaeshi-men wo* ***ute!***", "*kote wo* ***ute!***" "*Inko wo* ***tsuke***"... And any number of combinations, in any order... Note that "*ute*" is written here in bold as this word is accentuated when the command is given.

Chapter 3: Practical Drills Without a Partner

From *chudan-no-kamae*

Sune wo ute!
Kote wo ute!
Furiage(te)-sune wo ute!

Inko tsuke!

Group kihon practice.

Part 6: Defensive Blocks

Next, we will look at how to use the *ha-bu* or *e-bu to* defend or block against attacks. Learning how to block will enable training routines with a partner.

1. Blocking with the Ha-bu

a) Blocking *sokumen* and *do* (L&R)

1. From *chudan*,
2. *Kurikomi* while stepping back with *okuri-ashi*. The left elbow should be tucked lightly into the side of the body, and the back hand rests on the upper thigh. Block any strike to the *men*, *sokumen*, or *do* with the *shinogi* (side of the blade) at the *monouchi*.

Blocking a strike to sokumen

Blocking a strike to do

Blocking a strike to sokumen
(L) (R)

b) Blocking *sune* (L&R)

1. From *chudan*,
2. *Kurikomi* while stepping back with *okuri-ashi*. Drop the *kissaki* down (like *gedan*) and block the strike to *sune* with the *shinogi* (side of the blade) at the *monouchi*. Tighten your grip on impact.

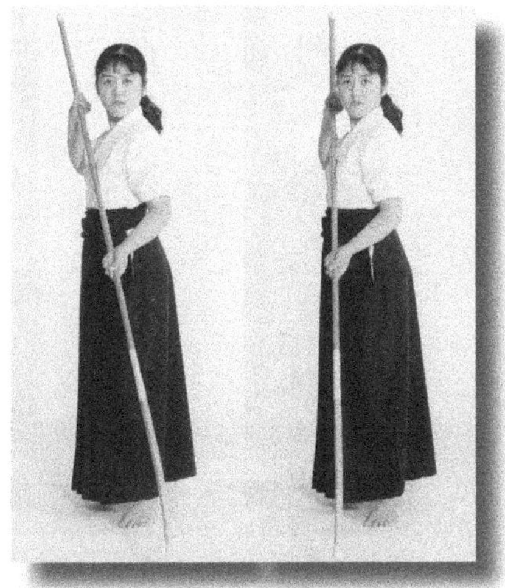

Blocking a strike to sune
(L) (R)

2. Blocking with the E-bu

a) Blocking *men*

1. From *chudan*,
2. Draw the front foot back to the same position as the back foot. At the same time turn the body to the front and lift the *naginata* above the forehead. Block the incoming *men* strike with the centre of the *e-bu*. The hands are not spread too far apart, nor are they too close together. Do not stretch the arms out too much in front of the forehead, or too high above it. Also, take care not to hold the *naginata* too low lest you be struck in the head by accident.

Blocking sokumen

b. Blocking *sokumen* & *sune*

1. From *chudan*,
2. Draw the front foot back while pivoting on the back foot and turning your body to face the opposite direction. At the same time, the *e-bu* is thrust out (*kuridashi*) and the *ishizuki* pulled in front of the face to block the strike to *men* with the *monouchi*. Tighten your grip on impact.

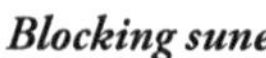

Blocking sune

Once you are able to strike and block, you will be able to train with a partner. This is called *sotai*. The next chapter will outline various practice patterns for training in pairs or in a group. Before delving into the techniques, it is necessary to know how to bow to your partner and show the necessary courtesies.

1. From *shizentai*, bow to your partner without dropping eye-contact.
2. Assume *ai-chudan* (mutual *chudan*).
3. Alternate between the striking role and the blocking role.
4. When finished, return to *ai-chudan*, then draw the front foot back and assume *shizentai*.
5. Bow once more, maintaining eye-contact from start to finish.

CHAPTER 4
PRACTICAL DRILLS WITH A PARTNER

A Naginata class for schoolgirls in the 1930s.

Part 1: Uchikaeshi

This chapter will outline how to employ the strikes and blocks in attacking and receiving sequences. To start with, *uchikaeshi* is one of the most basic exercises practised in Naginata. It helps the practitioner develop an understanding of *maai* (distancing), body movement and footwork, breathing technique, correct grip and application of power in the strike, and so on. These are all extremely important elements for using the *naginata* effectively. It also teaches the practitioner appropriate striking opportunities, precision in technique execution, and it helps develop the muscules and stamina necessary for training. Therefore, *uchikaeshi* is a fundamental exercise which is indispensable for beginners and advanced practitioners alike. It is usually practised at the beginning and end of the training session, and can be done with or without *bogu* (armour).

Order of the strikes for *uchikaeshi*:

Shomen ⇒ *Sayu-men* (L&R) ⇒ *Sayu-sune* ⇒ *Chudan* ⇒ *Shomen*
(*Furiage*) ⇒ (*Mochikae* x 2) ⇒ (*Mochikae* x 2) ⇒ (*Furiage*)
"Men!" *"Men-men!"* *"Sune-sune!"* *"Men!"*

The strikes are made while advancing. More advanced practitioners can repeat the same order while retreating as well. The attacker (*uchikata*) should continue striking as accurately as possible without stopping, preferably doing one sequence in one breath. The receiver (*ukekata*) is responsible for maintaining correct distance, and must assist the the attacker to strike vigorously with precision. The receiver moves back when the attacker is advancing, and moves forward when the attacker is retreating.

Uchikaeshi is an exercise designed to benefit both the attacker and the receiver. *Ukekata* is not just providing the targets for *uchikata* to hit, but must also consider and master many of the fundamentals of Naginata in order to receive the attacks properly. It is a learning experience for both sides, and cooperation is essential for safety and improvement.

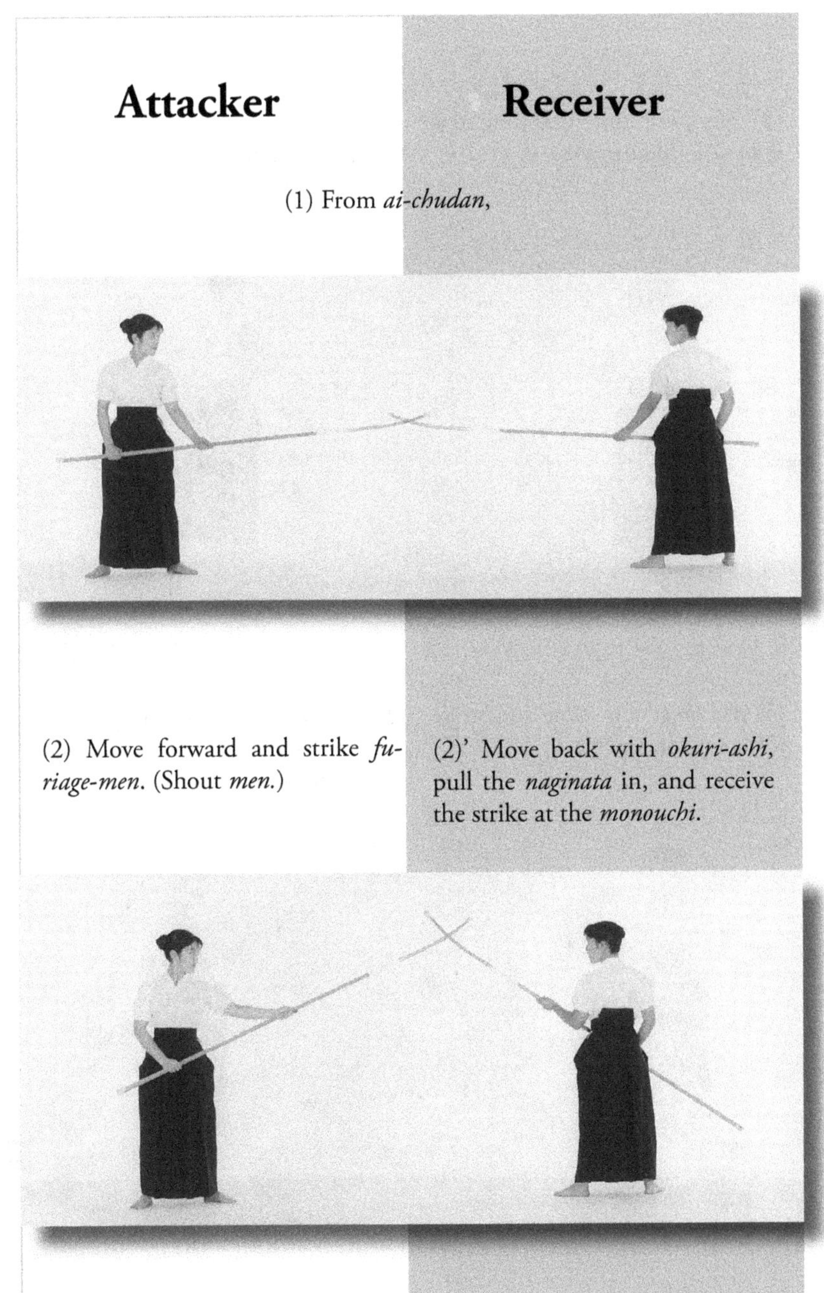

Attacker	Receiver
(1) From *ai-chudan*,	
(2) Move forward and strike *furiage-men*. (Shout *men.*)	(2)' Move back with *okuri-ashi*, pull the *naginata* in, and receive the strike at the *monouchi*.

(3) *Mochikae* into *hasso* and strike *sokumen*. (Shout *men*.)

(3)' Move back by pivoting on the right (back foot) and block *men* with the *monouchi* of the *e-bu*.

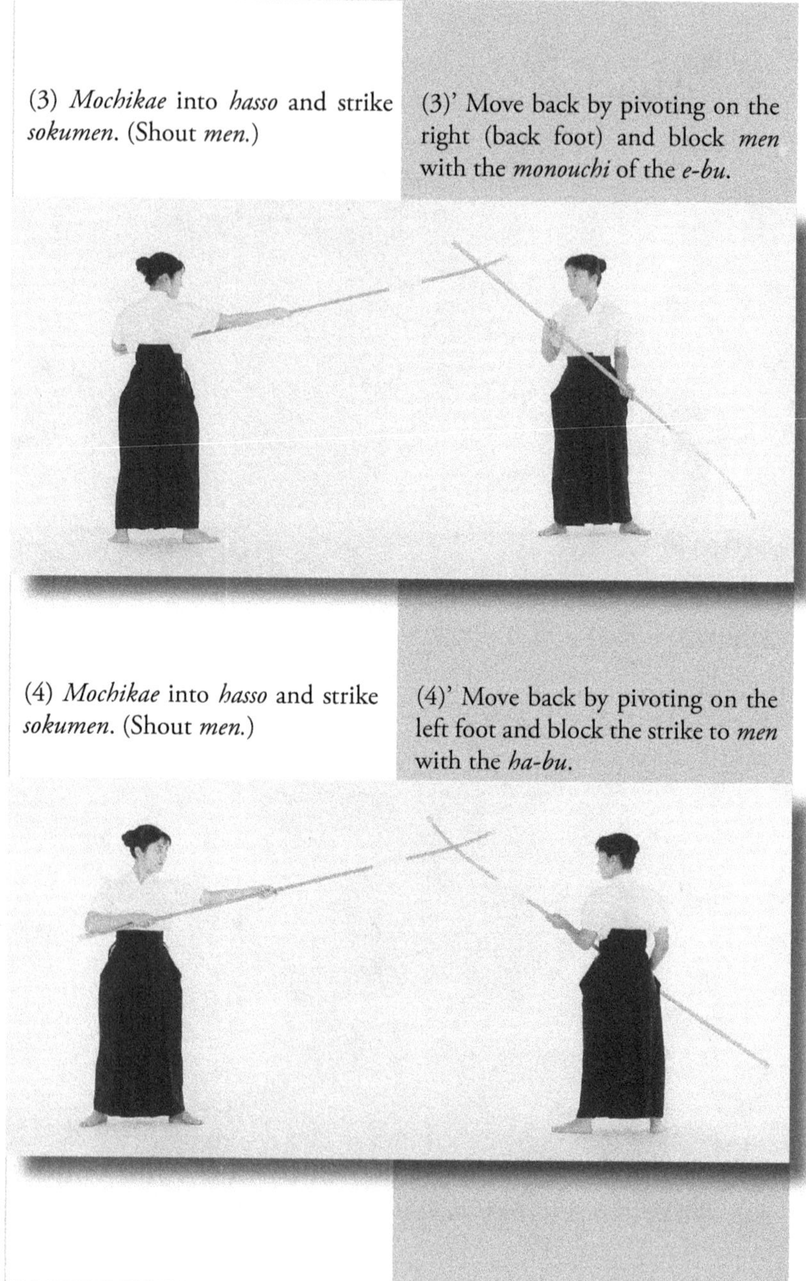

(4) *Mochikae* into *hasso* and strike *sokumen*. (Shout *men*.)

(4)' Move back by pivoting on the left foot and block the strike to *men* with the *ha-bu*.

(5) *Mochikae* into *hasso* and strike *sune*. (Shout *sune*.)

(5)' Move back by pivoting on the right foot and block the strike with the *monouchi* of the *e-bu*.

(6) *Mochikae* into *hasso* and strike *sune*. (Shout *sune*.)

(6)' Move back by pivoting on the left foot and block the strike to *sune* with the *ha-bu*.

(7) Lift the *kissaki* up and assume *chudan* on the spot.

(7)' Retreat to adjust the distance and assume *chudan*.

(8) Move forward and strike *furiage-men*. (Shout *men.*)

(8)' Move the front (left) foot back level with the right, and block the strike to *men* with the centre of the *e-bu*.

(9) Retreat to adjust the distance and assume *chudan*.

(9)' Drop the *kissaki* down and assume *chudan*.

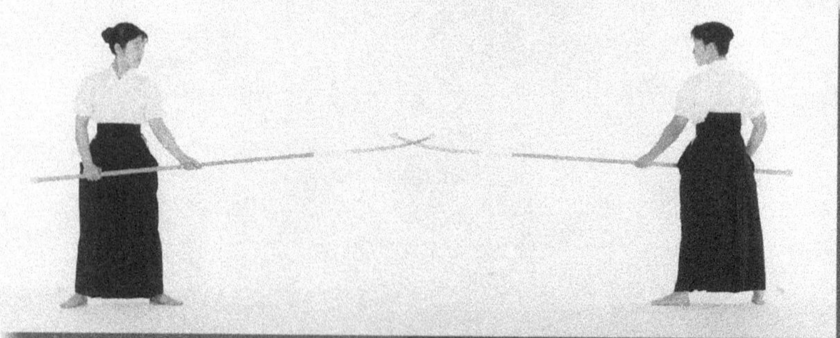

After finishing the sequence, either repeat the techniques in the same order while retreating, or change roles.

Chapter 4: Practical Drills With a Partner

Benkei's Pointers

Attacker:

1. Always maintain eye-contact, and don't look down at *sune* when striking.
2. Do *uchikaeshi* slowly and accurately rather than quickly and imprecisely. Make each movement as pronounced and exact as possible. For example, when assuming *hasso*, make sure that the body is side-on before launching in for the strike. This is not to say that you should stop each time you assume *hasso*. Try to make the sequence flow.
3. The cutting edge of the *ha-bu* should connect with the target on the correct angle. You can't cut with the side of the blade.
4. The *naginata* and body should move in unison. The strike should be made with the whole body, not just the arms.
5. Endeavour to complete the sequence in one breath. This will improve stamina and cardiovascular strength, and the practitioner will learn how to string techniques together rather than stopping and starting.

Receiver:

1. The receiver encourages the attacker to strike as cleanly as possible.
2. Always take care to maintain the correct striking distance. If the receiver is too close, the attacker's technique will become small, cramped, and deep rather than expansive and flowing. If the the attacker is too far away, striking will become disjointed, unbalanced, and shallow. The receiver should keep the distance just right to encourage large strikes but enabling the *monouchi* to reach the target. Work with attackers, not against them.
3. Do not move before the attack is made. Wait until the attacker has assumed the *kamae* and has sttarted to make the attack. This will teach you to observe the opponnet properly and move with speed.
4. When receiving with *bogu* on, make the targets clear and easy to hit. When practising without *bogu*, block each strike with the *monouchi* slightly off target. For example, when receiving the first *men* strike, move back with *okuri-ashi* and pull the *naginata* in (*kurikomi*) with the *monouchi* receiving the strike slightly off centre, at the point where your head was before moving. This is also applicable for the *sayu-men* and *sayu-sune* strikes.
5. Also, try to receive the sequence of strikes in one breath for the same reasons as the attacker.

1
2
3
4
5
6
7

Part 2: Naginata Techniques

This section will cover the plethora of techniques (*waza*) used in Naginata. All of the techniques can be practised with or without *bogu*. It is advisable to try without armour to begin with in order to learn the correct distance and timing. Naginata techniques can be divided into two broad categories: the first is *shikake-waza* (off-the-line techniques initiated by the attacker), and *oji-waza* (counterattacks). The following is a list of sub-categories of *waza* found in these two groups:

Shikake-waza:

• ***Fumikomi-waza:*** Direct attack, forwards and backwards.
• ***Nidan-waza & sandan-waza:*** Two or three consecutive strikes.
• ***Harai-waza:*** Deflecting the opponent's *naginata* then striking.
• ***Debana-waza:*** Technique of striking just as the opponent is about to.
• ***Hiki-waza:*** Striking while going backwards from *seriai*, or close-quarters.

Oji-waza:

• ***Uke-waza:*** Blocking the opponent's attack with the *ha-bu* or *e-bu,* then making an immediate counterattack.
• ***Nuki-waza:*** Dodging the opponent's attack by moving the whole body or the target out of range, and then making a counterattack.
• ***Uchiotoshi-waza:*** Striking the opponent's *naginata* down with the *ha-bu* or the *e-bu* when they are defending or making an attack, and then striking at their unbalanced posture.
• ***Makiotoshi-waza:*** Using the curvature of the blade (*sori*) to flick the opponent's *naginata* away prior to, during, or after their attack, and then executing a counterattack. (Depending on timing, this can also be classed as *shikake-waza.*)
• ***Ukenagashi-waza:*** Parrying the opponent's attack and letting their *naginata* slide away, using the momentum of the deflection to counterattack.

Shikake-waza must be executed with confidence and conviction. When employing *oji-waza*, the opponent's initial attack is nullified by being blocked, parried or avoided, followed immediately with a counterattack which takes advantage of the attacker's unbalanced posture. *Oji-waza* is only successful if the counterattack is a positive, calculated move as opposed to a passive reaction. Let us now look at possible training sequences for the techniques listed above. First, *shikake-waza.*

1. Shikake-waza

a) *Ni & Sandan-waza*

Nidan-waza and *sandan-waza* are techniques where two or three strikes are made continuously in one sequence. For example, if your opponent blocks or avoids your first attack, or your strike is inadequate, follow up immediately with another. Try to make each strike count using your legs well, and deliver the attack in a way that is vigorous and unrelenting. Ideally, you should be able to judge the failure of your initial attack and release another strike instantly without pausing to think about it. The following are some examples that can be practised with a partner, with or without *bogu.*

Attacker	Receiver
Men-sune-uchi	
(1) From *ai-chudan,*	
(2) Strike *furiage-men.* (Shout *men.*)	(2)' Retreat with *okuri-ashi, kurikomi,* and block *men* with *ha-bu.*
(3) *Mochikae* into *hasso* and strike *sune.* (Shout *sune.*)	(3)' Retreat by pivoting on the right foot and block with the *e-bu.*
(4) Separate. Both assume *migi-chudan.*	

(5) Strike *furiage-men.* (Shout *men.*)	(5)' Retreat with *okuri-ashi, kurikomi*, and block *men* with *ha-bu.*
(6) *Mochikae* into *hasso* and strike *sune* (Shout *sune.*)	(6)' Retreat by pivoting on the left foot and block with the *e-bu.*

(7) Separate. Both assume *chudan.*
Swap roles and repeat.

Sune-sokumen-uchi

(1) From *ai-chudan,*

(2) Strike *furiage-sune.* (Shout *sune.*)	(2)' Retreat with *okuri-ashi, kurikomi*, and block *sune* with *ha-bu.*
(3) *Mochikae* into *hasso* and strike *sokumen.* (Shout *men.*)	(3)' Retreat by pivoting on the right foot and block with the *e-bu.*

(4) Separate. Both assume *migi-chudan.*

(5) Strike *furiage-sune.* (Shout *sune.*)	(5)' Retreat with *okuri-ashi, kurikomi*, and block *sune* with *ha-bu.*
(6) *Mochikae* into *hasso* and strike *sokumen* (Shout *men.*)	(6)' Retreat by pivoting on the left foot and block with the *e-bu.*

(7) Separate. Both assume *chudan.*
Swap roles and repeat.

Men-sune-do-uchi

(1) From *ai-chudan*,

(2) Strike *men*. (Shout *men*.)

(2)' Retreat with *okuri-ashi*, *kuriko-mi*, and block *men* with *ha-bu*.

(3) *Mochikae* into *hasso* and strike *sokumen*. (Shout *men*.)

(3)' Retreat by pivoting on the right foot and block with the *e-bu*.

(4) *Mochikae* into *wakigamae* and strike *do*. (Shout *do*.)

(4)' Retreat by pivoting on the left foot and block with the *ha-bu*.

(5) Separate. Both assume *chudan*.

Sune-sokumen-sune-uchi

(1) From *ai-chudan*,

(2) Strike *furiage-sune*. (Shout *sune*.)

(2)' Retreat with *okuri-ashi*, *kurikomi*, and block *sune* with *ha-bu*.

(3) *Mochikae* into *hasso* and strike *sokumen*. (Shout *men*.)

(3)' Retreat by pivoting on the left foot and block with the *e-bu*.

(4) *Mochikae* into *hasso* and strike *sune*. (Shout *sune*).

(4)' Retreat by pivoting on the right foot and block with the *ha-bu*.

(5) Separate. Both assume *chudan*.

Devise your own combinations for *ni-dan* and *san-dan* techniques and incorporate them into your training.

Benkei's Pointers

Maai

When facing an opponent, the question of distance is of the utmost importance. *Maai* is the term used to refer to distance. It not only means the spatial gap between two opponents, but also timing. The standard *maai* is called *uchi-ma*. This is the distance in which you are able to strike your opponent by taking one step forward, or avoid an attack by taking one step back.

A closer interval is called *chika-ma*. From *chika-ma*, one's strikes can easily reach the opponent, but they can also reach you, and is thus a dangerous distance to engage from. The opposite of *chika-ma* is *to-ma*, or distant interval. It is very difficult for either to make a successful strike from this distance, and is considered to be relatively safe.

Each person has a different preferred distance for engagement. This depends on the height, reach, and dexterity of each individual practitioner. The establishment of *maai* and maintaining one's own preferred distance through the relationship with the opponent is very subtle, and is often the decisive factor in winning or losing a match. *Maai* should be studied carefully.

b) *Debana-waza*

Debana-waza are techniques in which the opponent is struck down just as they are starting an attack. In other words, it is to take the initiative and strike them first. A good indicator of an opponent's intention to strike is when their *kissaki* starts to move up, or strays away from the centreline. When employing *debana-waza* take care not to make the strike too small. Use your whole body in the strike, rather than just jabbing at the target with your hands.

Attacker	Receiver
(Rising *kissaki*)	
(1) From *ai-chudan*,	
(2) Start to strike *men*. (*Kissaki* begins to rise.)	(2)' Quickly *mochikae* into *hasso*, move to the side with *hiraki-ashi* and strike *sune* (Shout *sune*.)
(3) Move back and assume *hidari-chudan*.	(3)' Move back and assume *migi-chudan*.
(4) Start to strike *men*. (*Kissaki* begins to rise.)	(4)' Quickly *mochikae* into *hasso*, move to the side with *hiraki-ashi* and strike *sune* (Shout *sune*.)
(4) Separate. Assume *ai-chudan*.	
(Dropping *kissaki*)	
(1) From *ai-chudan*,	
(2) Start to strike *sune*. (*Kissaki* begins to drop.)	(2)' Quickly lunge forward and strike *men*. (Shout *men*.)
(3) Separate. Assume *ai-chudan*.	

Benkei's Pointers

1. To execute *debana-waza* successfully, you must be able to read your opponent's intention to attack before their movement even begins. This is a skill which requires intense concentration.
2. It is not a matter of seeing the start of the movement and then reacting. This will be too slow. Have the feeling of coaxing your opponent into making an attack, and pounce on them while they are taking the bate.
3. As soon as your opponent is about to strike, you must be bold and take the initiative to nip it in the bud without fear of being struck in the process.
3. Practice *debana-waza* in pairs with *bogu.*

c) *Harai-waza*

Harai-waza is the act of knocking the opponent's *naginata* from above or below on either the *ura* or *omote* side. (The *omote* side of the *naginata* is the right side when held in *hidari-chudan*). The moment the opponent's *kamae* is broken, an attack must be made immediately. If you stop after making the *harai*, the technique will be unsuccessful as the opponent will be able to reset their *kamae* .

Omote-harai

1. From *chudan*,
2. Use the curve of the blade (*sori*) to flick the *naginata* down while stepping back with *okuri-ashi*. The back hand should be in contact with the hip. Contact between the two *naginata* is made at the *shinogi* of the *monouchi*.

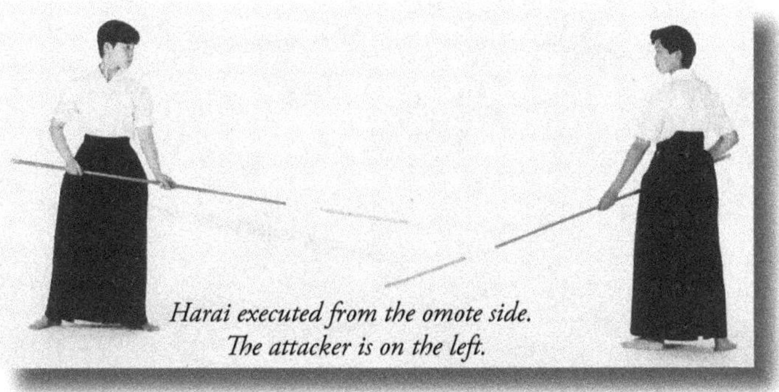

Harai executed from the omote side. The attacker is on the left.

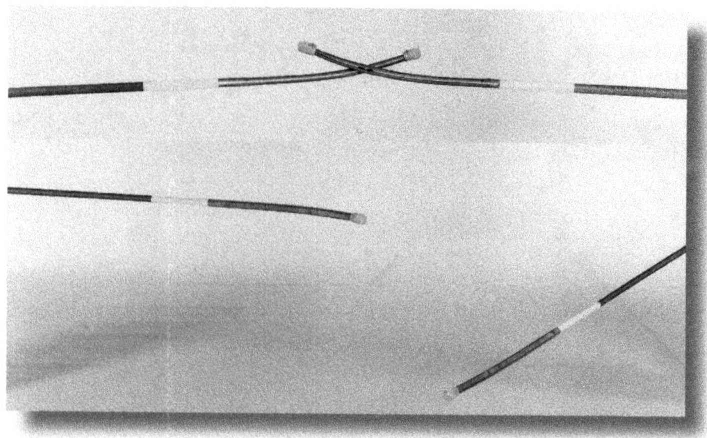

Ura-harai

1. From *chudan*,
2. Move the *kissaki* down and under the opponent's blade.
3. Using the curve (*sori*) of the *ha-bu*, flick the opponent's *naginata* down with the *shinogi* of the *monouchi* while moving back with *okuri-ashi*. The back hand should be touching the hip.

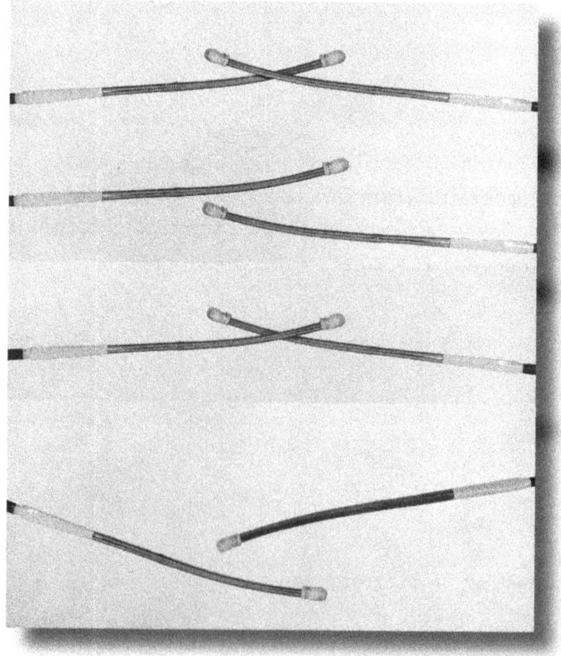

Harai with the e-bu

1. From *chudan*,

2. As you pivot on the front foot and turn to face the opposite side, strike the opponent's *naginata* on the *ura* side with the *monouchi* of the *e-bu*. The rear hand should rest lightly on the hip, and the front hand should slide in naturally as the *harai* is executed.

Harai with the ha-bu, then strike men

1. From *chudan*,

2. Lunge in and strike the opponent's *naginata* on the *omote* side with the *ha-bu*.

3. Immediately lift the *naginata* overhead and strike *men*. (Shout *men*).

4. Return to the starting position with *tsugi-ashi* while taking *chudan*.

Harai with the ha-bu, then strike kote

1. From *chudan*,

2. Bring the *kissaki* under and across the opponent's *naginata* and strike it on the *ura* side with the *ha-bu*.

3. Immediately lift the *naginata* overhead and strike *kote*. (Shout *kote*).

4. Return to the starting position with *tsugi-ashi* while taking *chudan*.

Benkei's Pointers

1. It is important to utilise the whole body when executing *harai-waza*, rather than just the arms.
2. Take care to not to use too much power in the arms as you will also find yourself unbalanced and unable to execute techniques after the *harai*. In the worst case scenario, the opponent may be able to take advantage of your unbalanced position instead.
3. Follow up with an attack the instant the *harai* is executed. In order to do this effectively, try not to deviate too far from the centreline when executing the *harai*. The point of *harai* is to unbalance the opponent and move their *kissaki* away from the centre, making it difficult for them to attack.

2. Oji-waza

a) *Uke-waza*

Uke-waza are techniques in which the opponent's attack is blocked with the *ha-bu* or *e-bu*, and immediately followed with a counterattack. As soon as the attack is started, move to an appropriate distance and receive the strike with the side of the *ha-bu* or *e-bu* at the *monouchi*. The instant the block is made, adjust the length of the *naginata* with *kuridashi* or *kurikomi* and finish with a counterattack.

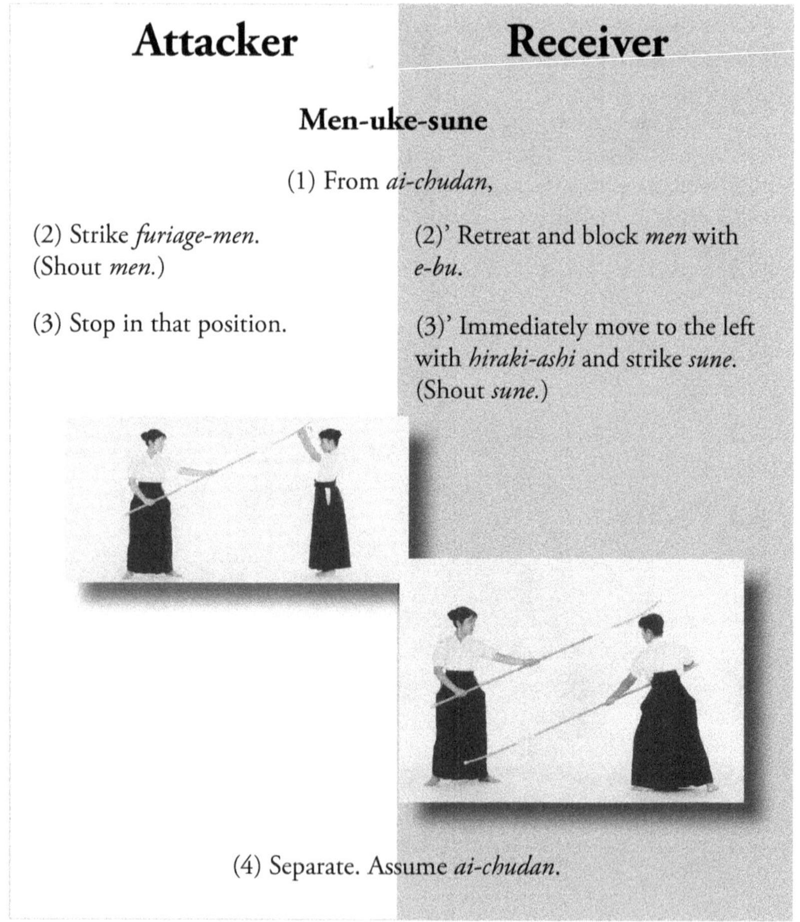

Attacker	Receiver
Men-uke-sune	
(1) From *ai-chudan*,	
(2) Strike *furiage-men*. (Shout *men*.)	(2)' Retreat and block *men* with *e-bu*.
(3) Stop in that position.	(3)' Immediately move to the left with *hiraki-ashi* and strike *sune*. (Shout *sune*.)
(4) Separate. Assume *ai-chudan*.	

b) *Nuki-waza*

Nuki-waza involves luring the opponent into making an attack, then dodging so that they "strike air" and immediately returning a counterattack. Timing is vital, and close observation of the opponent's movements is essential to execute *nuki-waza* effectively. As with all *oji-waza*, it is important that it is not merely reactive. The opponent must be coaxed into making an attack, which is then avoided and turned against them. In other words, the ability to control the opponent is a key element in the success of all *oji-waza*.

Attacker	Receiver
Sune-nuki-men	
(1) From *ai-chudan*,	
(2) *Mochikae* into *hasso* and strike *sune*. (Shout *sune*.)	(2)' Draw both feet back to dodge the strike while simultaneously lifting the *naginata* overhead.
(3)' Stay in that position.	(3) Immediately move forward with *okuri-ashi* and strike *men*. (Shout *men*.)
(4) Assume *migi-chudan*.	(4)' Assume *hidari-chudan*.
(5) *Mochikae* into *hasso* and strike *sune*. (Shout *sune*.)	(5)' Draw both feet back to dodge the strike while simultaneously lifting the *naginata* overhead.
(6) Stay in that position.	(6)' Immediately move forward with *okuri-ashi* and strike *men*. (Shout *men*.)
(7) Separate. Both assume *migi-chudan*.	

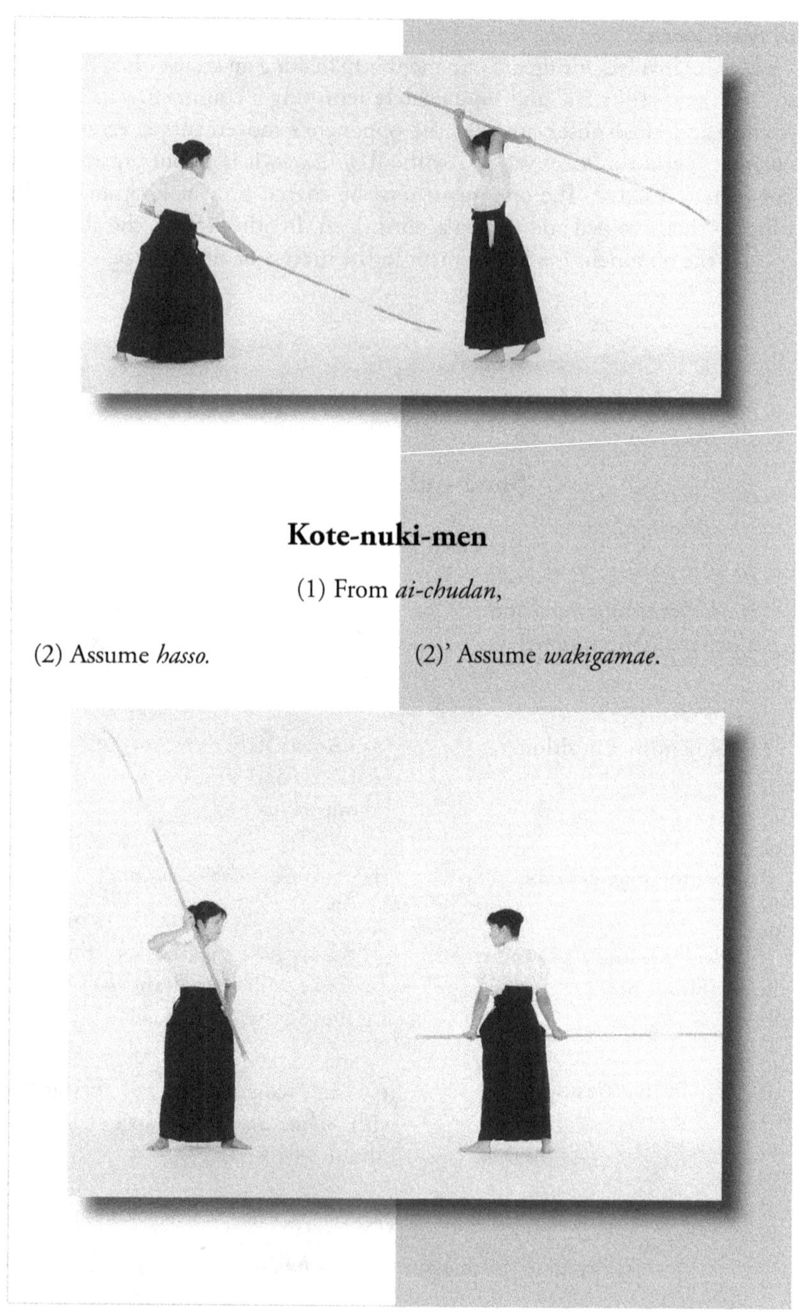

Kote-nuki-men

(1) From *ai-chudan*,

(2) Assume *hasso*.

(2)' Assume *wakigamae*.

(2) Step through with the back foot and strike *kote*. (Shout *kote*.)

(2)' Remaining in *wakigamae*, step back with *okuri-ashi* to avoid the strike to *kote*.

(3)' Stay in that position.

(3) Immediately step through with the back foot and strike *men*. (Shout *men*.)

(4) Move back and assume *hasso* again.

(4)' Move back and take *wakigamae* again.

(5) Step through with the back foot and strike *kote*. (Shout *kote*.)

(5)' Remaining in *wakigamae*, step back with *okuri-ashi* to avoid the strike to *kote*.

(6) Stay in that position.

(6)' Immediately step through with the back foot and strike *men*. (Shout *men.*)

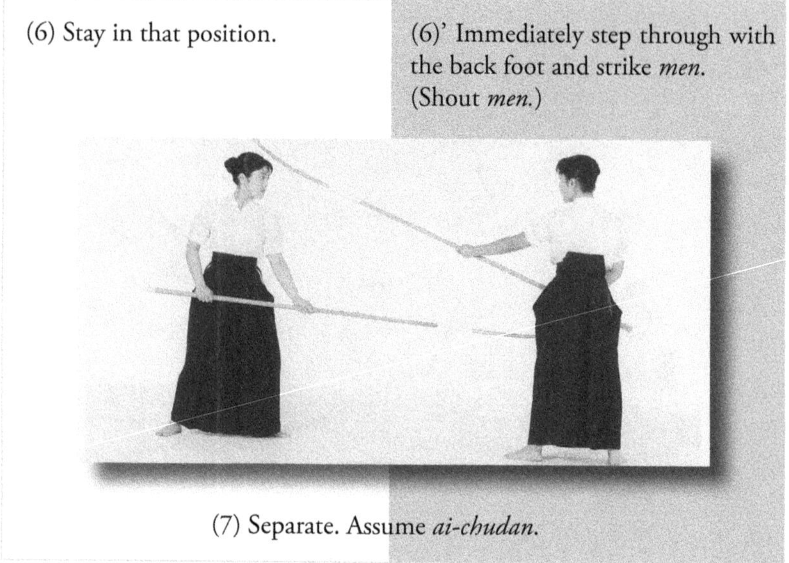

(7) Separate. Assume *ai-chudan.*

c) *Makiotoshi-waza*

Makiotoshi-waza utilises the *sori* of the *ha-bu* to force the opponent's *naginata* down. It is especially effective when the opponent has momentarily lost concentration, or just after they have blocked an attack. When executing *makiotoshi-waza*, use the whole body (not just the hands) and take care to maintain balance at all times.

Attacker	Receiver

Makiotoshi-men- uchi

(1) From *ai-chudan,*

(2) Strike *furiage-men.* (Shout *men.*)	(2)' Block with the *ha-bu.* Then step back as you flick the opponent's *naginata* down using the *sori.* The position of the back hand does not move.

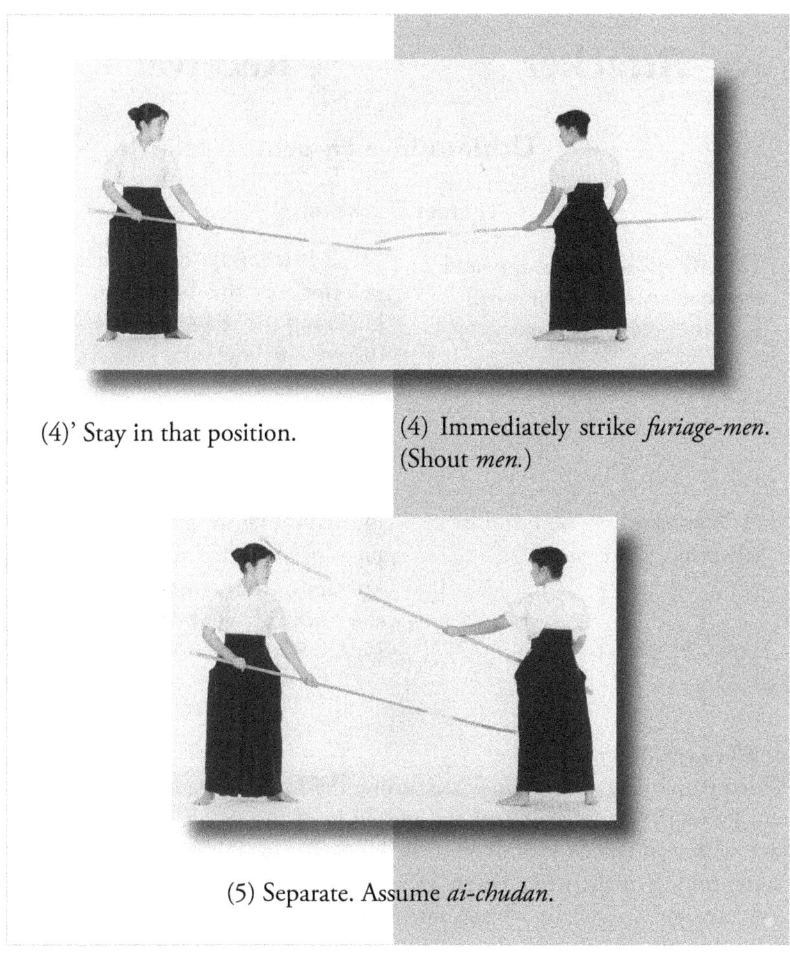

(4)' Stay in that position.

(4) Immediately strike *furiage-men*. (Shout *men.*)

(5) Separate. Assume *ai-chudan*.

d) *Uchiotoshi-waza*

When the opponent is about to attack, use this technique to hit the *naginata* down to the right or left using the *ha-bu* or *e-bu*. This will render the strike ineffective, and will provide an opportunity to counterattack. As with all techniques, it is important to use the *naginata* and body as a unified force.

Attacker	Receiver
Uchiotoshi-men-uchi	
(1) From *ai-chudan*,	
(2) *Mochikae* into *hasso* and strike *sokumen*. (Shout *men*.)	(2)' Move away from the strike pivoting on the back foot while knocking the *naginata* down with the *e-bu*. Follow up with a strike to *sune*. (Shout *sune*.)
(3) Both assume *migi-chudan*.	
(4) *Mochikae* into *hasso* and strike *sokumen*. (Shout *men*.)	(4)' Move away from the strike pivoting on the back foot while knocking the *naginata* down with the *e-bu*. Follow up with a strike to *sune*. (Shout *sune*.)

d) *Ukenagashi-waza*

When employing *ukenagashi-waza*, utilise the force of the opponent's strike and let their *naginata* slide off the *monouchi* of the *ha-bu*. Then counterattack with a *furikaeshi* technique. It is important to wait until the opponent is committed to the strike before executing this technique. *Uchiotoshi-waza* and *ukenagashi-waza* are advanced techniques which should attempted after mastering other basic techniques first.

The second part of this chapter will introduce the technical sequences called Shikake-Oji. Many of the techniques introduced so far are found in Shikake-Oji, which provides an effective way of learning all of the basic movements and *waza*, which can then be utilised in matches. It is easier to learn techniques without wearing *bogu*. It is necessary that practitioners learn the basic techniques of Naginata in accordance with the prescribed *kihon* methodology from the outset, otherwise there is a risk of developing bad habits which become increasingly difficult to unlearn.

Shikake-Oji
No. 1: Ippon-me

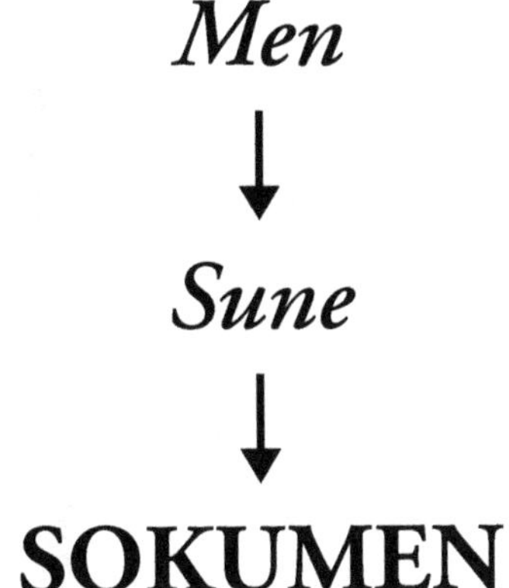

Ippon-me

Ippon-me

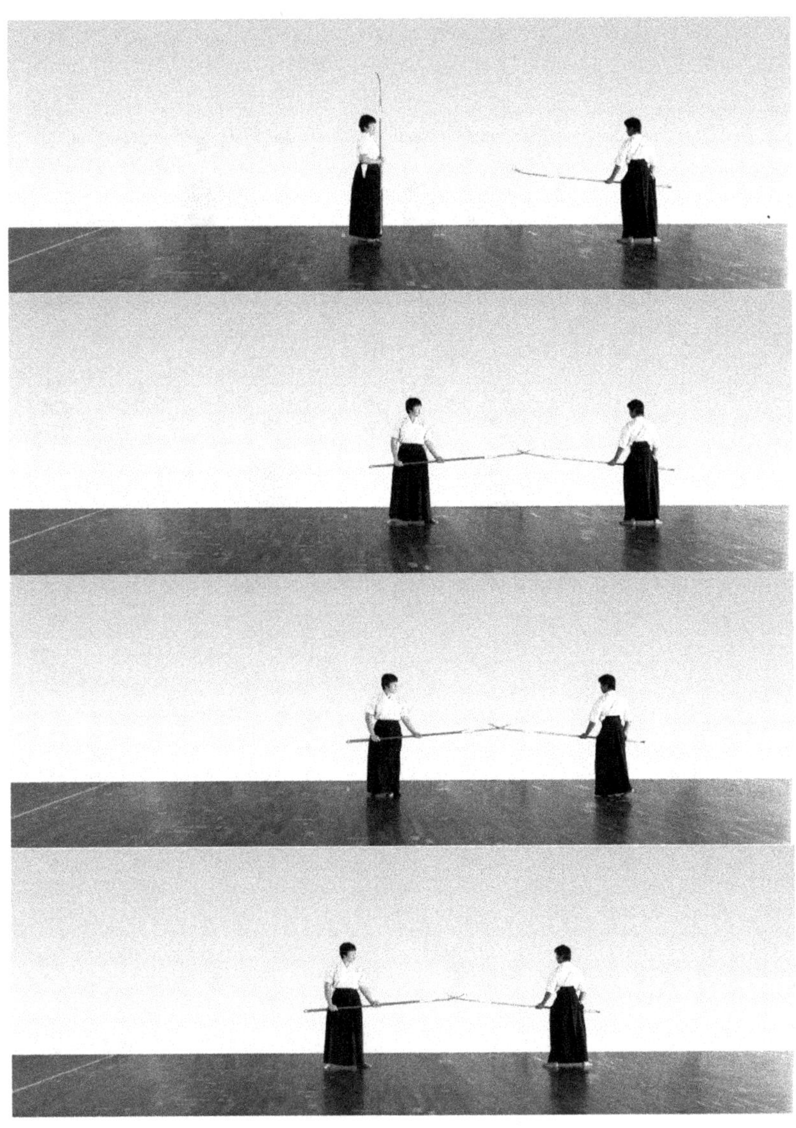

Ippon-me

All of the lessons in this book so far have been concerned with fundamental *kihon* movements and various techniques (*waza*) used in Naginata. These are combined and practised in set patterns called Shikake-Oji. By practising Shikake-Oji in pairs, practitioners learn correct etiquette, *kamae*, grip, footwork and body movement, *maai* (distancing), breathing technique, striking chances, *zanshin* (mental and physical state of alertness), correct posture, and so on. Shikake-Oji is also a competition event in *engi-kyogi*.

Always start and finish the set of Shikake-Oji in *shizentai*.

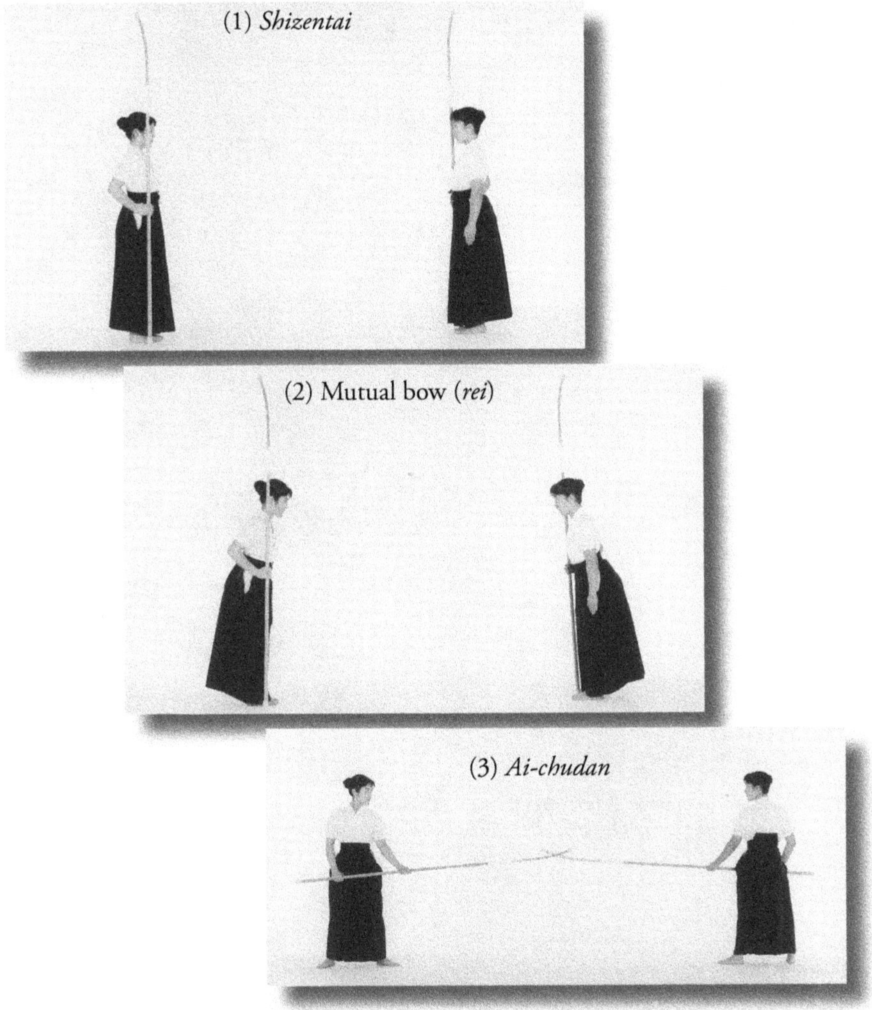

(1) *Shizentai*

(2) Mutual bow (*rei*)

(3) *Ai-chudan*

Shikake	**Oji**

From *ai-chudan*

(1) Strike *furiage-men*. (Shout *men.*)

Step through from the back foot (right) while lifting the naginata overhead, then step out with the left foot to strike men.

(1)' Pull in and block with the *ha-bu*.

Step back with okuri-ashi and block men with the ha-bu.

(2) *Mochikae* and strike *sune*. (Shout *sune.*)

Mochikae into hasso. Then step through from the back foot (right) and strike sune.

(2)' Block with the *e-bu*.

Stepping back, block sune with the e-bu.

(3) Remain in this position, but keep focussed on Oji. (*Zanshin*).

(3)' Assume *hasso* while stepping diagonally back, and then move in to strike *sokumen*.
(Shout *men. Zanshin*).

Oji assumes hasso while stepping back diagonally to the left.

Pivoting on the front foot (right) Oji steps through with the left foot and strikes sokumen.

(4) Return to *chudan*.

Oji assumes chudan while retreating from the front foot (left) first and then the right.

(5) Return to *chudan*.

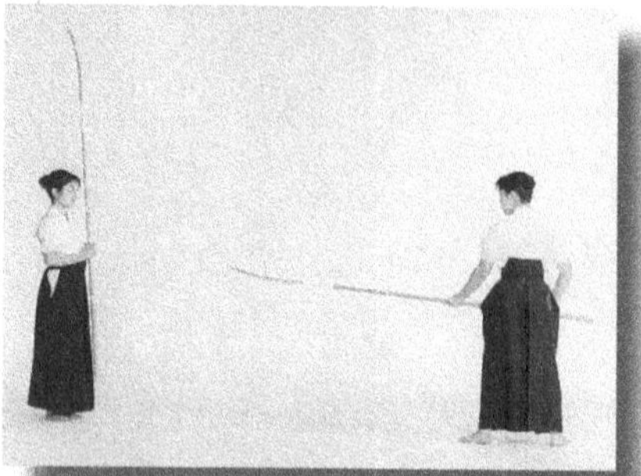

Shikake draws their front foot (right) back to the left and brings hands together while facing Oji, then steps out with the left foot into chudan.

(6) Return to original positions.

Without dropping concentration, Shikake moves back in sync with Oji with ayumi-ashi to the starting position (left, right, left, right).

Keeping in time with Shikake, Oji advances forward to the starting position with ayumi-ashi (right, left, right, left).

Important Points:

When receiving Shikake's attacks, Oji should wait until the last possible moment before reacting. Also, when executing blocks or attacks, the *naginata* and body should move in unison.

Shikake-Oji
No. 2: Nihon-me

Furiage-sune

↓

Sokumen

↓

SUNE

Nihon-me

Nihon-me

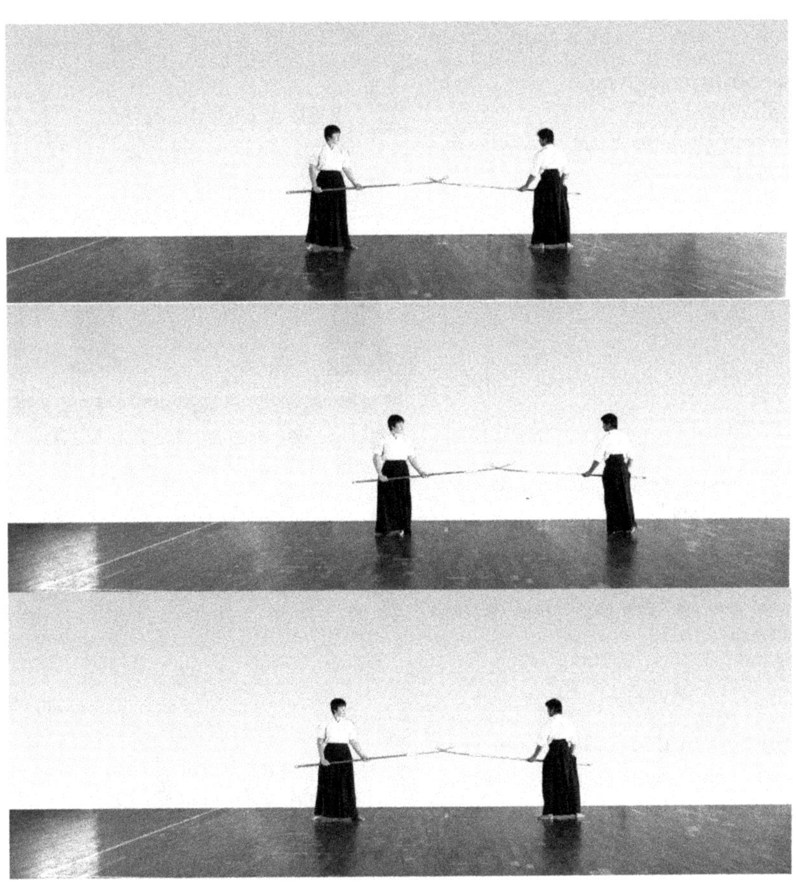

Shikake	**Oji**
From *ai-chudan*	
(1) Strike *furiage-sune*. (Shout *sune.*) *Same as ippon-me except strike sune instead of men.*	(1)' Block with the *ha-bu*.  *Move back with okuri-ashi as you block sune with the ha-bu.*
(2) *Mochikae* and strike *sokumen*. (Shout *men.*) *Mochikae into hasso and step forward with your back foot (right) to strike sokumen.*	(2)' Block with the *e-bu*.
(3) Stay in this position, but keep alert and maintain eye-contact. (*Zanshin.*)	(3)' Step back to the diagonal rear while taking *hasso*, and then move forward again to strike *sune*. (Shout *sune.*) 

Shikake	Oji

Pivoting on the right foot, Oji steps through with the left and strikes sune.

(4) Return to *chudan*.

Retreat into chudan moving from the front foot first.

(5) Return to *chudan*.

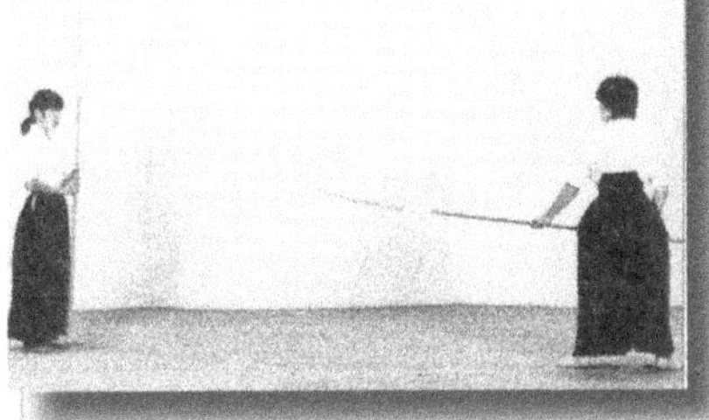

Draw the right foot back even with the left as both hands come together in front of the body. Then step out with the left foot into chudan.

(6) Return together to original positions.

Keep alert while moving back in ayumi-ashi (left, right, left, right).

Move forward with ayumi-ashi (right, left, right, left).

Shikake-Oji
No. 3: Sanbon-me

Do

↓

Furikaeshi-men

↓

MAKIOTOSHI-MEN

Sanbon-me

Sanbon-me

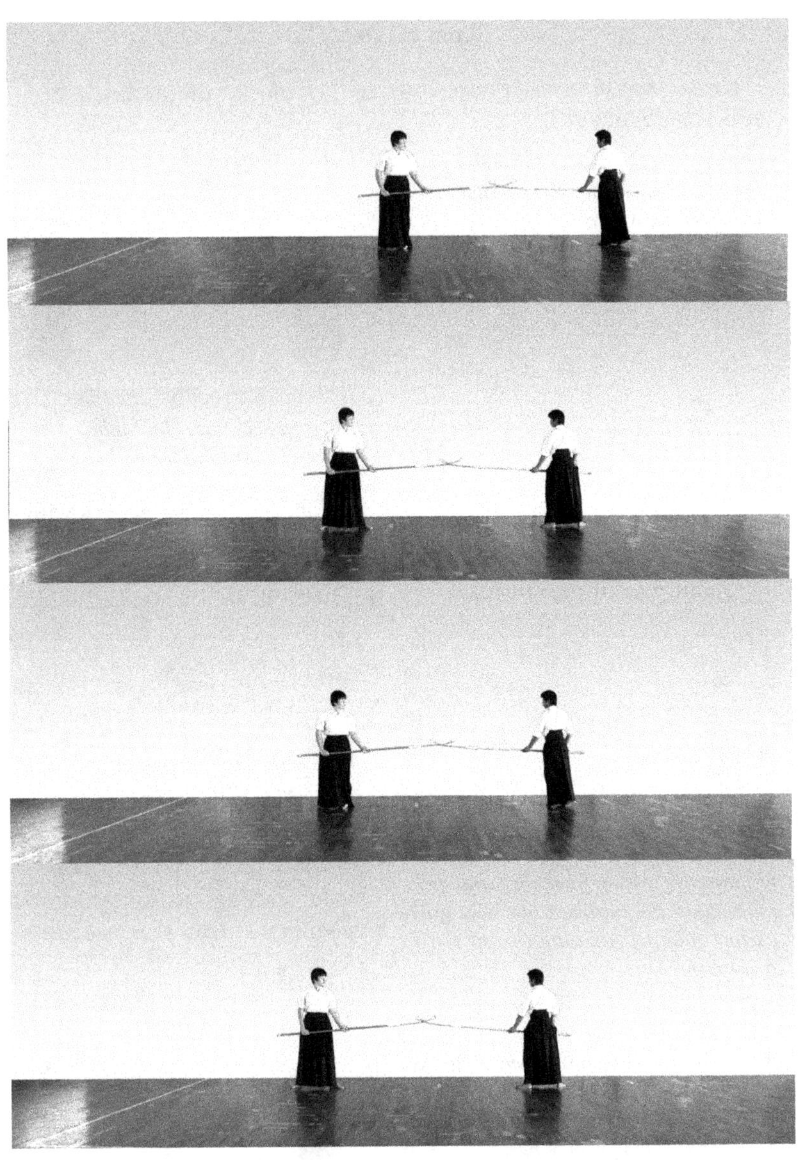

Shikake

Oji

From *ai-chudan*

(1) *Mochikae* into *wakigamae* and strike *do*. (Shout *do*.)

From wakigamae step forward with the right foot and strike do.

(1)' Block with the *ha-bu*.

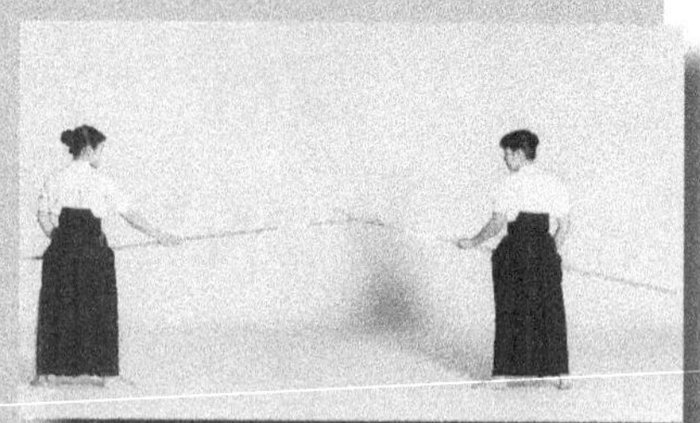

Step back with okuri-ashi and block with the ha-bu.

(2) Take one more step back with *okuri-ashi* and flick Shikake's *naginata* down (*harai*).

(3) Strike *furikaeshi-men*. (Shout *men*. Show *zanshin*.)

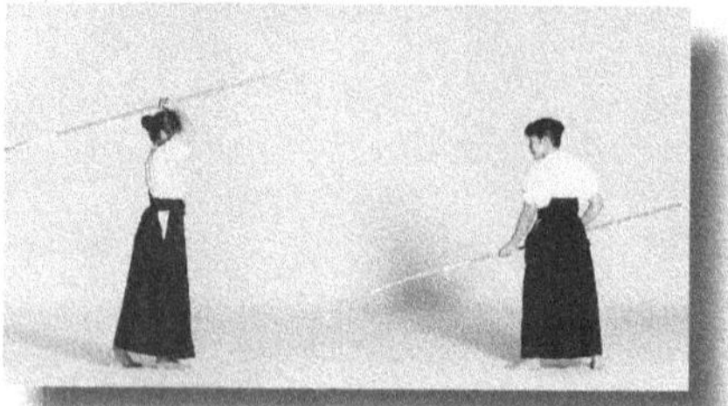

Utilising the power from the harai technique, spin the naginata overhead (furikaeshi), and step out with the left foot to strike men.

(3)' Block with the *ha-bu*.

Move back with okuri-ashi as you receive men with the ha-bu.

(4) Move back again with *okuri-ashi* while flicking Shikake's *naginata* down to the right with *makiotoshi*.

When your naginata is rendered ineffective with makiotoshi, the back hand (right) should keep contact with the body, and the front hand should grip the naginata lightly allowing it to slide.

Sanbon-me

Shikake	Oji
	(5) After executing *makiotoshi* move forward and strike *furiage-men.* (Shout *men. Zanshin.*)
	Stepping forward from the back foot (right) extend the naginata out (kuridashi) and lift it overhead (furiage), then strike men while stepping through with the left foot.

(6) Return to *chudan.*

Shikake	Oji
Lift the kissaki up to assume chudan.	*Assume chudan while retreating from the front foot (left) then the right.*

(7) Return together to original positions.

Shikake	Oji
Keep alert while moving back with ayumi-ashi (left, right, left right).	*Move forward with ayumi-ashi (right, left, right, left).*

Important Points:
Make sure the *do* cuts are not too high.
Block *do* properly before executing the *harai*.
The *harai* and *makiotoshi* do not require much power.

Shikake-Oji
No. 4: Yonhon-me

Sune

↓

NUKI-MEN

↓

FURIKAESHI-MEN

Yonhon-me

Shikake

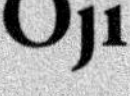

From *ai-chudan,*

(1) *Mochikae* into *hasso* and strike *sune*. (Shout *sune.*)

From hasso step forward from the right foot and strike at sune. The strike will be dodged, so the kissaki should continue through to the point slightly past where sune was.

(1)' Lift the *naginata* overhead while dodging the *sune* strike.

Step back with okuri-ashi to dodge the sune attack (nuki) as the naginata is lifted overhead. The hips are facing the front.

(2) Step forward and strike *men*.

After dodging sune, step forward immediately and strike men.

(2)' Step back with *okuri-ashi* and block with the *ha-bu*.

After missing the sune strike, pull back with okuri-ashi and lift the kissaki up to receive the attack to men.

(3) Move back with *okuri-ashi* as you flick Oji's *naginata* down to their left (*harai*).

(3)' Strike *furikaeshi-men*. (Shout *men*. Show *zanshin.*)

Shikake	Oji
Stay in this position and maintain eye-contact.	*Use the momentum of the harai to spin the naginata overhead (furikaeshi).*

Step forward from the back (right) foot and strike men.

(4) Return to *chudan*.

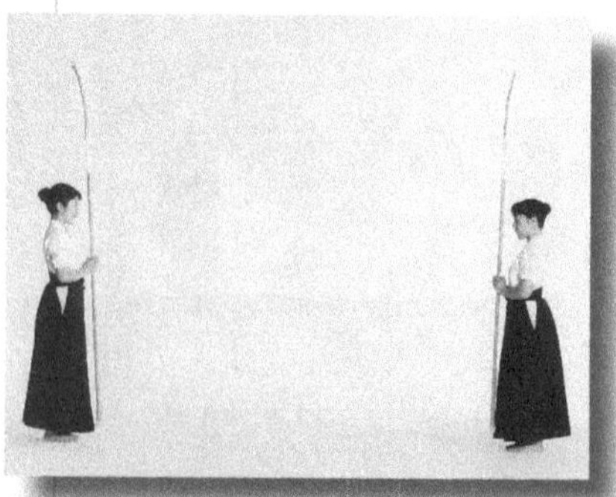

Both do mochikae and assume chudan together.

Assume chudan while retreating from the front foot (right) then the left.

Draw the front (right) foot back, mochikae, then assume chudan.

Important Points:

Shikake must make a large attack with the intention of hitting *sune*.
The *harai* should not be executed with excessive power.

Shikake-Oji
No. 5: Gohon-me

Do

↓

Furikaeshi-men

↓

HARAI-TSUKI

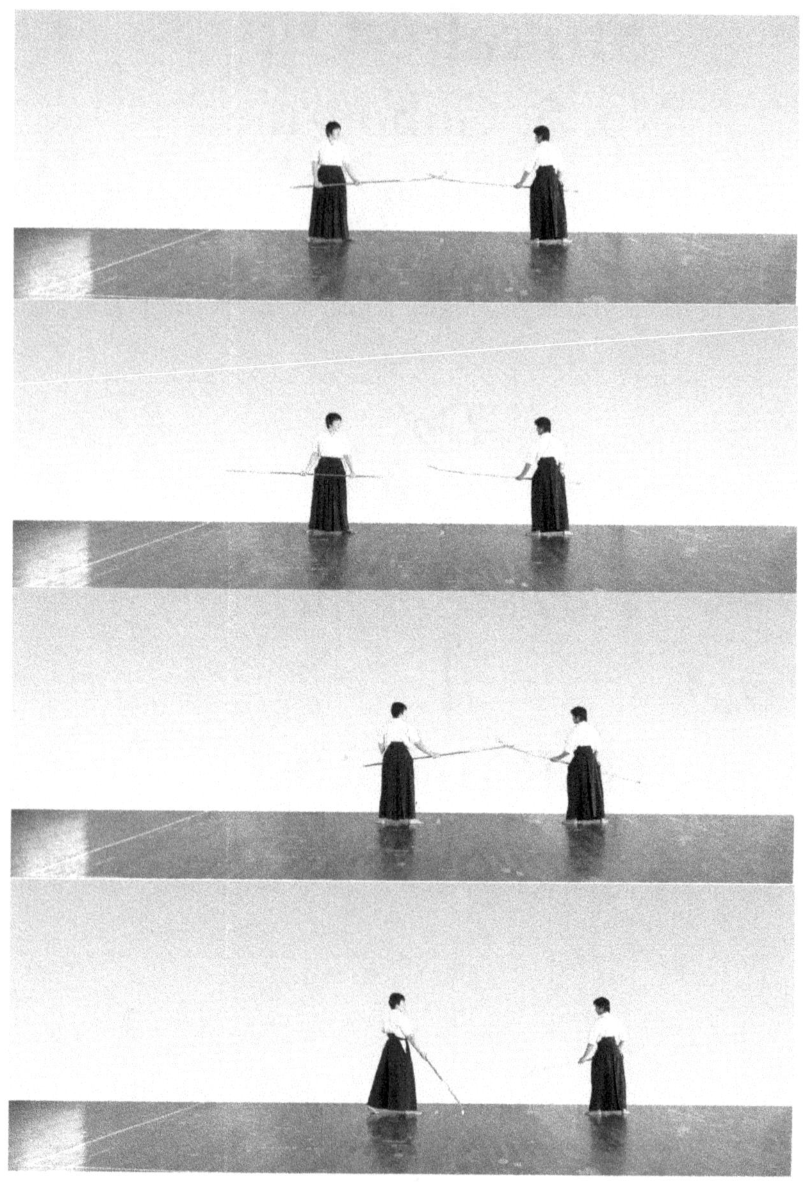

Gohon-me

Gohon-me

Shikake	Oji

From *ai-chudan,*

Shikake: (1) *Mochikae* into *wakigamae* and strike *do*. (Shout *do.*)

Oji: (1)' Block with the *ha-bu.*

From wakigamae step forward from the rear foot (right) and strike do.

Step back with okuri-ashi and block do with the ha-bu.

(2) Oji steps back again while flicking Shikake's *naginata* down to the left (*harai*).

(3) Strike *furikaeshi-men.* (Shout *men.* Show *zanshin.*)

(3)' Block with the *ha-bu.*

Using the momentum of the harai, spin the naginata overhead (furikaeshi), then strike men while stepping out with the left foot.

Move back again with okuri-ashi as the men strike is received with the ha-bu.

Shikake

(4)' When Shikake's *naginata* is rendered ineffective with *harai*, the back hand (right) should remain in contact with the body, and the front hand should grip the *naginata* lightly, allowing it to slide.

Oji

(4) Knock Shikake's *naginata* horizontally to the left with the *e-bu* (*harai*).

Rotate the body to the left using fumi-kae-ashi, and execute harai with the monouchi of the e-bu.

(5) Pull the *naginata* back (*kurikomi*) to prepare for the *tsuki* attack.

(6) Thrust the *ishizuki* into Shikake's side. (Shout *tsuki*. Show *zanshin*.)

Shikake | Oji

(7) Return to *chudan*.

Maintaining alertness, Oji steps back from the front foot (right) with ayumi-ashi then the left and assumes wakigamae.

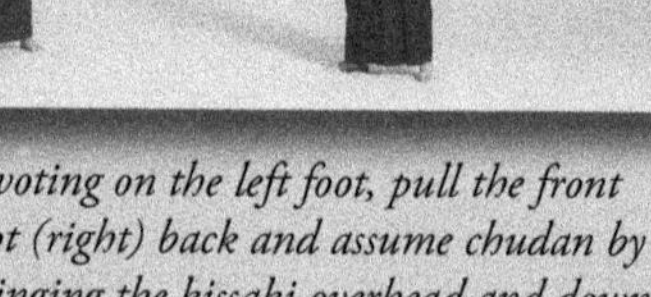

Assume chudan.

Pivoting on the left foot, pull the front foot (right) back and assume chudan by bringing the kissaki overhead and down the centreline.

(8) Return to original positions.

Move back with ayumi-ashi (left, right, left, right).

Move forward with ayumi-ashi (right, left, right, left).

Important Points:

The *harai* executed by Oji should be executed with the whole body (*fumikae-ashi*), not just the arms.

Shikake-Oji
No. 6: Roppon-me

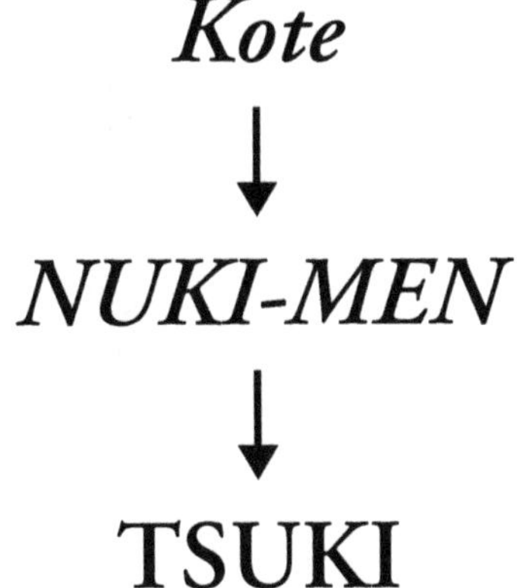

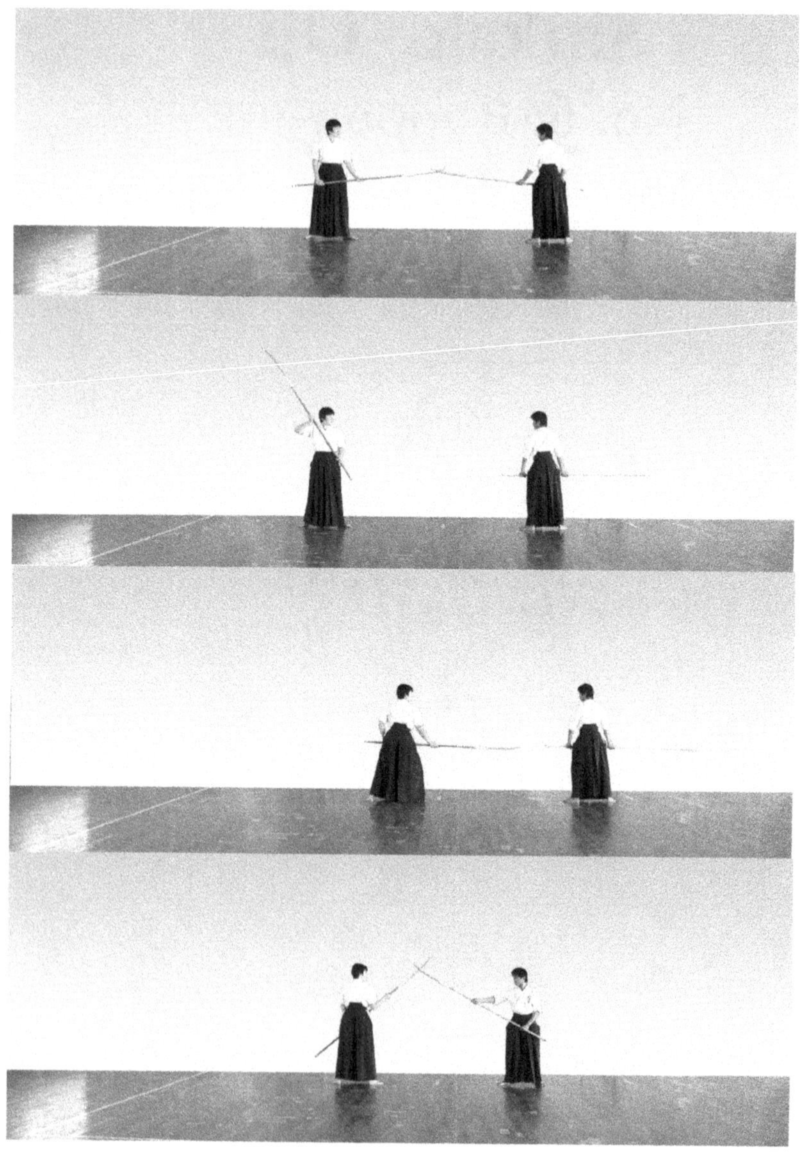

Roppon-me

Shikake	**Oji**

From *ai-chudan,*

Assume *hasso.*

Assume *wakigamae.*

(1) Strike *kote.* (Shout *kote.*)

Pivoting on the front foot, step forward with the back foot (right) and strike kote. As the attack is dodged, the kissaki should continue to slightly below the height of kote.

(1)' Dodge the *kote* attack (*nuki*).

From wakigamae, step back with okuri-ashi and dodge the kote strike (nuki).

(2) Pivoting on the front foot, immediately step forward with the back foot (right) and strike *men.* (Shout *men.*)

(2)' Block the *men* strike with the *ha-bu* while moving back with *okuri-ashi.*

Shikake

(3) Move back with *okuri-ashi* while flicking Oji's *naginata* down to the left (*harai*).

Oji

(3)' Using the momentum from the *harai*, pivot on the front foot (right) and spin the body around to the opposite side while pulling the *naginata* back and in (*kuriko-mi*), and prepare to unleash a *tsuki* attack with body weight resting on the pivot foot.

(4) Stepping forward with the left foot, thrust the *ishizuki* into Shikake's side. (Shout *tsuki*. Show *zanshin*.)

(5) Return to *chudan*.

Draw the front foot (right) back level with the rear foot so that the hips are facing the front. Bring the hands together in the middle of the e-bu and then step out with the left foot to assume hidari-chudan.

Assume wakigamae while stepping back with the left foot then the right. Then bring the hands together in the middle of the e-bu and assume chudan.

Shikake | **Oji**

Shikake and Oji should be already in the original starting positions when assuming ai-chudan, so there should be no necessity to move.

Important Points:

From Roppon-me, both Shikake and Oji assume their respective *kamae* in synchronisation from *chudan*, and then begin the sequence. All attacks by Shikake and Oji must be straight ensuring that the *naginata* comes through the centre. As with all *harai* movements done in the Shikake-Oji sequences, the *harai* by Shikake must not be executed with excessive physical power. In the final *tsuki*, Oji places their body weight on the pivot foot (right), and spinning around to the right, finishes the attack after a slight pause. Eye-contact must be maintained at all times.

Shikake-Oji
No. 7: Nanahon-me

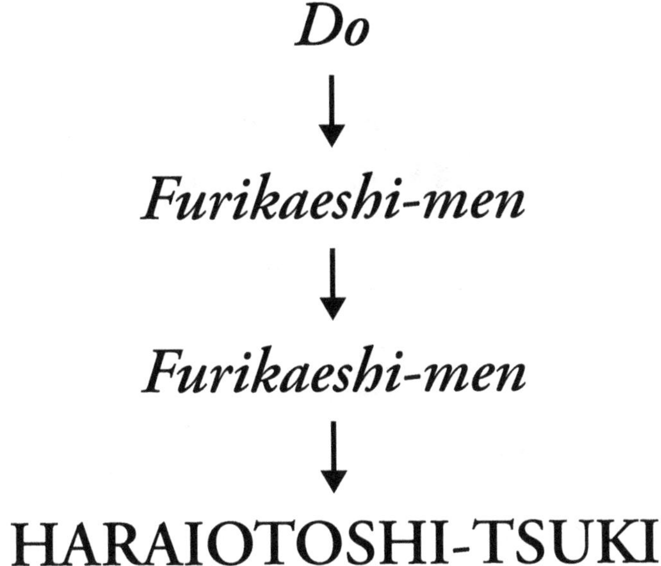

Nanahon-me

Nanahon-me

Nanahon-me

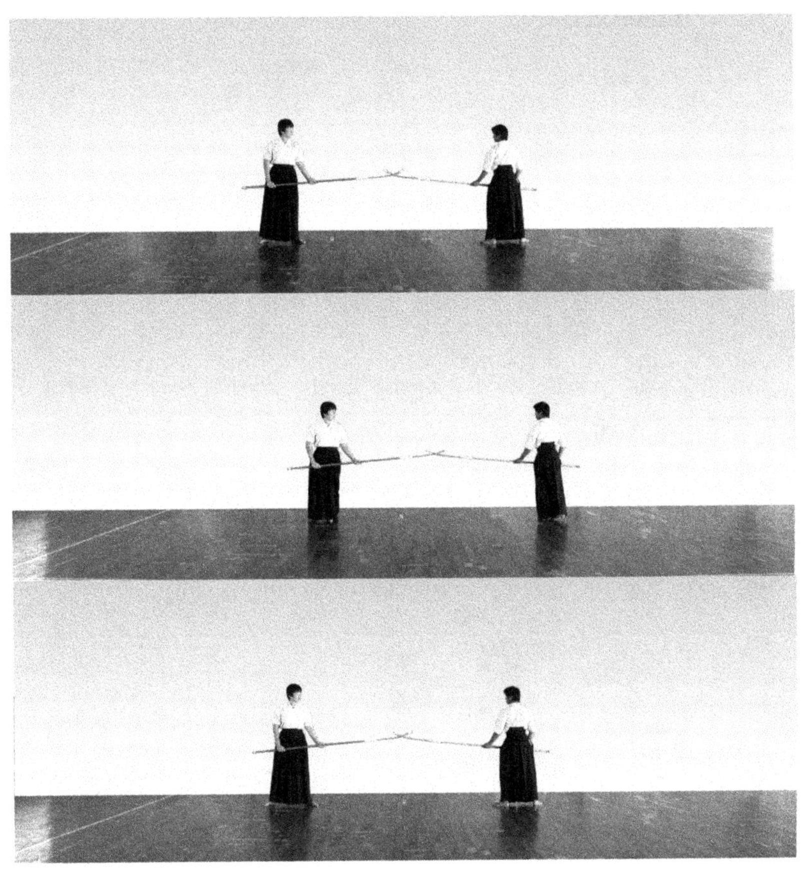

Shikake

From *wakigamae.*

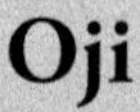

Oji

From *jodan.*

(1) Step through with the back foot (right) and strike *do*. (Shout *do*.)

(1)' Block the *do* strike with the *monouchi* of the *ha-bu.*

From jodan, pull the front foot (left) back and block the do strike with the ha-bu.

(2) Move back with *okuri-ashi* and flick Shikake's *naginata* to the left (*harai*).

(3) Using the momentum from the *harai*, strike *furikaeshi-men*. (Shout *men.*)

(3)' Block with the *ha-bu.*

Move back with okuri-ashi as the men strike is blocked with the ha-bu.

Shikake

Oji

(4) Move back with *okuri-ashi* while flicking Shikake's *naginata* down to the right (*harai*).

(5) Using the momentum from the *harai*, strike *furikaeshi-men*. (Shout *men.*)

(6) Rotate around to the left with *fumikae-ashi* and knock (*harai-otoshi*) Shikake's *naginata* down with the *e-bu*. Immediately pull the *naginata* in (*kurikomi*), then lunge forward from the left foot for *tsuki*. (Shout *tsuki*. Show *zanshin.*)

(6)' When the *naginata* is rendered ineffective with *haraiotoshi*, the back hand (right) should maintain contact with the body, and the front hand should grip the *naginata* lightly, allowing it to slide.

Turn on the spot with fumikae-ashi.

Knock Shikake's naginata down with the e-bu (haraiotoshi).

Shikake	Oji

After executing the haraiotoshi, pull the naginata back (kurikomi) primed to make the final tsuki attack.

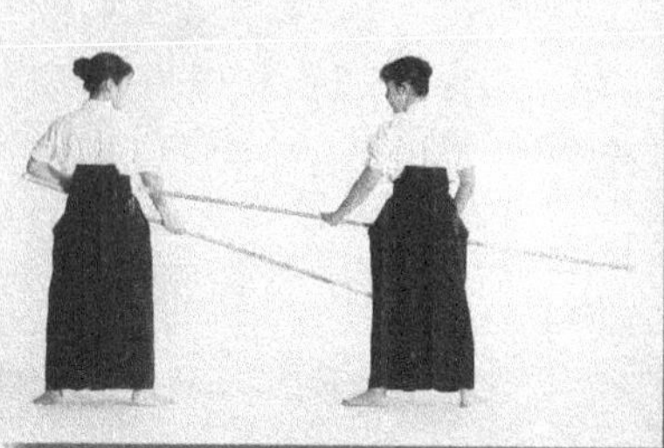

Lunging forward from the left foot, thrust at Shikake's side with the ishizuki. The blade should be facing outward

(7) Return to *chudan.*

Shikake	Oji
Draw the front foot (right) back level with the back foot so that the hips are facing the front. Bring the hands together in the middle of the e-bu and then step out with the left foot to assume chudan.	*Assume wakigamae while stepping back from the left the right foot. Then bring the hands together in the middle of the e-bu and step out with the left foot to assume chudan.*

(8) Return to original positions.

Shikake	Oji
Move back with ayumi-ashi (left, right, left, right, left, right).	*Move forward with ayumi-ashi (right, left, right, left, right, left).*

Important Points:
In executing the *haraiotoshi*, Shikake's *naginata* is knocked down by striking the *monouchi* and then pulling the *naginata* in (*kurikomi*) to prepare for the thrust. The rear hand (right) should be touching the hip at point of impact, and should not move until the *naginata* is pulled back.

Shikake-Oji
No. 8: Hachihon-me

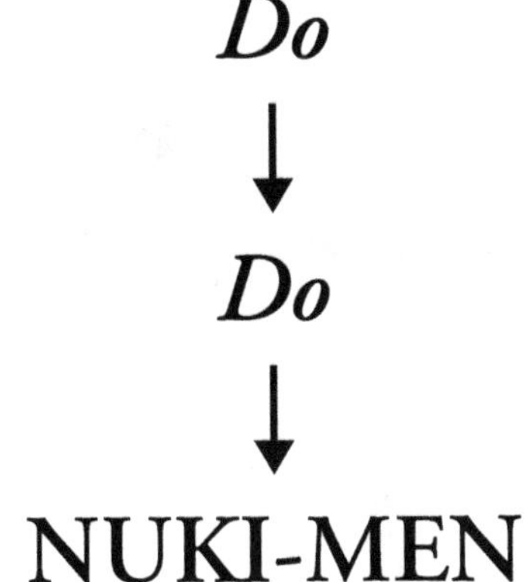

Hachihon-me

Hachihon-me

Shikake

From *wakigamae*.

Oji

From *hasso*.

(1) Step forward with the back foot (right) and strike *do*. (Shout *do*.)

(1)' Stepping back from the front foot (left) block the *do* attack with the *ha-bu*.

Draw the front foot (right) back and rotate the body to face the other way as the kissaki is pulled behind to avoid the do attack.

(2) *Mochikae* into *wakigamae* and immediately make another attack to *do*. (Shout *do*. Show *zanshin*.)

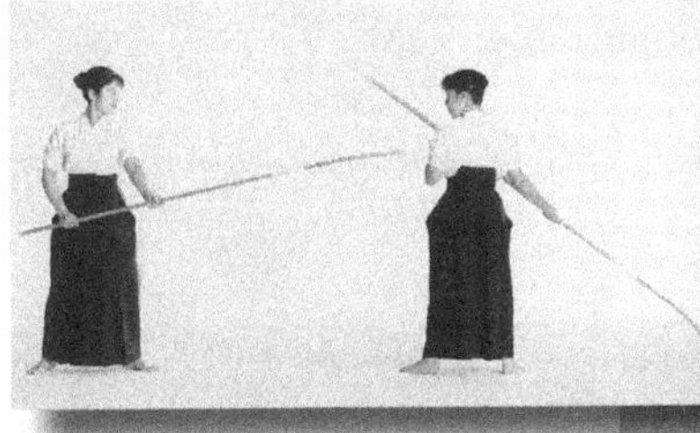

As the attack will be dodged, the strike should carry on slightly past the target. Maintain eye-contact and remain in that position.

(2)' Step back and dodge the *do* strike.

Pulling the front foot back, the body turns and faces the opposite direction as the do strike is blocked with the mon-ouchi of the ha-bu.

Shikake	Oji
	(3) Strike men. (Shout *men.* Show *zanshin.*)

Step forward from the back (right) foot, pull the ishizuki down through the centre as the final men strike is made.

(4) Return to *chudan.*

Shikake	Oji
Assume chudan in time with Oji.	*Retreat two steps from the left the foot (ayumi-ashi) as the naginata is brought down into migi-chudan. Then change to hidari-chudan.*

(5) Return to original positions.

Shikake	Oji
Move back with ayumi-ashi in time with Oji (left, right, left, right).	*Move forward with ayumi-ashi (right, left, right, left).*

Important Points:

Make sure that the attacks to *do* are strong, but not too high. As is the case with all of the Shikake-Oji sequences, Oji should wait until the last possible moment before blocking or dodging Shikake's attacks.

Chapter 5
Drills With Bogu

Photo from *Kokumin Naginata-do Kyohon,* 1941.

Part 1: First Things First

In competition or sparring with *bogu*, you are essentially putting all of your *kihon* into practise in the cauldron of combat. To be good at Naginata, movement and execution of techniques has to be second nature. There is no time to think about what you should be doing when your opponent is trying to strike you. This is why constant repetition of *kihon* techniques is the cornerstone of Naginata.

It is useful to train with as many different people as possible to become accustomed to opponent's with different timing, distance, and technical idiosyncrasies. One must learn to strike the targets with an upright posture, good *kamae*, confidence, strong *kiai*, appropriate *maai*, and *zanshin*.

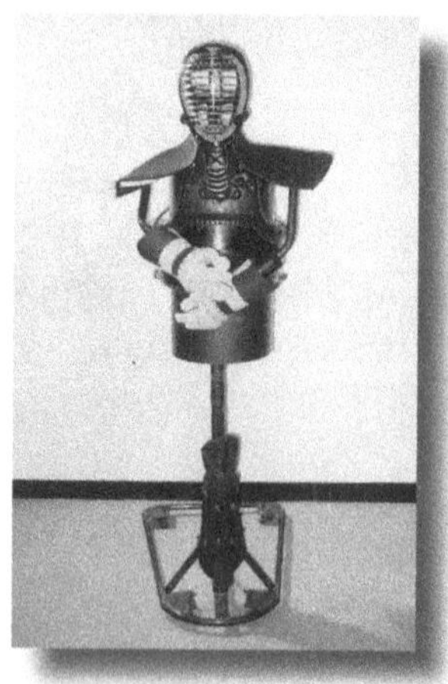

When you wear *bogu* for the first time it will feel very awkward at first. Until you are able to move freely without distraction, it is helpful to practise striking against hit dummies or other such equipment. It is also a good idea not to put all the *bogu* on straightaway. Get used to striking and moving piece by piece.

As you will now be making full-contact strikes, you must be considerate to your training partner, and be careful not to hurt them with careless or overly powerful strikes. In the course of any training session, you will accidentally strike and be struck on uncovered parts of the body. This is inevitable, and is an important part of your training. Try not to do it, but soak it up when it happens to you. It goes both ways.

Obviously, the less it happens the better, but as long as you execute your attacks with correct posture and without using too much superfluous power, you will not injure your partner in an accidental miss. The golden rule is to strike slowly and accurately at first, then gradually build up speed and power as you become more proficient. Eventually, you will be able to make spirited and vigorous attacks with confidence, and without being a danger to your peers.

CHAPTER 5: Drills with Bogu

Injury prevention

Compared to the basic training methods we have covered so far, training in *bogu* is considerably more rigorous. The techniques are executed with full force, and as each training partner will have different characteristics and be unpredictable in their movements, the risk for injury is increased. Warm up exercises should be conducted at the beginning of each session to prepare for the rigours of training, and followed by cool down exercises at the end to aid recovery.

Students warming up and stretching in the background before putting bogu on.

In many Naginata dojo, the standard procedure is to warm up with stretches, then move on to *happo-buri*, and then striking practice. This will often be followed by some sets of Shikake-Oji before *bogu* training begins. In other dojo, *bogu* training may be started straight away. In either case, make sure that you are completely warm and stretched before putting *bogu* on. Once on, it is difficult to stretch properly, so it is advisable to stretch properly before doing so.

Some practitioners mistakenly think that Shikake-Oji and the other *kihon* exercises constitute a warm up. Stretches and limbering of joints will enhance the quality of your training, and will also help prevent injury.

An often overlooked aspect of injury prevention is taking care of your equipment, and putting it on properly. *Bogu* is designed to protect the wearer from blows to the body. If any part of your armour is loose or becomes untied during the course of training, one risks receiving painful blows to uncovered areas, and it certainly is not the fault of the hitter.

Be sure to tie armour securely. This applies to the *sune*, *do*, and *men* cords. Learn how to attach *bogu* quickly but in a way that it is can be removed quickly if need be. Ensure that your *bogu* and *naginata* are always kept in perfect order, not only for your own safety, but also for the people you will be training with. This is a basic courtesy in Naginata, and should be strictly observed at all times.

Part 2: Putting Bogu On

Before a competition or training, *bogu* should be placed to the side of the *dojo,* ready to put on when necessary. Place the *sune-ate* down first, then the *kote* on top of the *sune-ate*, followed by the *men* face down on top of the *kote*. Fold the *men* cords and place them inside the *men*. The *tenugui* (*men* towel) is placed over the back of the *men*. The *tare* is wrapped around the *do*, and they are both placed in front of the other equipment. *Bogu* is attached in the following order:

1) *Tare*

Align the large centre *tare* panel in the centre of the body with the top at waist level. Pass the *tare* cords around to the back, cross below the *hakama's koshi-ita*, then pulling firmly, bring the chords back to the front and tie in a bow under the centre panel.

2) *Do*

Place the *do* against the torso. Pass the *himo* through the loops from back to front (see diagram). Adjust the positioning of the do by pulling the *himo* up or down, and then tie at the same height on both sides. Do not tie in a knot. The *himo* should not come undone during training, but should still be easy to unfasten. Tie the shorter cords in a horizontal bow at the back.

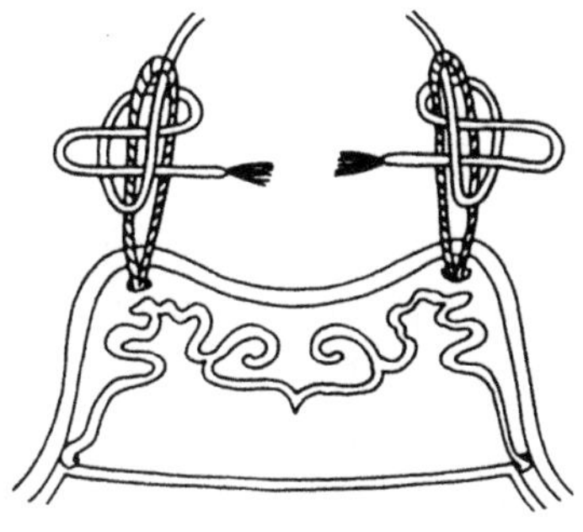

Tighten the knot by pulling the cords firmly on each side. There should not be a large gap between the top of the *do* and the *men*. The bottom of *nodo-dare* should be approximately the same height as the top of *do*.

3) *Sune-ate*

Place the *sune-ate* over the *hakama* with the bamboo slats facing the outside. (Try to keep the pleats of the *hakama* as straight as possible.) Wrap the top and bottom cords around the leg twice and tie in secure bows. Tuck the remainder of the cords out of the way. When you put the *sune-ate* on, it is considered good manners to face away from the dojo's *shomen*.

4) *Tenugui*

The *tenugui* is put on under the *men* in order to prevent chafing and to absorb sweat, stopping it from getting in your eyes. There are various ways of putting the *tenugui* on, but the following method is the most common.

Take hold of the *tenugui* from the top corners and hold it open. Place the *tenugui* on your face and slide it back over your forehead, so that the edge held by your fingers comes down to cover the back of your head at the top of the neck.

Fold each corner of the *tenugui* across your forehead, so that they reach the opposite side behind your ears.

Take hold of the lower edge hanging in front of your face, lift it over the top of your head, then flatten it down.

The *tenugui* should not be too tight as this will cause discomfort during training. Care must also be taken so that it is not loose. If it slips down over your eyes during sparring or a match, you will make an easy target, or even be in danger of injury. It is also inconvenient to have to cease activity temporarily in order to take off the *men* and re-fasten the *tenugui*. For the sake of hygiene, be sure to wash it after each training session. Please...

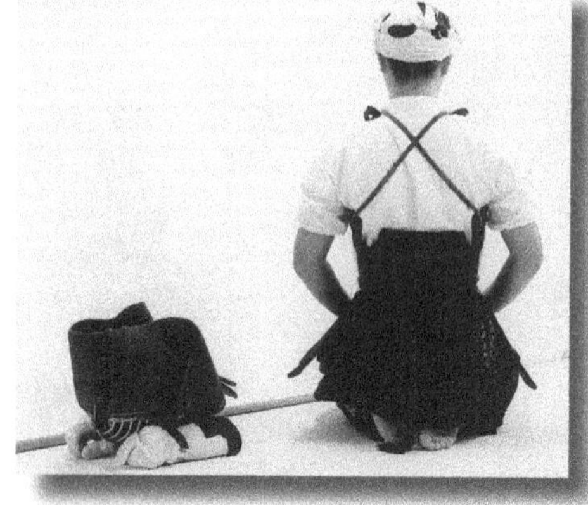

5) *Men*

There are two ways to secure the *men*: at the top or at the bottom. The *men* should fit snugly on the chin and forehead. One should be able to see clearly from the space between the sixth and seventh bars from the top. Wrap the *men* cords around to the back, front, then back again, as shown in the photos. Before tying at the back, the cords should be threaded through the very top bars, and then around to the back where they are tied in a bow. The cords dangling at the back should be of equal length.

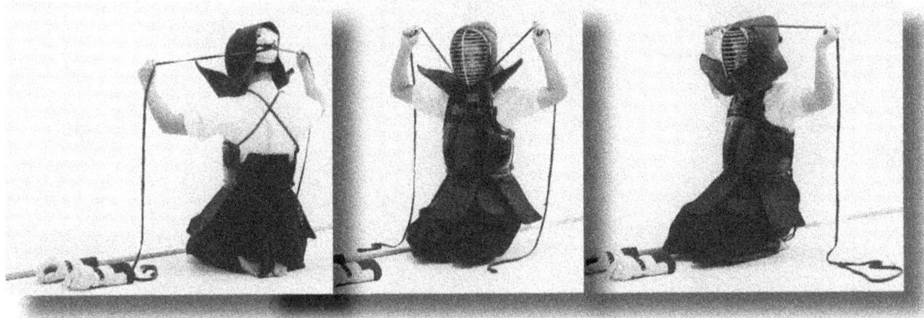

1. From the front, take around and cross at the back.

2. From the back, bring around and cross under the chin.

3. Take around and cross at the back again.

4. Thread through the top bars.

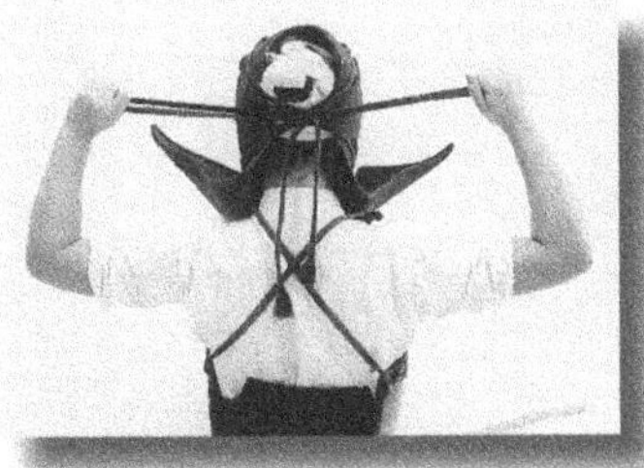

5. Take around to the back and tie in a bow.

Good example

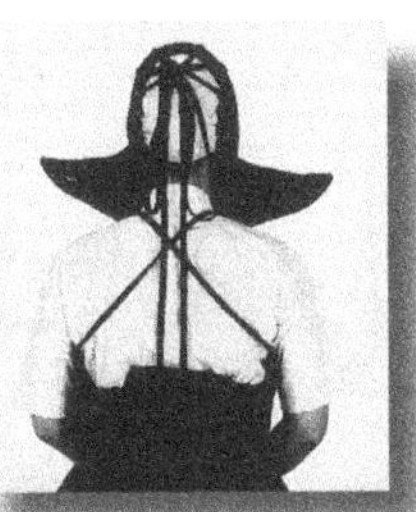

Bad example

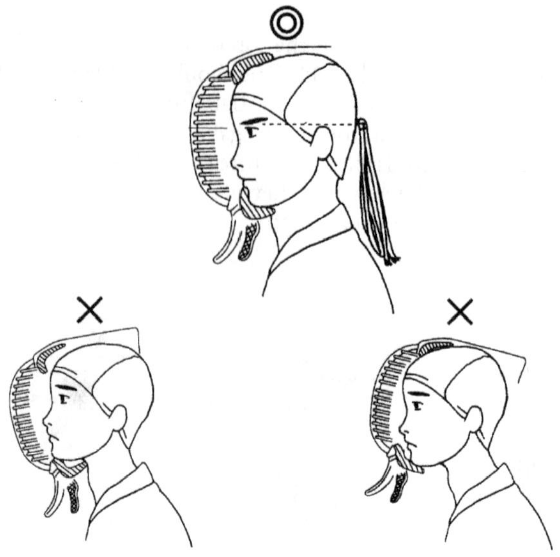

6) *Kote*

Put the left *kote* on first, followed by the right. Take off from the right when removing *kote*. Do not pull from the fist as this will weaken the *kote* at the wrist. Make sure that the laces are tied neatly and securely.

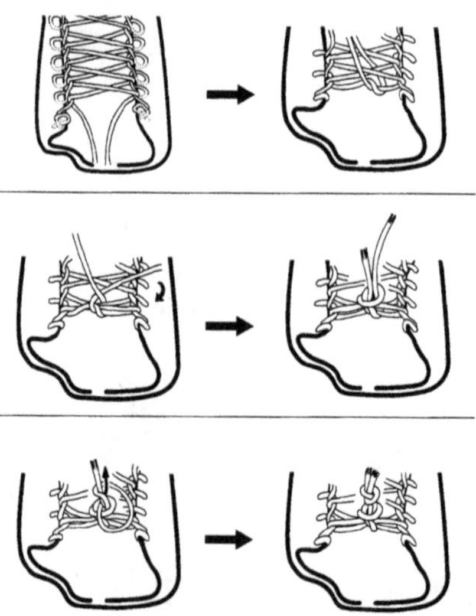

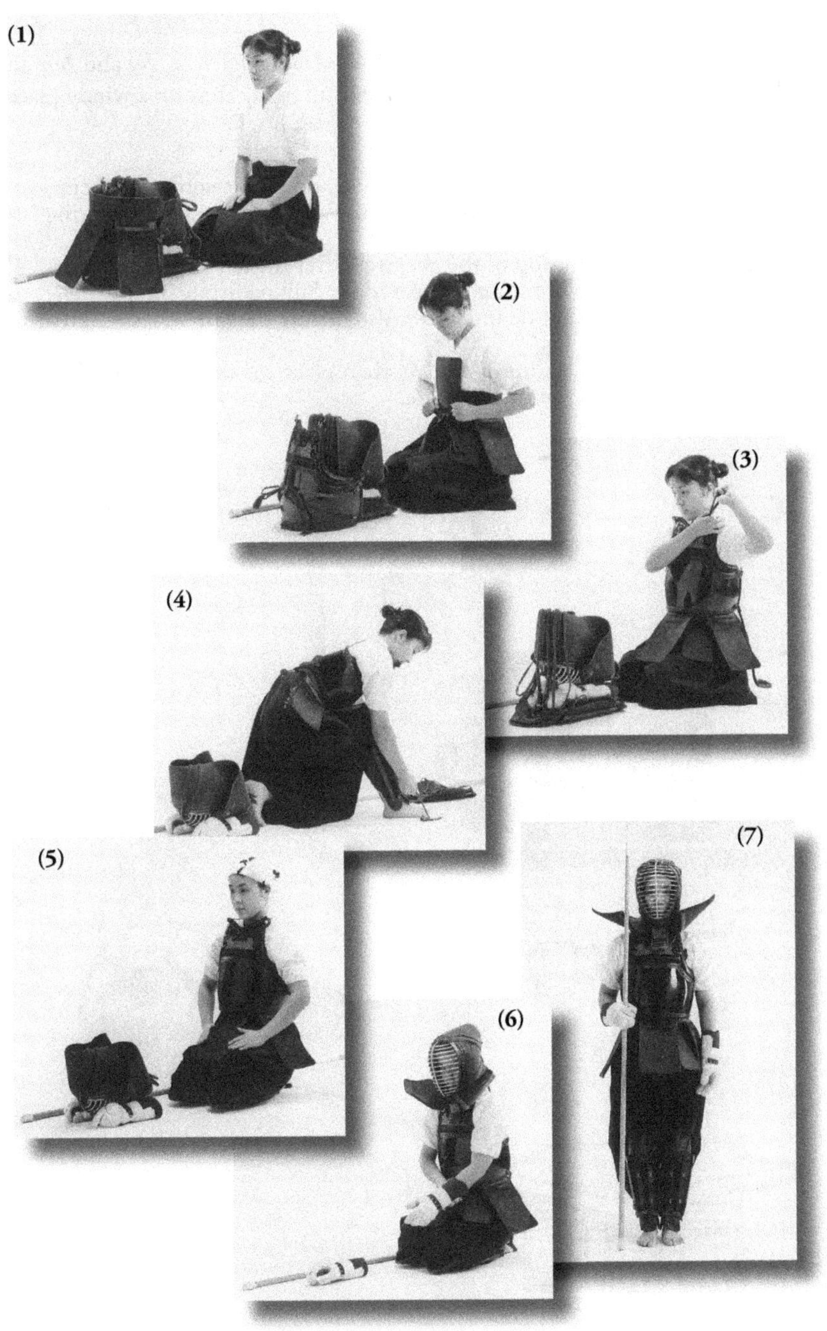
(1)
(2)
(3)
(4)
(5)
(6)
(7)

Putting it Away

When you remove the armour, take off *kote*, *men*, *sune-ate*, *do*, and *tare* in that order. Avoid placing the *bogu* in direct sunlight. Store in a windy place to dry it.

1. Place the *sune-ate* bamboo to bamboo and tie the cords together.
2. Wipe the sweat from inside the *men* and fold the cords, placing them inside.
3. Place the *tare* on top of the *do*. Cross over the left and right *mune-himo* (long cords) of the *do* in the middle. Pulling firmly on the *himo*, turn the *do* over and tie in a bow. Also, secure the *tare* straps as illustrated below.
4. Place the *sune-ate* inside the *do*, then place the *men* on top of the *sune-ate* with one *kote* in each side.

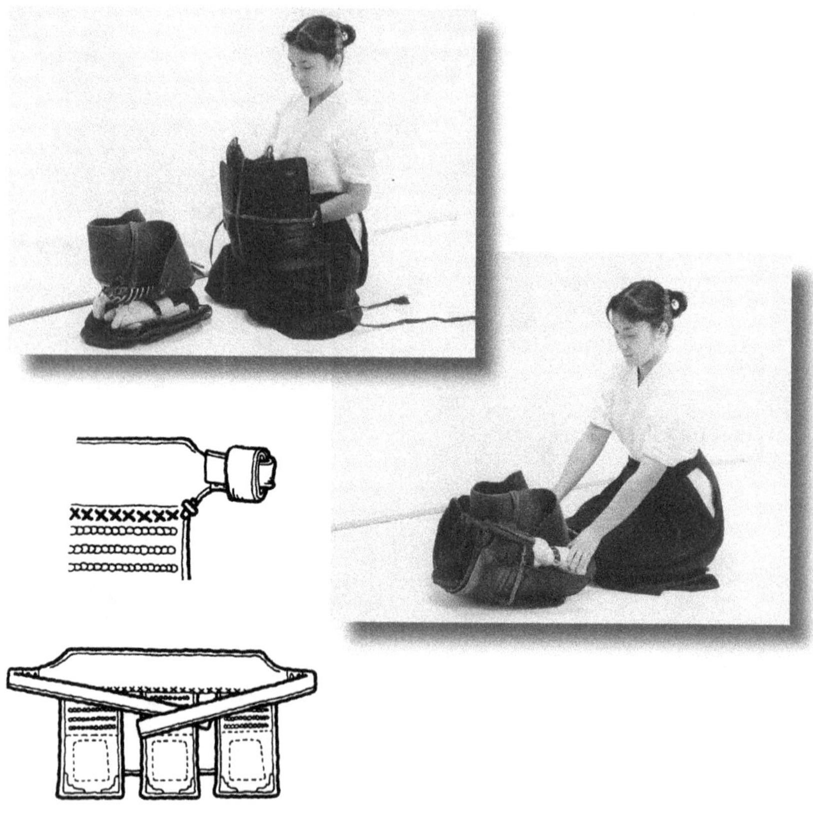

Part 3: Training Sequences

Other points to keep in mind:

1. *Chudan-no-kamae* is the standard stance to train in.
2. The receiver (*motodachi*) should adjust the distance and clearly indicate where the attacker should strike. Learning how to receive attacks is an important step in improving your attacking skill and understanding of Naginata principles.
3. Make sure that you use the whole body when striking, and not just the hands. You should aim to strike with *ki-ken-tai-itchi* (Spirit-*naginata*-body as one united entity).
4. Maintain intense concentration and attack as soon as you see an opening.
5. Do not just attack aimlessly or randomly.
6. *Shikake* (offensive) techniques are usually the focus of training, but don't neglect *oji* techniques.

How to seme

Seme refers to the act of assailing or applying pressure on the opponent to force an opening. *Seme* is to take the initiative in closing the distance between you and the opponent in order to strike. This has the effect of putting the opponent off balance physically and psychologically, and prevents them from moving freely. In this sense, it is important to assail with intention, and not just rely on chance.

1. *Seme* the *kissaki* – An effective way of forcing an opening on your opponent is to knock (*harai*) or force (*makiotoshi*) the opponent's *kissaki* out of the way, thereby leaving the opponent with no recourse for attack.
2. *Seme* with *waza* – Take the initiative and attack your opponent first. This will agitate opponents, and make them vulnerable by creating openings.
3. *Seme* with *ki* – Overwhelming opponents with a positive and vigorous spirit will dash their confidence, leaving them susceptible to attack. Keep these points in mind when you are training with *bogu*. A good understanding of these concepts will not only enhance your performance in matches, but will also lead to developing a strong, confident, and astute mind.

1. Shikake-waza

It is a good idea to learn to strike while wearing *bogu* by starting with *sune*. This way, the practitioner will gradually get used to moving with armour on.

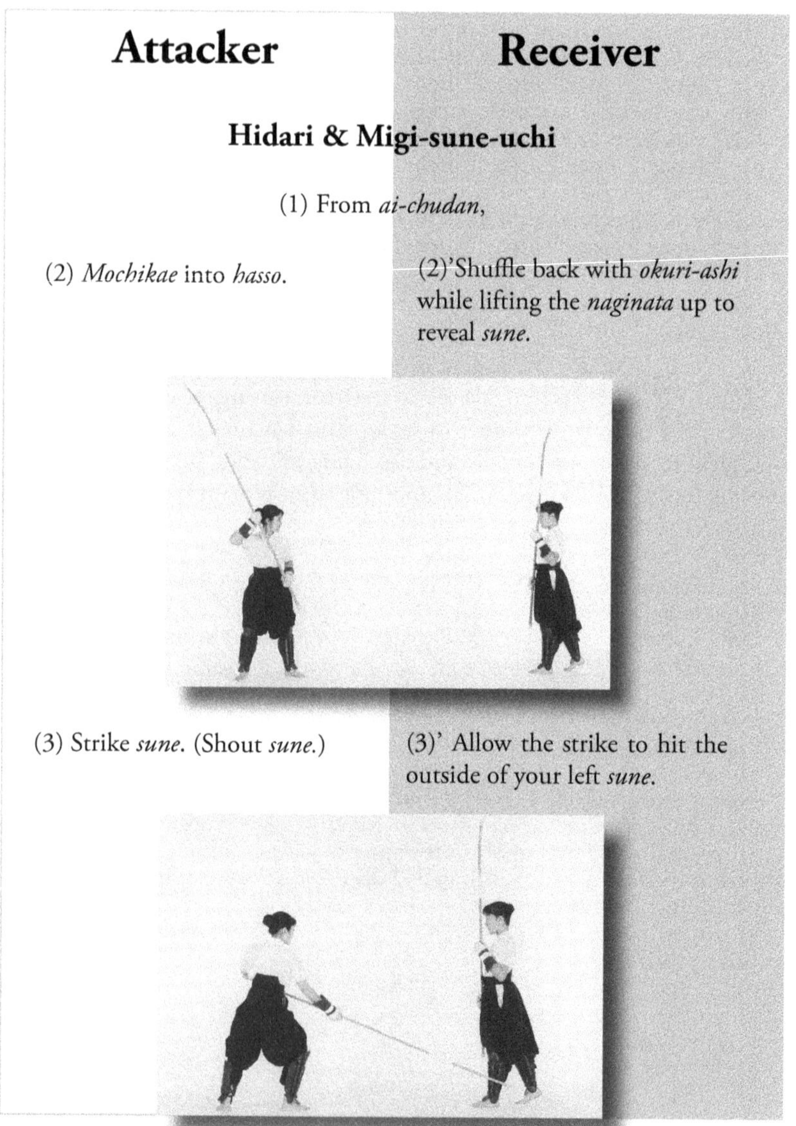

Attacker	Receiver

Hidari & Migi-sune-uchi

(1) From *ai-chudan*,

Attacker	Receiver
(2) *Mochikae* into *hasso*.	(2)'Shuffle back with *okuri-ashi* while lifting the *naginata* up to reveal *sune*.
(3) Strike *sune*. (Shout *sune*.)	(3)' Allow the strike to hit the outside of your left *sune*.

(4) *Mochikae* into *hasso* again, and strike the other *sune*. (Shout *sune*.)

(4)' Draw the left foot back while lifting up the *ishizuki* to allow the strike to hit the outside of the right *sune*. The eceiver should be facing the front.

Return to *ai-chudan* and swap roles.

Important Points:

1. Practise moving in all directions rather than just in a straight line. The receiver takes the initiative in controlling direction.
2. Be relaxed when striking. Maintain eye-contact avoiding the temptation to look down at the target.
3. The striker's feet and knees should be pointing in the direction of the target. Be perfectly side-on at the completion of each strike.
4. Aim for the middle of the *sune-ate*.
5. You are trying to strike the target with the whole body, not just the hands. Too much power in the arms will make the strike difficult to control. This is not good for the receiver's knees or ankles!
6. If struck accidentally, don't make an issue out of it. It may sting, but grin and bear the pain without showing it. The odd wayward strike is a fact of life in Naginata.

Furiage-sune-uchi

(1) From *ai-chudan*,

(2) Lift the *naginata* overhead (*furiage*) while stepping forward from the back foot.

(2)'Stepping back, lift the *ishi-zuki* or *ha-bu* end of the *naginata* to reveal the *sune-ate*.

(3) Strike *sune*. (Shout *sune*.)

Return to *ai-chudan* and swap roles.

Important Points:

1. Practise striking from both *migi-chudan* and *hidari-chudan*.
2. When the *naginata* is lifted overhead, the body should face the front, and then spun around to the side in time with the strike as it is made.
3. The receiver may take strikes on either *sune*, inside or outside.

E-bu-sune-uchi

(1) From *ai-chudan*,

(2) Step forward from the back foot and thrust the *ishizuki* end of the *naginata* out (*kuridashi*) while pivoting around to strike *sune*. (Shout *sune*.)

(2)'Step back while lifting the *ishizuki* or *ha-bu* end of the *naginata* to reveal the *sune-ate*.

Important Points:

1. Learn to strike from both *migi-chudan* and *hidari-chudan*.
2. The *motodachi* may receive the strikes on either *sune*, inside or outside.
3. Make sure that the strike is not too deep or shallow. The *monouchi* (20cm~25cm from the *ishizuki*) should make contact with the target.
4. As the *e-bu* is made from hard wood as opposed to bamboo, there is more danger of injury with a missed or overly forceful strike. Thus, only practitioners of a high level of technical proficiency, and who are at least 16 years old, should attempt this technique.
5. Power from the strike comes from the momentum gained through rotating the hips.
6. This technique is particularly effective when employed at close quarters while attempting to move away. (*Hiki-waza*.)

After becoming accustomed to moving with the *sune-ate* and other pieces of armour on, move to the next step in full armour. It will take a while to get used to the *men*. It will feel awkward, but you will get used to it as you learn to put it on properly. Make sure that the *men* size is right for you.

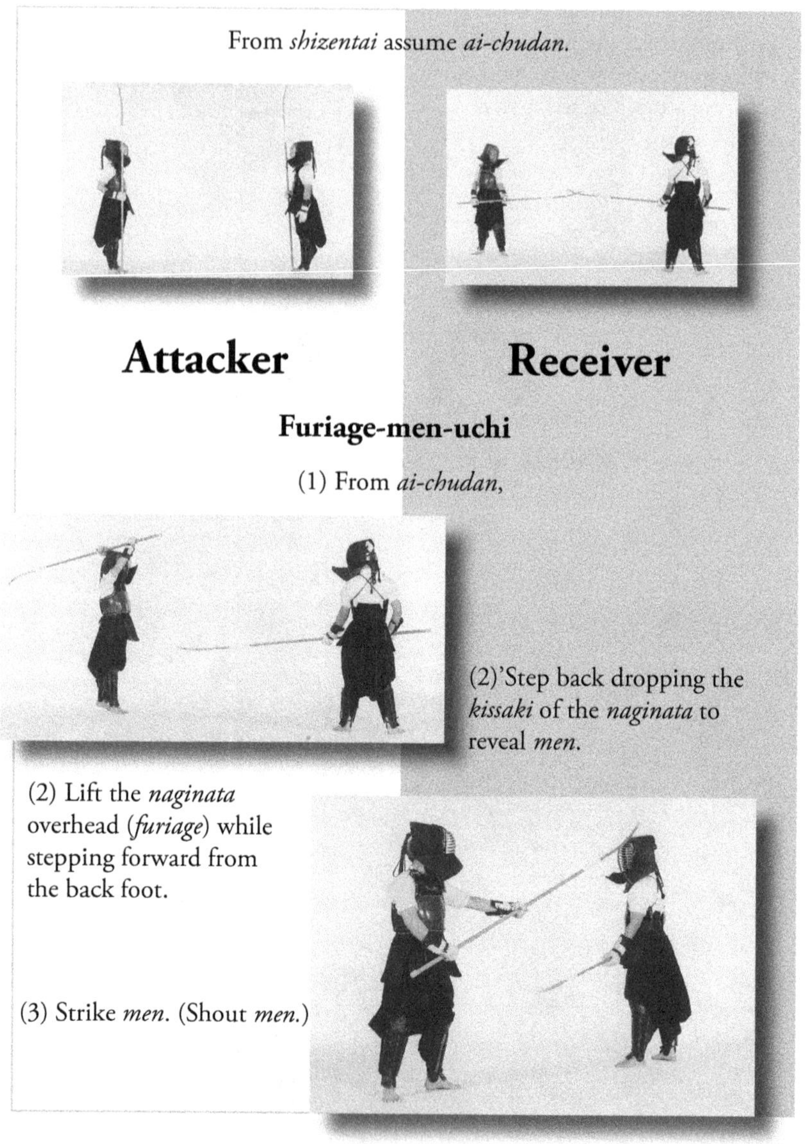

From *shizentai* assume *ai-chudan*.

Attacker **Receiver**

Furiage-men-uchi

(1) From *ai-chudan*,

(2)'Step back dropping the *kissaki* of the *naginata* to reveal *men*.

(2) Lift the *naginata* overhead (*furiage*) while stepping forward from the back foot.

(3) Strike *men*. (Shout *men*.)

Sokumen-uchi

(1) From *ai-chudan*,

(2) *Mochikae* into *hasso*.

(2)' Move back and lower the *kissaki* to reveal *men*.

(3) Strike *sokumen*. (Shout *men*.)

(4) *Mochikae* into *hasso*.

(4)' Move back with the *kissaki* lowered to reveal *men*.

(5) Strike *sokumen*. (Shout *men*.)

Return to *ai-chudan* and swap roles.

Do-uchi

(1) From *ai-chudan*,

(2) *Mochikae* into *wakagamae*.

(2)' Move back and lift the *naginata* overhead revealing the *do*.

(3) Strike *do*. (Shout *do*.)

(4) *Mochikae* into *wakigamae* and strike *do*. (Shout *do*.)

(4)' Move back maintaining the same open posture.

Return to *ai-chudan* and swap roles.

Kote-uchi

(1) From *ai-chudan*,

(2) Lift the *naginata* overhead (*furiage*) while stepping forward from the back foot.

(2)' Lift the *kissaki* up to the right to reveal the *kote*.

(3) Strike *kote*. (Shout *kote*).

Return to *ai-chudan* and swap roles.

Tsuki

(1) From *ai-chudan*,

(2) Twist the blade while stepping in to thrust at the throat.

(2)' Drop the *kissaki* to the left, face the front and receive the thrust.

Return to *ai-chudan* and swap roles.

2. Oji-waza

Men-uke-sune

(1) From *ai-chudan*,

(2) Strike *men*.

(2)' Block *men*.

(3) Move forward to the left with *hiraki-ashi* and strike *sune*.

Return to *ai-chudan* and swap roles.

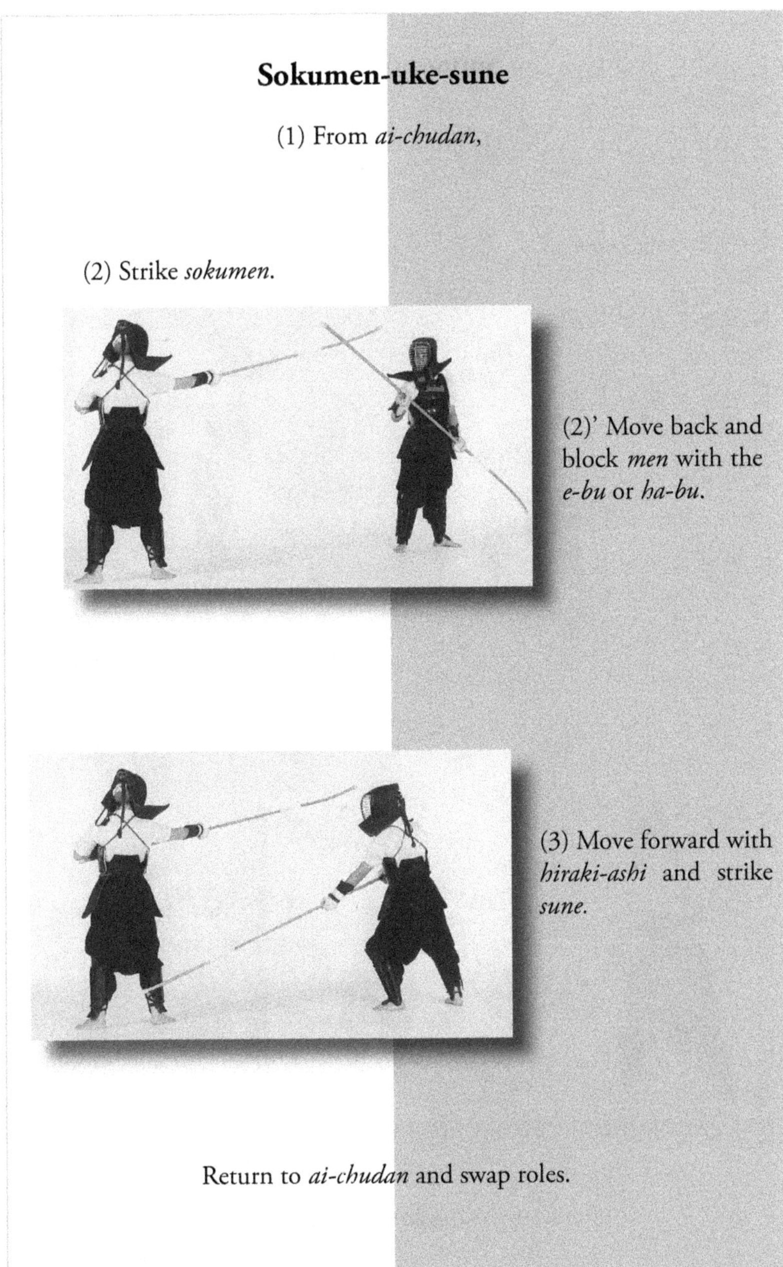

Sokumen-uke-sune

(1) From *ai-chudan*,

(2) Strike *sokumen*.

(2)' Move back and block *men* with the *e-bu* or *ha-bu*.

(3) Move forward with *hiraki-ashi* and strike *sune*.

Return to *ai-chudan* and swap roles.

Sune-nuki-men

(1) From *ai-chudan*,

(2) Strike *sune*.

(2)' Move back with *okuri-ashi* to avoid the strike (*nuki*).

Move forward and strike *men*.

Return to *ai-chudan* and swap roles.

Do-nuki-kote

(1) From *ai-chudan*,

(2) Strike *do*.

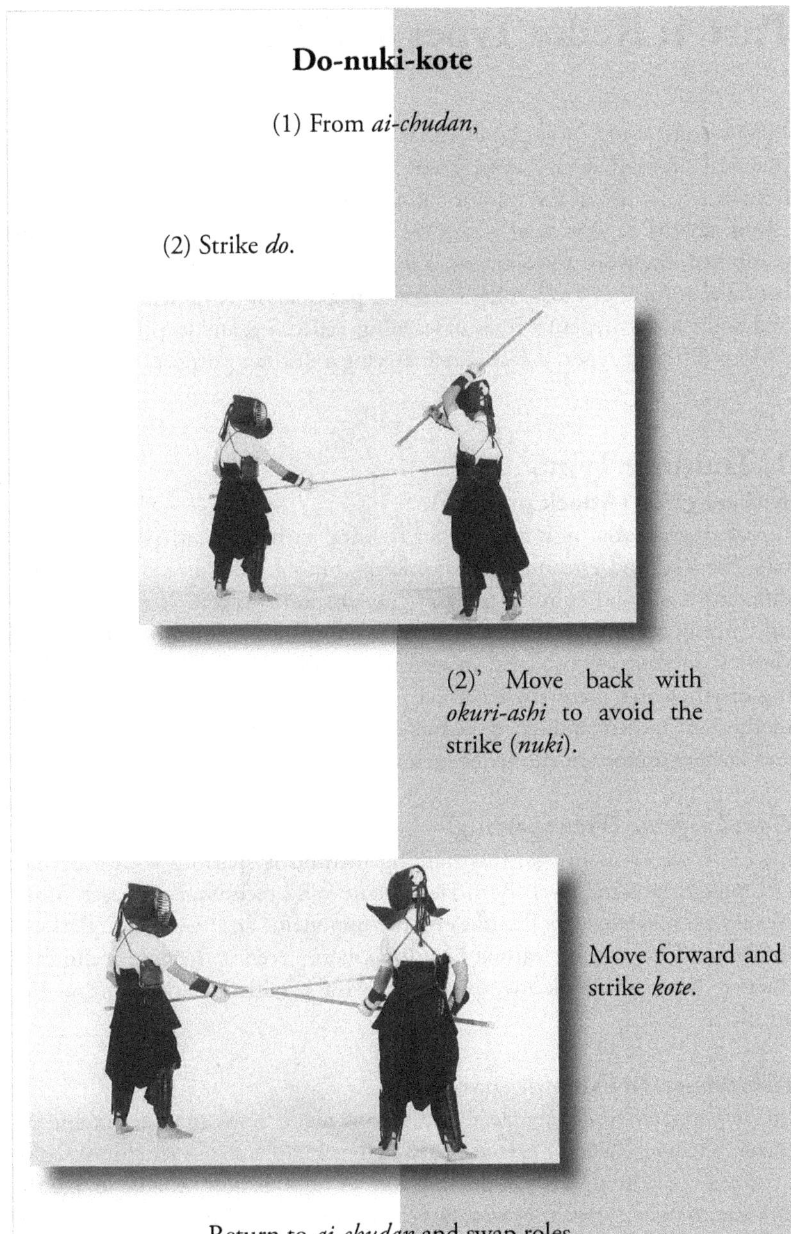

(2)' Move back with *okuri-ashi* to avoid the strike (*nuki*).

Move forward and strike *kote*.

Return to *ai-chudan* and swap roles.

Part 4: Keiko Types and Attitude

Now we are ready to apply all the techniques in the previous lessons in a practical situation such as *shiai-geiko*. For many centuries, the word used to describe the study of the traditional martial arts is *keiko*. *Kei* (稽) means to "think about" or "consider". *Ko* (古) means "old", or "olden times". Thus combined, the word *keiko* means to learn the wisdom of the ancients. It also contains a nuance of self-cultivation and personal development of the mind and body. It is a perpetual circle of learning, reflecting, and learning. There are various different types of *keiko*, each serving a distinct purpose.

1. Training Types

Kakari-geiko (Attack practice)

In *kakari-geiko* you must attack your training partner relentlessly, while they take the lead and encourage you to keep coming. You should try as many different *waza* and combinations as you can until told to stop. Never give up halfway even if your strikes are deflected or avoided. Although pushing yourself to your physical and mental limits, always gauge the correct striking distance and maintain a correct posture. This is an invaluable training method for understanding *maai*, building a strong spirit (*kiai*) and stamina, and honing important subtleties such as effective grip etc.

Gokaku-geiko (Free sparring)

Also referred to as *jigeiko*, this training method is sparring with a partner of roughly the same level. Both vie to score valid techniques on each other. Always acknowledge good strikes by the opponent, and use it as a platform to learn. Much can be learned from opponents even if they are technically inferior. Never overlook any openings. Take the initiative and be primed to attack.

Hikitate-geiko (Mentor sparring)

In *hikitate-geiko*, there are clear distinctions made between attacker, and receiver. The *motodachi* for *hikitate-geiko* is, in principle, the instructor or senior member(s) of the dojo. It is the *motodachi*'s responsibility to encourage the attacker to fight as best they can, not to destroy them with their own superior skill. *Hikitate* means to "support" or to "draw out". This means that it is an instructional style of sparring, and designed to encourage development through positive attacking. It is not *kakari-geiko*, but the bout will often build up to *kakari-geiko* to cap things off.

Shiai-geiko (Match practice)

Match practice affords practitioners the opportunity to try all of their techniques in a competitive situation. Abiding by the rules of Naginata competition, match practice should be conducted with Shinpan (referees) deciding valid points. It is beneficial to compete against many different people, and the instructor should encourage everybody to participate.

Tokubestu-geiko (Special training)

The following training methods conducted for specific purposes:

- *Kan-geiko* (Mid-winter training)
Kan-geiko training is traditionally conducted early in the morning of the coldest time of the year. The purpose is to boost mental strength and technical improvement through training in immensely uncomfortable circumstances. In this case, extreme cold.
- *Shochu-geiko* (Mid-summer training)
Shochu-geiko is conducted for the same purpose as *kan-geiko*, however, it is carried out at the hottest time of the year instead.
- *Hitori-geiko* (Solitary training)
It is beneficial to also train by yourself to work on technique and strategy. Practising in front of a mirror is a good way to identify problems with technique and *kamae*, etc.
- *Mitori-geiko* (Observing)
Watching others train is a sure path to improvement. Scrutinise individual styles, good or bad habits, successful or unsuccessful techniques, and try to incorporate your observations into your own training.

2. Mind and Attitude in Training

When training or competing, the practitioner must not be fixated, and be lucid enough to respond to any situation without becoming distracted. This liberated state of mind is called *hoshin*. Without *hoshin*, the mind gets stuck on some superfluous detail, and this preoccupation makes the practitioner freeze. Hands and feet will stop moving freely, and it will become difficult to execute *waza* effectively. The practitioner will unable to respond appropriately to any given situation. This restricted state is referred to as *shishin*. *Shishin* is the self-destructive state of mind that prevails if one is unable to sustain the state of *hoshin*.

It is also important to remember that even though we have covered *shikake-waza* (attacking) and *oji-waza* (counter-attacking), offence and defence are inseparably combined. This is described by the term *ken-tai-itchi* (different to *ki-ken-tai-itchi*). Here, *ken* means to attack or strike the opponent, and *tai* means to wait while observing the opponent's movement calmly. In other words this is referring to the importance of always being mentally prepared and physically ready to defend while attacking, and counterattack while defending.

The ideal way of using the mind or body when facing an opponent in a match or during the course of training is expressed by the term *do-chu-sei*. This is the state where the mind calmly watches the opponent even though the body is moving rapidly in attack or defence. The contrasting term is *sei-chu-do*, which refers to the state where even though the body outwardly appears to be still, inwardly the mind is fully ready to respond at any time.

3. Shiai Attitude

Before

1. Plan ahead so that you are peaking physically and mentally by the time of the match.
2. Have confidence in your ability, and work on some of your favourite techniques.
3. Always make sure that your equipment is in order.
4. Know beforehand what kind of match it is going to be.
5. When you know who your opponent is going to be try to find out as much as you can about their style of Naginata, and work out a game plan.
6. Find out how to get to the venue, and what public transport is available.
7. Remain calm and composed, confirm your match court, and the time your matches will begin.
8. Warm up well, and try to relax.

During

1. Try your best to win the match.
2. Concentrate, and observe your opponent calmly.
3. Even if the odds seem against you, give it your best shot.
4. The harder it becomes the more effort that is required.
5. Try not to become engulfed by your opponent's pace. Take your time and stay composed.

6. Abide by the rules.
7. Always aim to get the first point.
8. Try to ignore the commotion of the spectators and supporters watching the match. Do not react to any comments made by a spectator.

After

1. Stay calm in victory and defeat. It is considered bad manners to jump up and down happily or to display any other such antics when you win a match.
2. Do not be arrogant, or openly complain about the referee's decisions.
3. Learn from each match, and try to improve in future matches.
4. Pack your equipment away neatly when it's all over.

4. Examination Attitude

Attitude

1. You may decide to take an examination of your own accord to test your progress, or you may have been advised to by your teacher. In either case, it is important when sitting an examination to keep an open mind and be as objective as possible.
2. When it comes time to take the examination, try to relax and do the best that you can.
3. If you pass, you have a responsibility to continue living up to the level expected of the grade you receive.
4. If you fail, you should endeavour to understand the reason why. Seek advice from your seniors, and continue to evaluate your own level of Naginata, both the strong points and your weaknesses. It is this process which enables the individual to progress.

Appearance & Equipment

1. Make sure that your equipment and attire is clean and in order. The *keiko-gi* must be clean and white, and the cords tucked on the inside.
2. You should be wearing an *obi* that is wrapped twice around the waist and tied in a bow or a knot at the back.
3. The pleats in the *hakama* should be straight and pronounced. It should be slightly raised at the back as the *koshi-ita* sits on top of the *obi* knot. Make sure that it is not too short or too long.
4. Always use a clean *tenugui*.
5. Fasten your equipment securely so that it doesn't come undone during the examination.
6. All the cords should be in good order and fastened neatly.
7. Check that your *naginata* is safe. There should be no splinters in the bamboo, or splits in the *sendan-maki* tape, and that the leather caps on the *kissaki* and *ishizuki* are secure.

Appendix 1

Naginata Match Regulations

(競技規定)

The following is a translation of the most recent AJNF "Naginata Match Regulations" (January 10, 2014) which the INF adheres to.

CONTENTS

Appendix 1: Match Regulations

CHAPTER 1: Naginata Matches (Shiai-kyogi)

Match Outline

ARTICLE 1

A Naginata match is conducted in a stipulated area, and is contested by two competitors (*shiai-sha*), each holding a *naginata*, who vie to score valid points on each other by successfully striking designated targets.

Types of Matches

ARTICLE 2

Naginata *shiai-kyogi* consists of individual matches (*kojin-shiai*) and team matches (*dantai-shiai*).

Match Method

ARTICLE 3

Individual Matches (Kojin-shiai)

1. In principle, individual matches shall be decided by the best of 3 points (*sanbon-shobu*).
2. The *shiai-sha* who scores 2 points within the designated time shall be the winner. However, in the case whereby only 1 point is scored by the conclusion of match time, the scorer of that point shall be the winner.
3. In case a match is not decided within the designated time with both competitors having 1 point each, or no points at all, an extended period of play (*encho*) will be conducted wherein the *shiai-sha* who scores 1 point first shall be the winner. If the match is still not decided after *encho*, the outcome will be determined by *hantei* (Referees' decision). Depending on the kind of match, however, the end result may also be declared a draw (*hikiwake*).

ARTICLE 4

Team Matches (Dantai-shiai)

1. A series of matches shall be contested by individuals in a predetermined order to decide victory or defeat of the team.
2. The team with the majority of individual winners shall be the overall winner. If the number of individual match winners is equal, the team that has the higher number of points scored shall be the winner. Furthermore, if the number of points scored happens to be equal, one individual from each team will face off to decide the victor in a representative match (*daihyosha-sen*).

3. Depending on tournament circumstances, a match may be declared a draw (*hikiwake*).

Match Area (Shiai-jo)

ARTICLE 5

The match area (court) should be a square measuring 12mx12m inclusive of the lines. (See Fig. 1.)

ARTICLE 6

An extra area of 2m or more from the boundary line should be provided outside the court.

ARTICLE 7

The boundary lines should be marked in white, with each line measuring 5cm in width. The length of each side of the court should be measured from the outer edge of the lines.

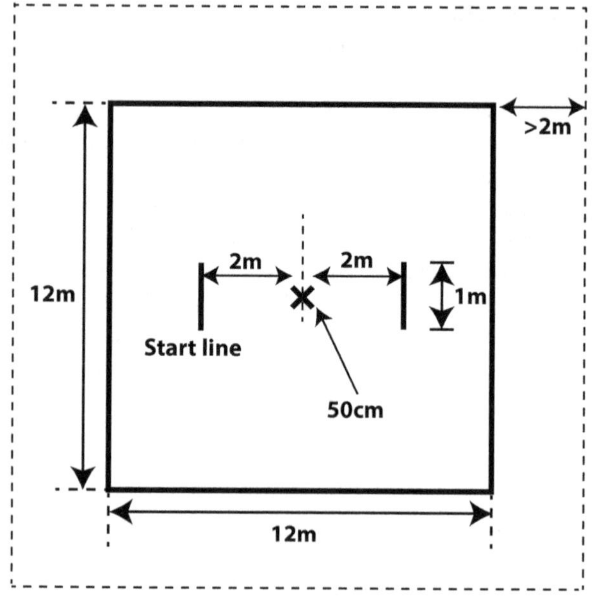

(Fig. 1) Shiai-jo

Equipment

ARTICLE 8

The *naginata* shall be the same length, weight, and made of the same materials shown in Fig.2. The shaft (*e-bu*) should be oval in shape.

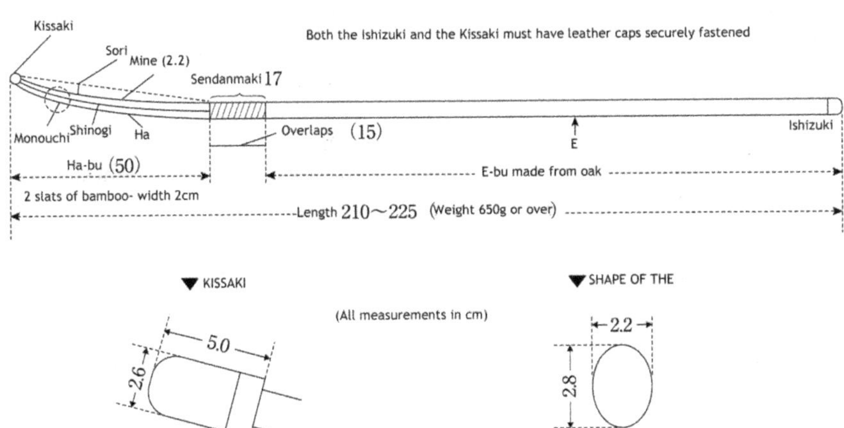

(Fig. 2) Structure of the Naginata

- The *kissaki* should be rounded by inserting some strips of cloth under the leather.
- The *sendan-maki* should 15cm with 1cm of tape at each end to anchor it, thus making a total length 17cm.
- The *naginata* should not be coloured or ornately engraved.

ARTICLE 9

Protective equipment (*bogu*) used in Naginata shall consist of a mask (*men*), gauntlets (*kote*), plastron (*do*), waist protector (*tare*), and shin protectors (*sune-ate*).

ARTICLE 10

The attire shall consist of a white top (*keiko-gi*) secured with a white sash (*obi*), and a black or navy blue split-skirt (*hakama*).

Match Duration

ARTICLE 11

Match time shall be no longer than 5 minutes.

ARTICLE 12

In principle, a time extension (*encho*) shall be no longer than 2 minutes.

ARTICLE 13

Match time will commence with the pronouncement of "*Hajime*" by Shushin

(Head Referee), and finish when the Time Keeper (Tokei-iin) signals that time is up.

ARTICLE 14
Match time will not be included in the following situations:

1. From the time when a valid point (*yuko-datotsu*) is pronounced by the Shushin until the match is resumed again.
2. From the time when the match is suspended until it is resumed again.

ARTICLE 15
The time that it takes for Shushin to separate *shiai-sha* in *seriai* shall be included in the match duration.

Starting, Finishing, Suspending, and Extending Matches
ARTICLE 16
The match shall commence with the pronouncement of "*Hajime*" by Shushin.

ARTICLE 17
The match shall conclude with Shushin's declaration of "*Shobu ari*" (victory decided), or "*Hikiwake*" (draw).

ARTICLE 18
The match shall be suspended in the event of foul play (*hansoku*), or accident etc., with Shushin's pronouncement of "*Yame*".

ARTICLE 19
Encho (time extension) is enacted when the match cannot end in a draw and victory or defeat must be decided. The prolongation of match time will begin with Shushin's pronouncement of "*Encho. Hajime*".

Requesting Suspension of a Match

ARTICLE 20
Shiai-sha may request stoppage of the match if unable to continue due to an accident or some other reason. *Shiai-sha* must signal their desire for suspension of the match by raising their hand and obtaining permission from the Shinpan-in.

Appendix 1: Match Regulations

Striking Targets (Datotsu-bui)

ARTICLE 21

***Datotsu-bui* (Striking Targets)**

Men	*Shomen* (centre of the *men*); *Sayu-sokumen* (left and right men—between 25°~30° to the left and right of the centre of *shomen*)
Kote	Left and right *kote* (5cm from the wrist)
Do	Left and right sides of the plastron
Sune	Left and right *sune*, inside left and right *sune* (the section between the knee and ankle)
Inko	Throat (prohibited for high school students and below)

(Fig. 5) *Datotsu-bui*

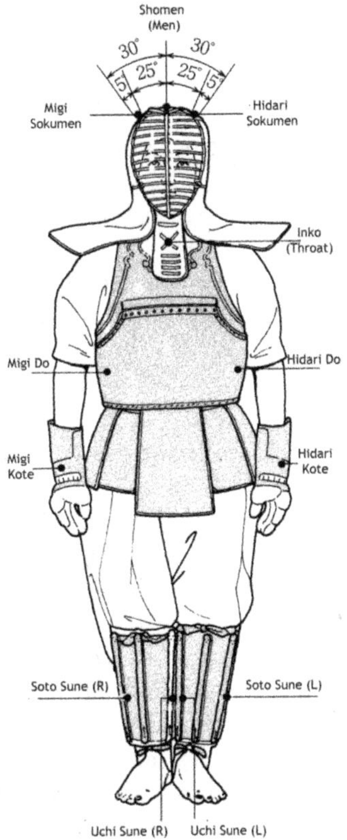

Target Areas (Datotsu-Bui)

Valid Strike (Yuko-datotsu)

ARTICLE 22

A valid strike (*yuko-datotsu*) is defined as an accurate strike or thrust made onto targets (*datotsu-bui*) with the striking section (*datotsu-bu*) of the *naginata* in high spirits and correct posture while simultaneously vocalising the name of the target, and followed with continued alertness (*zanshin*).

Datotsu-bui	Datotsu-bu of the naginata	Vocalisation
Men	15cm~20cm from the *kissaki* (*monouchi*)	*Men*
Kote	Same as above	*Kote*
Do	Same as above	*Do*
Sune	Same as above, and also with the *e-bu* (shaft) 20cm~25cm from the *ishizuki*	*Sune*
Inko	*Kissaki*	*Tsuki*

* *Tsuki*, and striking *sune* with the *e-bu* is prohibited for high school students or below.

Judging a Match

ARTICLE 23

A strike or thrust (*datotsu*) shall awarded as a 1 point (*ippon*) when at least two Shinpan-in recognise its validity.

ARTICLE 24

Referees' consultation (*gogi*) will be convened to question the validity of a strike, confirmation of foul play (*hansoku*), or when unforeseen circumstances arise.

ARTICLE 25

A strike or thrust (*datotsu*) shall be recognised as valid and awarded *ippon* in the following cases:

1. A strike made while going forward even if it is slightly weak or light. Or, an accurate strike made while retreating.
2. An accurate strike against a *shiai-sha* who breaks *kamae* and lets their guard down, or stops after making a strike.
3. An accurate strike made against a *shiai-sha* who has no intention of attacking and merely holds the *naginata* on the opponent.
4. An accurate strike made immediately against a *shiai-sha* who has dropped their *naginata*, or who has fallen over.
5. An accurate strike made at the same time as the time-up signal.

ARTICLE 26

In the case of injury or accident, a match shall be decided in accordance to the procedure stipulated below, and 2 points will be awarded to the victor. However, only 1 point will be awarded if *ippon* has already been scored. If the defeated competitor has scored *ippon*, that point will remain valid.

1. A *shiai-sha* who defaults will lose the match.
2. An injured *shiai-sha* who refuses to resume even though the injury is considered to be slight and it feasible to continue will forfeit the match.
3. If the match cannot continue due to the occurrence of injury, the *shiai-sha* who caused it shall be judged the loser. If the cause of the accident is unable to be determined, the *shiai-sha* who is unable to continue will be the loser.
4. In a team match (*dantai-shiai*) any *shiai-sha* who is unable to continue due to the above three situations, or requests termination of the match, will not be permitted to participate in the tournament thereafter.

ARTICLE 27

If a match is not decided in the designated time, Shinpan-in shall simultaneously make a decision (*hantei*), and 1 point will be awarded to the superior *shiai-sha.*

Hantei criteria – the following factors should be taken into consideration when making a *hantei* decision:

1. Superior level of offence and defence
2. Standard of posture and manner
3. Fouls committed

Fouls (Hansoku)

ARTICLE 28

A *shiai-sha* who is disrespectful and insults the opponent or Shinpan-in will be penalised.

ARTICLE 29

Stepping out of bounds (*jogai-hansoku*) will be penalised in the following occurences:

1. When one foot completely steps out of the match area. If both competitors step out of bounds, the first one will be penalised; and both *shiai-sha* will be penalised if they step out of match area at exactly the same time.
2. When a *shiai-sha* falls and a part of the body touches outside the match area.

3. When a *shiai-sha* props the body up with the *naginata* outside the match area.

ARTICLE 30

The following actions will be penalised as *hansoku*:

1. Striking *men* with the shaft (*e-bu*) of the *naginata*.
2. Intentionally or repeatedly hitting around the ears, or any area not protected by *bogu*.
3. Gripping the opponent's *naginata*, or wedging it between some part of the body.
4. Illicitly pushing the opponent, or stopping the match needlessly.
5. Showing no will to fight by remaining in *seriai* (close-quarters), or ignoring calls for *wakare* (separate).
6. Unnecessary vocalisations.
7. Dropping the *naginata*.
8. When a piece of *bogu* comes untied and falls off.
9. Other actions considered dangerous.
10. Committing prohibited acts.

Penalties

ARTICLE 31

Any *shiai-sha* who commits a foul stipulated in ARTICLE 28 shall be expelled from the match (*taijo*), and the opponent shall be awarded 2 points. Only 1 point will be awarded if *ippon* has already been scored. The expelled *shiai-sha* will be disqualified from any further participation.

ARTICLE 32

Any *shiai-sha* who commits a foul stipulated in ARTICLES 29–30 shall be penalised with *hansoku* each time. If penalised 2 times, *ippon* (1 point) will be awarded to the opponent.

Protesting (Igi no moshitate)

ARTICLE 33

Protests cannot be made against Shinpan-in decisions.

CHAPTER 2: Engi-kyogi

Outline of Engi

ARTICLE 1

The objective is to encourage the correct diffusion and development of Naginata. *Engi* is conducted in a stipulated match area, with pairs of competitors who perform sequences of *waza.*

Types of Engi

ARTICLE 2

The types of *engi* competition are All Japan Naginata Kata and Shikake-Oji.

Engi Method

ARTICLE 3

The methods for deciding victory in *engi* are *hata-keishiki* (decision by raising flags), and *saiten-keishiki* (decision by point scoring).

1. The forms to be contested will be designated from the All Japan Naginata Kata or Shikake-Oji.
2. In *hata-keishiki*, the superior pair shall be indicated by the Shinpan-in is red or white *shinpan-ki.*
3. In *saiten-keishiki*, the superior pair shall be decided by Shinpan-in scores. Exceeding or falling short of the stipulated performance time will result in a loss of points.

Engi Court

ARTICLE 4

The *engi* court shall be the same dimensions as those shown in the following diagrams (Fig. 16–Fig. 18). An area of 2m or more should be provided outside the court. The boundary should be marked with white lines 5cm in width. The length of each side should be measured from the outer-edge of the line.

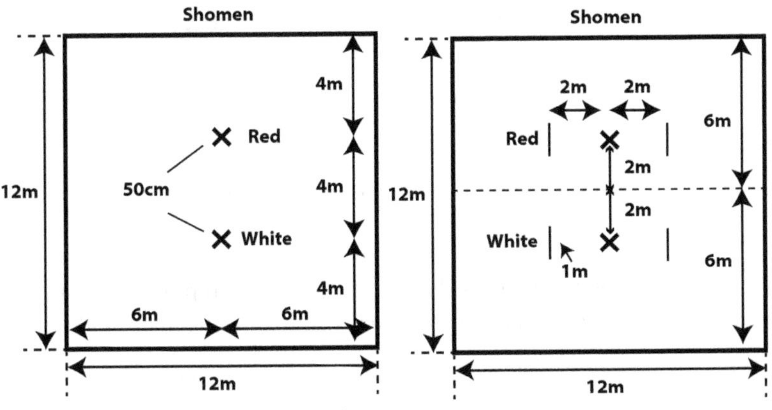

(Fig. 16) Kata (Hata-keishiki)

(Fig. 17) Shikake-Oji (Hata-keishiki)

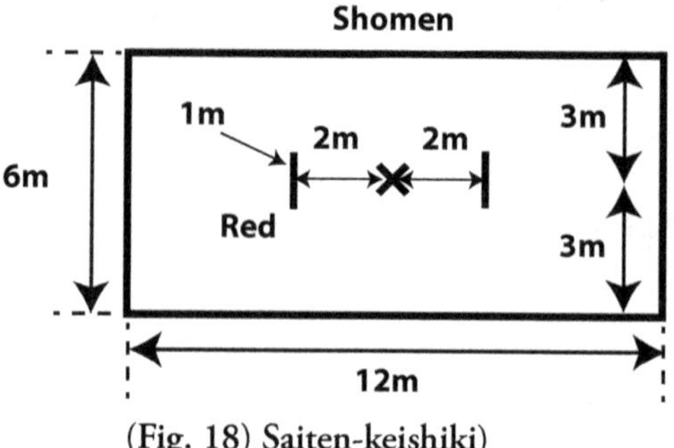

(Fig. 18) Saiten-keishiki)

Equipment

ARTICLE 5

All Japan Naginata Kata shall be performed with Kata *naginata*. (Fig. 19–Fig. 21). Shikake-Oji performed with match *naginata*. (Fig. 2–Fig. 4.) The Kata *naginata* should correspond to the length, weight, and materials indicated in the diagrams, and the shaft should be oval in shape. The *naginata* should not be coloured or engraved.

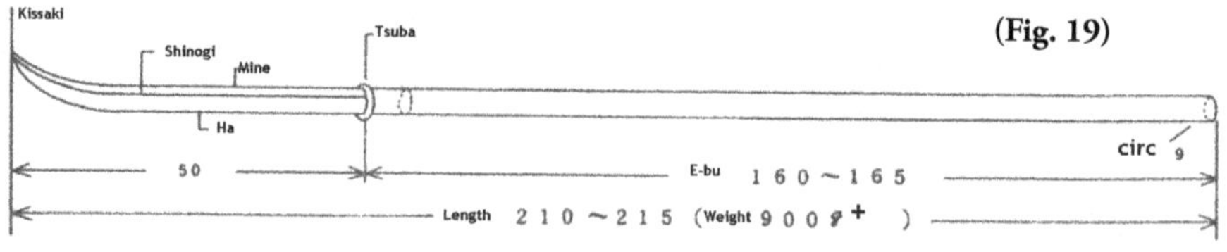

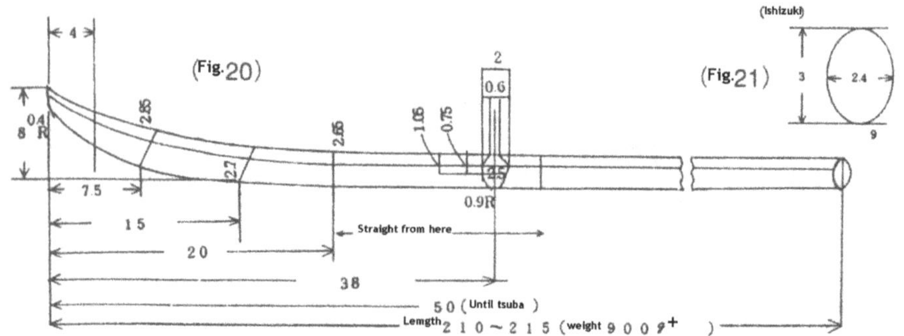

ARTICLE 6

The attire worn by competitors shall consist of a white top (*keiko-gi*) fastened with a white sash (*obi*), and a black or navy blue split-skirt (*hakama*).

Appendix 1: Match Regulations

Engi Time for Saiten-keishiki

ARTICLE 7

The time for *saiten-keishiki* shall depend on the assignment, and will begin with Shushin's signal and finish when the court is exited.

ARTICLE 8

The time required for stoppage due to accident (or breakage of a *naginata*) shall not be included in the performance time.

Starting, Finishing, and Suspending Engi Matches

ARTICLE 9

Engi starts with the signal for "*Nyujo*" (enter court), and finishes when all the competitors have exited the court.

ARTICLE 10

In the case of an accident, Shushin shall suspend the match by calling "*Yame*". In this case, it shall be done at the beginning of the technique.

Striking Targets (Datotsu-bui)

ARTICLE 11

Datotsu-bui **(Striking targets)**

Men	*Shomen* (centre) *Sayu-sokumen* (25°–30° either side of the centre)
Kote	Left and right *kote* (5cm from the wrist)
Do	Left and right sides of the torso
Sune	Left and right *sune*, inside left and right *sune* (the section between the knee and ankle)
Wakibara	Left and right side of the body
Mizoochi	Pit of the stomach
Inko	Throat

Deciding Victory and Defeat, or Ranking

ARTICLE 12

In *hata-keishiki*, victory and defeat is decided by the majority of the five Shinpan-in decisions. In *saiten-keishiki*, rankings are decided by the median score of five Shinpan-in. (Precision of time is also taken into account when scoring.)

Protesting (Igi no moshitate)

ARTICLE 13

Protests cannot be made against Shinpan-in decisions.

Appendix 2
Naginata Shinpan Regulations
(審判規定)

The following is a translation of the most recent AJNF "Naginata Shinpan Regulations" (January 10, 2014) which the INF adheres to.

CONTENTS

Appendix 2: Shinpan Regulations

CHAPTER 1: Shinpan-in

1. The Importance of Shinpan
Those tasked with adjudicating have the important responsibility of guiding Naginata by ensuring that matches are conducted in accordance with the principles of Naginata and exhibit its special characteristics, and by seeing that all matches are contested fairly and judged properly without prejudice.

2. The Function of Shinpan-in*
The function of Shinpan-in is to oversee Naginata competitions in accordance with the All Japan Naginata Federation's (AJNF) official "Match Regulations" and "Shinpan Regulation", and adjudicate matches to decide the outcome. In *shiai-kyogi*, Shinpan-in will determine victory and defeat by judging valid strikes or thrusts (*yuko-datotsu*) and fouls (*hansoku*) in strict observance of the stipulated rules. In *engi-kyogi*, Shinpan-in confirm that *engi* is performed in accordance with the regulations, and will determine the outcome of the contest by assessing the quality of *waza* (techniques).

(*Shinpan-in is the collective term for refereeing officials.)

3. Shinpan-in Qualifications
The "Shinpan-in Certification System" authorises those persons deemed most suitable to serve as Shinpan-in in anticipation of impartial adjudication and continual improvement of refereeing skills to assist in the advancement of Naginata competitions.

There are four categories of Shinpan-in certification:

- *Meiyo Shinpan-in* (Honorary Referee) – Those who hold the *shogo* title of *Hanshi.*
- *Isshu* (Class-1): Persons who hold the title of *Renshi* or above, and who have a high level of technical proficiency.
- *Nishu* (Class-2): Persons who hold the title of 5-dan and above, who have a high level of technical proficiency.
- *Sanshu* (Class-3): Persons who are 3-dan and above, who have a high level of technical proficiency.

4. Training and Approving Shinpan-in
Certified Shinpan-in are those who have been recommended by their federation of affiliation, have completed the mandatory units through participation in seminars, and have successfully passed the final examination.

5. Required Knowledge for Shinpan-in

1. Shinpan-in must be versed in the concept, purpose, and characteristics of Naginata, and have a high level of technical proficiency.
2. Shinpan-in must know the "Match Regulations" and "Shinpan Regulations"
3. Shinpan-in must have a thorough understanding of principles (*riai*) of Naginata.
4. Shinpan-in must be skilled in the techniques of refereeing.
5. Shinpan-in must be impartial.
6. Shinpan-in must be in good health.
7. Shinpan-in must be responsible.

6. Outline of the Shinpan-ki (Flags)

Shinpan-ki should not be thought of simply as tools, but as symbolic of the authority and responsibilities intrinsic to refereeing.

7. The Function and Duties of the Shinpan Director (Shinpan-cho)

(1) Function

The Shinpan-cho (Shinpan Director) makes sure that the Shinpan-in conduct their refereeing duties in strict accordance to the "Match Regulations", and must resolve any issues that may arise during the course of matches that are not stipulated in the regulations. Further, the Shinpan-cho decides the outcome of any protest (*igi-no-moshitate*).

(2) Duties

① The Shinpan-cho shall take all necessary measures to facilitate smooth administration of the tournament through maintaining close communication with the Kyogi-Iincho (Contest Chairperson).

② The Shinpan-cho shall prepare a chart delegating refereeing duties, and notify Shinpan-in of the roster before the commencement of the matches (usually distributing copies at the Shinpan Meeting). Shinpan-in for the semi-finals, third-place playoff, and the finals will be notified immediately before those matches.

③ The Shinpan-cho will make any changes to the Shinpan-in roster when required.

8. The Function and Duties of the Court Managers (Court Shinpan-shunin)

(1) Function

Court Managers (Shinpan-shunin) will be appointed when there are two or more courts in the competition venue. Shinpan-shunin will assist by overseeing the refereeing at their designated court, and resolve any issues that may arise during the course of matches that are not stipulated in the regulations.

(2) Duties

① Shinpan-shunin shall prepare a chart delegating refereeing duties in their respective court, and notify Shinpan-in of the roster before commencement of the matches.

② Shinpan-shunin will make any changes to the Shinpan-in roster when required.

9. Transferral of the *Shinpan-ki*

① Shinpan-cho will pass the *shinpan-ki* to the Shinpan-shunin (Court Managers) before commencement of the matches.

② Shushin (Head Referee) of the first match will receive the *shinpan-ki* from the Shinpan-shunin, and carry them to the Shinpan-in waiting in the standby area and present one set of *shinpan-ki* to each of the Shinpan-in starting from the *kamiza*.*

③ After all of the matches have been concluded, the Shinpan-in will return to the Shinpan seats, and Shushin will collect the *shinpan-ki* from each of the Shinpan-in individually, starting at the *shimoza*. Then, the three Shinpan-in will return together in single-file to the standby position, upon which Shushin takes the *shinpan-ki* and passes them back to the Shinpan-shunin.

④ Shinpan-shunin will receive the *shinpan-ki* and return them to the Shinpan-cho after the conclusion of the matches.

(*In this case, *kamiza* refers to the Fukushin (Sub-referee) who is standing on the side closest to the venue *shomen*. *Shimoza* is the opposite side to this.)

10. Holding the *Shinpan-ki*

① When moving, the *shinpan-ki* should be rolled together and held down the side of the body in the right hand with the edge of the cloth pinned securely with the index finger to prevent it from unrolling (Fig. 2).

② When refereeing, the handle of the *shinpan-ki* is held in the palm of the hand with the index finger extended to touch the edge of the cloth. The index finger should remain in this position when indicating decisions, with the flag handle and arm extended in a straight line (Fig. 2).

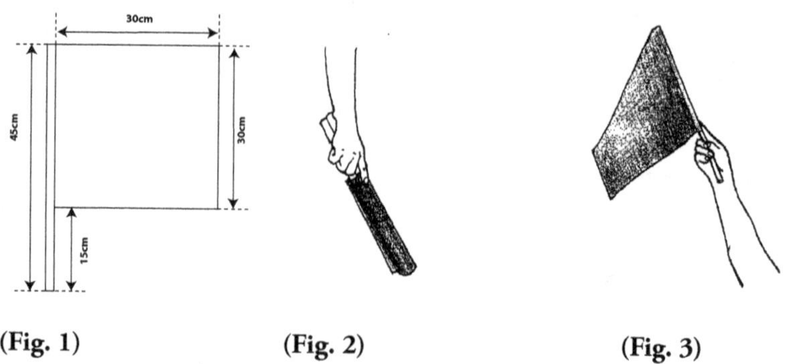

(Fig. 1) (Fig. 2) (Fig. 3)

11. Rolling the Shinpan-ki

The white flag should be rolled once before being placed together with the red flag. The two should then be rolled together (white on the inside), so that only the red cloth is visible when completed.

12. Changing Shinpan-in Positions in the Court

When Shinpan-in change positions during individual matches, a formal bow is conducted first, and then both *shinpan-ki* are held together down the side of the body in the right hand, and not swung as while walking to the new position.

13. Passing and Receiving the Shinpan-ki

① Passing the *shinpan-ki*:

When passing the flags which are rolled together and held in the right hand, pass them over using both hands while turning the handles to the left for ease of receiving. The right hand holds the cloth section from the bottom, and the left hand is placed on top of the handle (Fig. 4a.)

② Receiving the *shinpan-ki*:

When receiving the *shinpan-ki*, grasp the handle from the top with the right hand first, and the cloth section from the bottom with the left hand. (When lowering the flags to the side of the body, the index finger of the right hand should secure the edge of the cloth to stop it from unrolling). (Figs. 4a, b, c).

Note: The *shinpan-ki* should be delivered in the same way in bundles of three (*shiai*) or five (*engi*). (Figs. 5 & 6.)

Appendix 2: Shinpan Regulations

(Fig. 4)

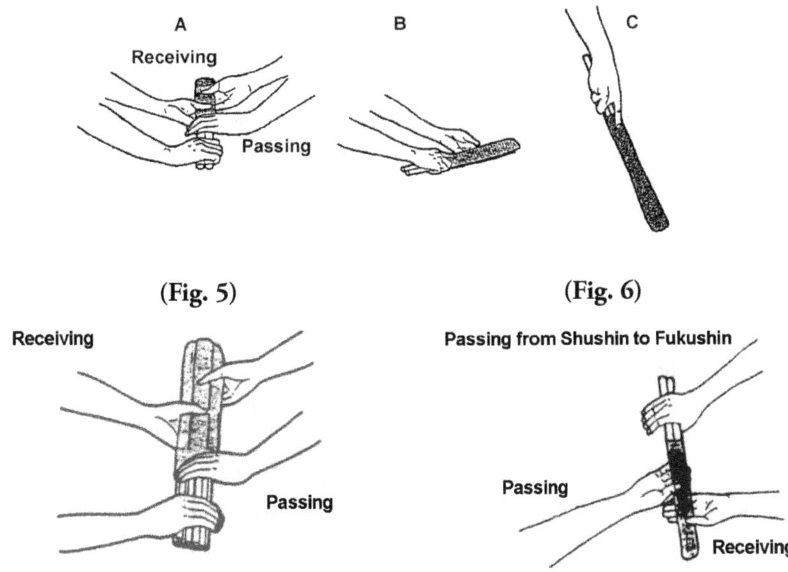

14. Venue Layout

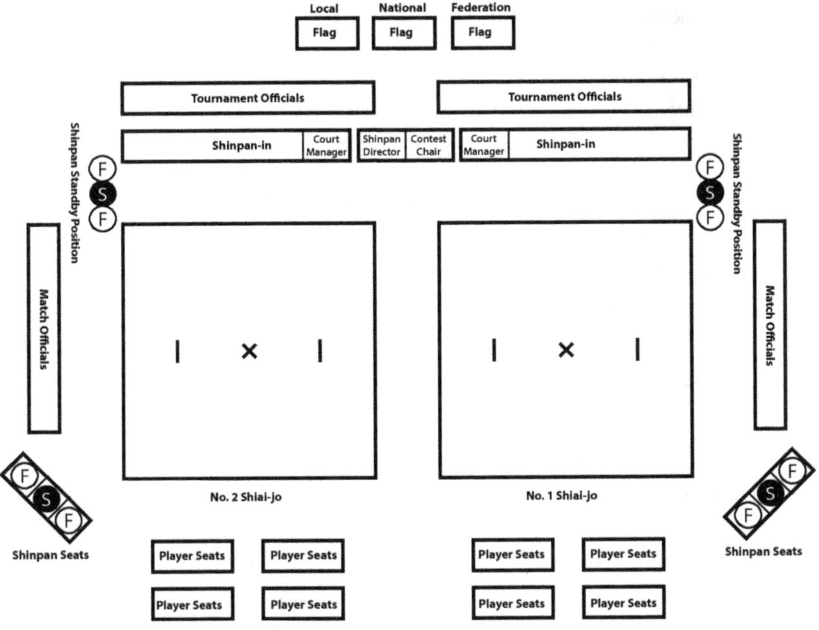

15. Method of Shinpan-in Entry

Shinpan-shunin will receive the *shinpan-ki* from Shinpan-cho. The Shinpan-in rostered for the first match line up at the Shinpan standby area. Shushin receives the *shinpan-ki* from the Shinpan-shunin. The Shinpan-in then proceed to the Shinpan seats in single file. Upon reaching the seats, Shushin will take one step forward, about-turn to the right, bow, and then pass the *shinpan-ki* to the Shinpan-in starting from the upper position (*kamiza*), and then return to the original position in the line. The three referees conduct one more bow and then sit down. The Shinpan-in all stand up in time with Shinpan-cho, march to the centre area of the court along the boundary line, and then enter the court following Shushin's signal.

16. Method of Shinpan-in Exit

At the conclusion of the matches, a mutual bow is conducted, the *shinpan-ki* are rolled up, and the Shinpan-in line up facing the *shomen*. A bow is made at Shushin's signal, and all return in single file to the Shinpan seats. Shushin takes a step forward, about-turns to the right and bows. The *shinpan-ki* are collected by Shushin from the lower position (*shimoza*), a mutual bow is made, and Shushin returns to the original position in the line. The Shinpan-in then proceed in single file to the Shinpan standby area. Shushin returns the *shinpan-ki* to the Shinpan-shunin and then returns to the standby area.

17. Starting the Competition

(1) Shiai-kyogi

① Team matches (*Dantai-sen*):

The *shiai-sha* line up in the court. (Taisho stands closest to the *shomen*, with only Senpo holding their *naginata*.)

The Shinpan-in step into the court from the left foot and bow at the command of "*Shomen ni rei!... Otagai ni rei!*" by Shushin. The Shinpan-in move to their designated positions. Shushin holds the red *shinpan-ki* in the right hand and the white one in the left. The Fukushin have the white *shinpan-ki* in the right hand and the red one in the left. When the *shinpan-ki* are unrolled a mutual bow is performed, and Shushin starts the match with the command "*Hajime*".

Note: When the referees are to be substituted, the next cohort of Shinpan-in stand in a line behind the incumbent group. When the next teams are lined up behind the preceding teams, Shushin pronounces "*Otagai ni rei. Shomen ni rei*", everybody bows, and then the first group of Shinpan-in about turn to the right, pass the *shinpan-ki* to their counterpart in the incoming group, and then exit the court.

② Individual matches (*Kojin-sen*):
The Shinpan-in bow to the *shomen*, then move to their positions before the commencement of the match. The *shiai-sha* proceed to the starting line at the call of the Scoreboard Official (Saiten Keiji-iin), bow to each other, and assume *ai-chudan* (the face-off position). The match commences with the announcement of "*Hajime*" by Shushin.

(2) *Engi-kyogi* (*Hata-keishiki*)
After proceeding to the court and conducting a bow to the *shomen* in the same method as *shiai-kyogi*, the Shinpan-in then move to their positions. Shushin, Nishin (②) and Sanshin (③) about turn to the right and hold the red *shinpan-ki* in the right hand, and the white *shinpan-ki* in the left. Isshin (①) and Yonshin (④) hold the white *shinpan-ki* in the right hand and the red *shinpan-ki* in the left. All bow together and then sit down. Both *engi* teams enter the court, and start with the signal of Shushin's whistle.

18. Movement Parameters for Shinpan-in
(1) Shiai-kyogi

(2) Engi-kyogi

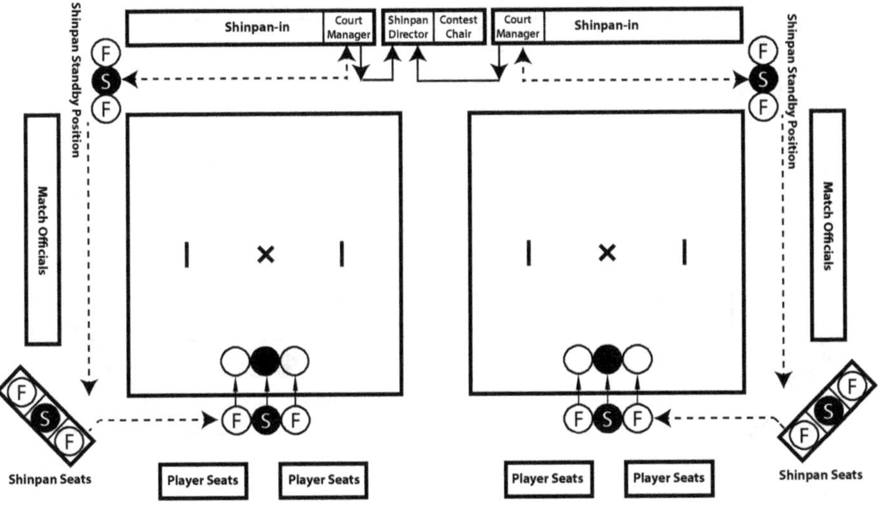

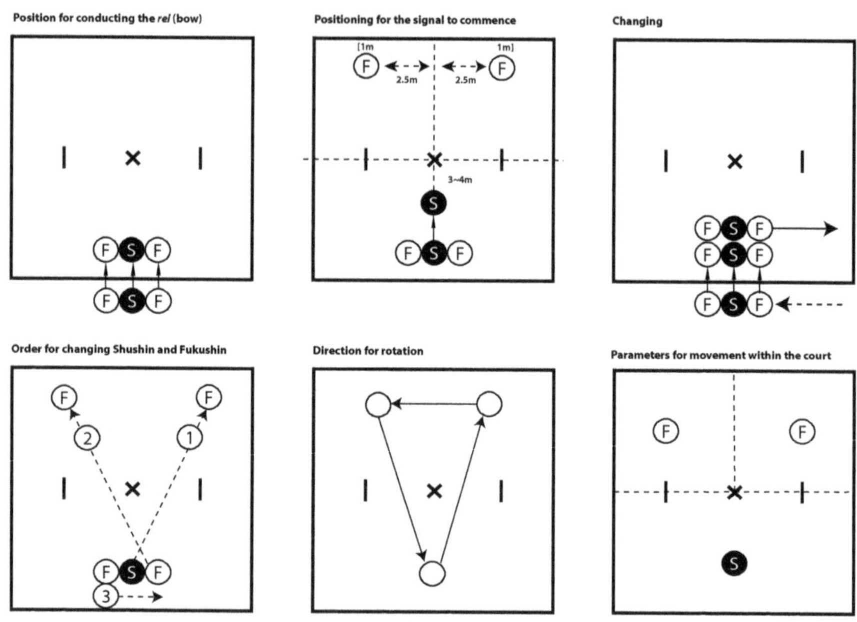
Position for conducting the *rei* (bow)
F
S
F
Positioning for the signal to commence
[1m
1m]
2.5m
2.5m
3~4m
Changing
Order for changing Shushin and Fukushin
1
2
3
Direction for rotation
Parameters for movement within the court

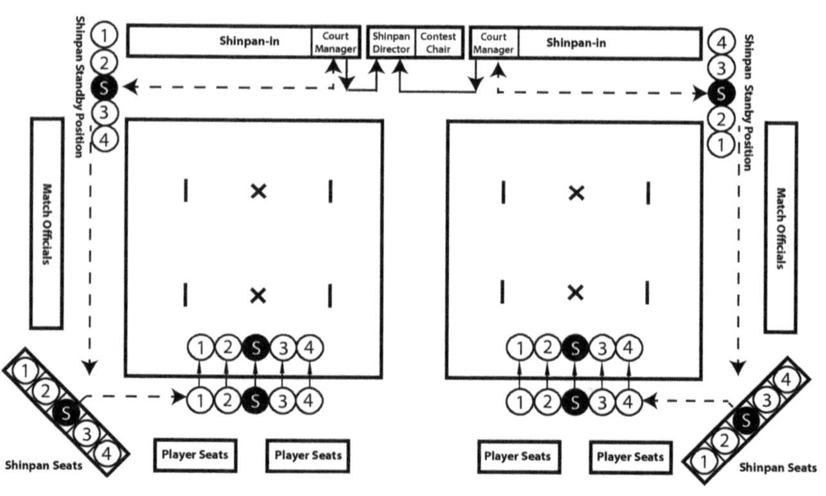
Shinpan-in
Court Manager
Shinpan Director
Contest Chair
Court Manager
Shinpan-in
Shinpan Standby Position
Shinpan Stanby Position
Match Officials
Match Officials
Shinpan Seats
Shinpan Seats
Player Seats
Player Seats
Player Seats
Player Seats

Appendix 2: Shinpan Regulations

Position for conducting the *rei* (bow)

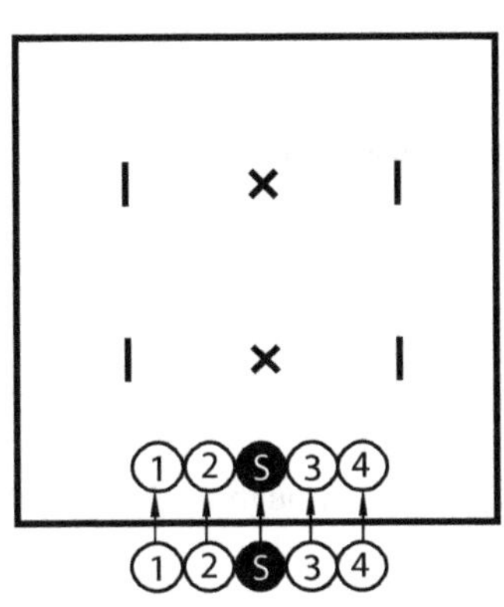

Take one step into the court from the left foot.

Positions

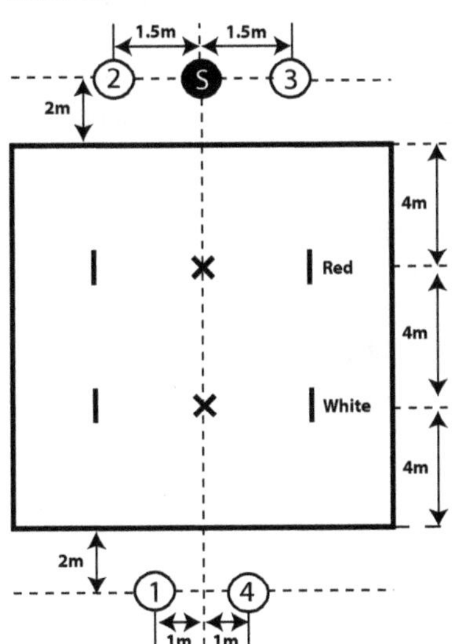

CHAPTER 2: Shiai-kyogi

ARTICLE 1
Shinpan-in shall adjudicate matches in accordance with the All Japan Naginata Federation "Shiai-kyogi Regulations".

ARTICLE 2
In principle, a refereeing cohort will consist of one Shushin (Head Referee) and two Fukushin (Sub-Referees).

ARTICLE 3
The function of Shinpan-in is to determine valid strikes (*yuko-datotsu*).

ARTICLE 4
Shinpan-in shall indicate their decision for *yuko-datotsu* through the use of red or white *shinpan-ki*.

ARTICLE 5
Yuko-datotsu will be determined in the following manner:

1. Shushin shall, with overall authority to administer the match, be positioned suitably to observe both *shiai-sha* equally, and using the *shinpan-ki* will pronounce the decision of *yuko-datotsu*, *hantei* (referees' decision), and the match outcome. Shushin will also announce *hansoku*.
2. Fukushin will mostly stand opposite to the Shushin in a suitable position to observe the match without overlapping, and will have equal authority and responsibility to Shushin in determining *yuko-datotsu*, *hansoku* and *hantei*. Fukushin will assist Shushin in administrating the match.

ARTICLE 6
Shinpan-in will motion their decision for *yuko-datotsu* based solely on their own judgement. If two or more Shinpan-in indicate *yuko-datotsu* with their flags, it shall be determined as one point (*ippon*).

ARTICLE 7
Shinpan-in will adjudicate matches in the following way:

1. Shushin will start the match by announcing "*Hajime*" when both *shiai-sha* are ready after performing a mutual bow and have assumed *chudan*.
2. When one Shinpan-in motions *yuko-datotsu*, the other two must react by indicating their decision.
3. When a foul (*hansoku*) has been committed, the match must be suspended and the *shiai-sha* returned to the start lines by Shushin. Shushin will clarify

the infringement and pronounce *hansoku*, and then restart the match.

4. If a *shiai-sha* falls over and the opponent does not immediately attempt to strike, Shushin will suspend the match, return the *shiai-sha* to the start lines for resumption of the match.

5. If a *shiai-sha* drops their *naginata* and the opponent does not immediately attempt to strike, Shushin will suspend the match, return both back to the starting lines, and pronounce *hansoku*.

6. Shushin will separate *shiai-sha* in the *seriai* position if it is prolonged and neither *shiai-sha* is attempting to attack by pronouncing "*Wakare*", and then immediately resume the match at the same location.

7. In the case of match time expiration, accident, or other reasons in which the match must be suspended, Shushin will pronounce "*Yame*" and return the *shiai-sha* to start lines. Shushin will pronounce "*Hajime*" to resume the match. In the case whereby match time will be extended (*encho*), Shushin will pronounce "*Encho. Hajime*".

8. Shinpan-in may decide victory or defeat through *gogi*.

9. Use of *Shinpan-ki*:

a. When starting a match, both *shinpan-ki* are extended in front of Shushin's body and parallel to the floor, and lowered while pronouncing "*Hajime*". (Fig. 8).

b. In the case whereby *yuko-datotsu* is acknowledged, the Shinpan-in will raise the applicable *shinpan-ki* on an angle of 45°. (Fig. 9.)

c. In the case whereby a Shinpan-in determines a *datotsu* in question is not valid, the *shinpan-ki* shall be crossed repeatedly in front of the body 2 or 3 times with arms stretched downwards and with the red flag in front of the white. (Fig. 10.)

d. When pronouncing *yuko-datotsu*, Shushin raises the applicable *shinpan-ki* on an angle of 45°. (Fig. 9.)

e. Both *shinpan-ki* are raised straight up to suspend a match. (Fig. 11.)

f. When separating two *shiai-sha* in *seriai*, Shushin extends both arms out to the sides and parallel to the floor while pronouncing "*Wakare*", then brings both *shinpan-ki* to the front and lowers them down while pronouncing "*Hajime*". (Fig. 12→Fig. 8.)

g. For *gogi*, Shushin raises both *shinpan-ki* in the right hand and calls "*Gogi*", to which the Shinpan-in move to the centre. (Fig. 13)

Note: In the case of danger, foul play, or the expiration of match time and so on, Fukushin may also signal to Shushin by raising the *shinpan-ki* and pronouncing "*Yame*". Shushin will immediately pronounce "*Yame*" also, and return the *shiai-sha* to the starting lines. However, only Shushin can resume a match by pronouncing "*Hajime*".

(Fig. 8)  **(Fig. 9)**  **(Fig. 10)**

(Fig. 11)  **(Fig. 12)**  **(Fig. 13)**

10. Making Pronouncements:

a .

(Fig. 14)

(Fig. 15)

Appendix 2: Shinpan Regulations

Pronouncing the commencement of a match – "*Hajime*". (When both competitors are ready in *chudan-no-kamae.*) (Fig. 8.)

b. Pronouncing *yuko-datotsu* – "*Men* (*kote, do, sune, tsuki*) *ari*". (Pronounced on the spot.) (Fig. 9)

c. Pronouncing match commencement for the second point – "*Nihon-me*". (*Shiai-sha* returned to start lines.)

d. Pronouncing match commencement for the final point (when each competitor has 1 point) – "*Shobu*". (*Shiai-sha* returned to start lines.)

e. Pronouncing victory and defeat – "*Shobu ari*" (victory decided). (*Shiai-sha* returned to start lines.)

f. Pronouncing victory through the absence of the opponent – "*Fusen-sho*". (*Shiai-sha* at the start line.)

g. Pronouncing a single point victory – "*Ippon-gachi shobu ari*" (victory decided by a single point). (*Shiai-sha* returned to start lines.)

h. Pronouncing extended match time – "*Encho. Hajime.*" (*Shiai-sha* returned to start lines.)

i. Suspending a match – "*Yame*". (*Shiai-sha* stop and return to the start lines.)

j. In the case of *seriai* – "*Wakare*" (break) and then "*Hajime*". (*Shiai-sha* stay where they are and resume on the spot.) (Fig. 12→Fig. 8)

k. Pronouncing *hansoku* – "*Hansoku …kai*". (*Shiai-sha* returned to start lines.)

Note: Pronounce while indicating the offending *shiai-sha* using the hand. (Fig. 14.)

l. Pronouncing a point created by the accumulation of two *hansoku* – "*Ippon ari.*" (*Shiai-sha* returned to start lines.)

Note: An pronouncement of "*Hansoku nikai*" (2x) is made to the violator, and then the flag is raised for the opponent to which one point is awarded with the declaration of "*Ippon ari*". (Fig. 14→Fig. 9.)

m. Pronouncing victory and defeat after a point gained through two *hansoku* – "*Shobu ari*". (*Shiai-sha* returned to start lines.)

Note: An pronouncement of "*Hansoku nikai*" is made to the violator and then "*Ippon ari. Shobu ari*" shall be declared and indicated with the applicable flag.

n. When a *shiai-sha* requests a suspension of stop the match – "*Yame*". (Fig. 11.)

Note: Shushin raises both *shinpan-ki* straight up and pronounces "*Yame*", and must then verify the reason for stoppage.

o. When a match is not decided – "*Hikiwake*" (draw). (*Shiai-sha* returned to start lines.)

Note: Shushin pronounces "*Hikiwake*" with both *shinpan-ki* crossed overhead. (The red flag should be placed in front of the white). (Fig. 15.)
p. In the case of *hantei* (deciding a winner when scores are even) – "*Hantei. Shobu ari.*" (*Shiai-sha* returned to start lines.)
Note: Upon the pronouncement of "*Hantei*" by Shushin, all Shinpan-in simultaneously raise the *shinpan-ki* indicating their judgement, after which Shushin declares "*Shobu ari*" and indicates with the applicable *shinpan-ki.*
q. In the case where a *shiai-sha* defaults (*kiken*) the match – "*Kiken. Shobu ari*". (*Shiai-sha* returned to start lines.)
Note: Shushin holds both flags in one hand points to the withdrawing *shiai-sha* while announcing "*Kiken*" and then raises the applicable flag to indicate "*Shobu ari*" in favour of the opponent. (Fig. 14→Fig. 9.)
r. In the case where a *shiai-sha* is expelled (*taijo*) from the match – "*Taijo. Shobu ari*". (*Shiai-sha* returned to start lines.)
Note: Shushin holds both flags in one hand points to the *shiai-sha* to be expelled while announcing "*Taijo*" and then raises the applicable flag to indicate "*Shobu ari*" in favour of the opponent. (Fig. 14→Fig. 9.)

11. Fukushin must not lower their *shinpan-ki* until Shushin's next pronouncement after indicating *yuko-datotsu.*

ARTICLE 8

Shinpan-in must arbitrate matters not outlined in the preceding articles in mutual consultation (*gogi*) and seek the approval of Shinpan-cho (or, Shinpan-shunin).

CHAPTER 3: Engi-kyogi

ARTICLE 1

Shinpan-in shall decide placings according to the "All Japan Naginata Federation Engi-kyogi Regulations".

ARTICLE 2

In principle, a refereeing cohort will consist of one Shushin (Head Referee) and four Fukushin (Sub-Referees).

ARTICLE 3

The function of Shinpan-in will be as follows:

1. Shinpan-in must judge competitors fairly on the quality of their technique, fullness of spirit, and correctness of posture. Shinpan-in will be seated in designated positions and make their decisions independently.
2. In *hata-keishiki* (flag method) standings will be determined by the majority decision of Shinpan-in. At the completion of the *engi* match, Shinpan-in will indicate their decisions on the signal (whistle) from Shushin.
3. To ensure consensus of assessment criteria in *saiten-keishiki* (point method), Shinpan-in will all consult with Shushin after the first *engi* match has been completed. Thereafter, Shinpan-in will fill out and submit scorecards to Shushin.
4. Shushin will confirm disparities in the scorecards. If Shushin decides that there is too much inconsistency in the scores, Shushin's assessment shall become the benchmark, and a meeting may be convened even while *engi-kyogi* is still in progress. If a meeting of Shinpan-in fails to find consensus, the matter shall be settled by Shinpan-cho.
5. Shushin must issue a warning if Shinpan-in do not score in accordance with the "Regulations", or are not objective.

ARTICLE 4

The following method shall be applied in order to score with accuracy and in a straightforward manner:

1. Matches for *engi* shall be judged out of 10 points.
2. Scoring shall be based on attire and attitude, spirit, vocalisation, breathing, grip (*tenouchi*), striking (*datotsu*), distance (*maai*), posture, position of hands, attentiveness (*zanshin*), and gaze. Faults in any of these aspects will result in the deduction of 0.1–1 point. For each mistake that is made, 1 point will be deducted each time. Deducted points will be subtracted from the initial 10 points to determine the final score. The method for assessment is based on subtraction rather than addition.

ARTICLE 5

The final score shall be calculated as the median of the five Shinpan-in scores, and also from the accuracy of the time taken to complete the forms. If the timing is not perfect, 0.1 of a point shall be deducted from the median score for every five seconds out (under or over).

ARTICLE 6

Declaration of the score will be done in the following manner:
Score ranking will be established. If the scores are equal, Shushin's scores will become the basis for referees' consultation (*gogi*).

(Revised January 10, 2014)

Appendix 2: Shinpan Regulations

1. Engi Score Sheet

Engi Perspectives

Perspective	Category		Criteria
Attitude	Attire		Dressed properly
	Posture, attitude		Natural, unforced posture
	Etiquette (*reiho*)		Correct, composed etiquette
Precision	Process	*Furiage*	Good coordination of body movement and *naginata* handling
		Mochikae	
		Furikaeshi	
	Datotsu (Strike)	Posture	(*Taisei*) – Good turns and body movement
		Distance	(*Maai*) – Precise distancing and solid striking and receiving
		Hands	Correct hand positioning at completion of strikes
		Grip	(*Tenouchi*) – Accurate blade trajectory (*hasuji*)
		Voice	Strong, energetic vocalisation
		Gaze	Imperturbable and perceptive gaze (*kan-no-me*)
		Alertness	(*Zanshin*) – Strong sense of vigilance accompanying strikes
Proficiency	Partner harmony		Partners (Shikake-Oji / Uchi-Shi) show technical symmetry
	Respiration		Breathing is in sync
	Technical skill		Techniques are spirited and crisp (*sae*)
	Understanding		Techniques are executed in accordance with principles

(February 25, 2015)

Engi-kyogi Scoring Criteria Chart

Attire	Wearing non-regulation attire	Unclean	Tidiness
Posture Attitude	Incorrect posture Not serious	Incorrect manners	Unsettled
Hands		Hand position is imprecise	*Ai-chudan* is not exact
Grip	Dropping the *naginata* Striking with the top or side of the blade Incorrect trajectory (*hasuji*)	Letting go with one hand Receiving is not accurate Not sliding properly	*Furiage* is imprecise Grip is incorrect
Voice	Mistaking target name	Not loud enough Unclear	Too long
Breathing		Breathing not in sync	Techniques are flat
Vigour		Little energy or vigour	
Strikes	Striking the wrong target	Striking is inaccurate	
Body Movement		Loud stamping	Footwork is inadequate Superfluous foot movement
Gaze	Unable to focus on partner	Looking at the target	Dropping eye-contact
Distance		Incorrect distance	
Attentiveness		Loss of focus after striking	
Other	Stopping mid-technique Performance of non-stipulated techniques Whispering	Stepping out of bounds	
Treatment	Point deduction		
	Big (0.6–0.5)	Middle (0.4–0.3)	Small (0.2–0.1)

(October 8, 1997)

Appendix 2: Shinpan Regulations

Engi Scoring (Stipulated, Free) Part 1

Treatment	Assessment Elements		
	Criteria		
	Big 0.6–0.5	Middle 0.4–0.3	Small 0.2–0.1
Attire Attitude	Non-regulation attire Not serious	Unclean	Unsettled
Spirit		No vigour	
Voice	Mistaking target name	Not loud enough Unclear	
Breathing		Breathing not in sync	Techniques are flat *Ai-chudan* is not exact
Grip	Dropping the naginata Striking with the top or side of the blade Unable to execute *harai*	Letting go with one hand when receiving *harai* Receiving is not accurate Not sliding properly	*Furiage* is imprecise Letting go during *harai* and immediately fixing grip
Striking Distance	Striking or thrusting the wrong targets	Inaccurate striking Inaccurate target	
Posture			Inadequate footwork Bad posture (chin, neck, foot width, hand width)
Hands		Incorrect hand positioning	
Attentiveness		Loss of focus after striking	Not returning to right position
Gaze		Looking at the target	
Other	Performance of non-stipulated technique (Big 1 point) Stopping mid-technique (Big 0.7) Whispering	Clear hesitation Loud stamping Stepping out of bounds	Superfluous foot movement

Engi Scoring (Free Engi) Part 2

Scoring Elements			
Treatment	**A**	**B**	**C**
Difficulty (2)	2–1.6	1.5–1.0	0.9–
Composition (3)	3–2.4	2.3–1.6	1.5–
Execution (5)			

December, 1981

Appendix 3
Handbook for Administering Tournaments
(大会運営の手引き)

The following is a translation of the most recent AJNF "Handbook for Administering Tournaments" (January 10, 2014) which the INF adheres to.

CONTENTS

Appendix 3: Tournament Handbook

Handbook for Administering Tournaments

CHAPTER 1: Criteria for Administering a Tournament

1. Tournament Type

Scale: National; Prefecture (State); Town/City; Club level.
Participants: Elementary school; Junior high school; High school; University; Open.

2. Scheduling

Scheduling the tournament depends largely on the kind of participants. For example, tournaments for school children should be held in the weekend or during school holidays.

3. Venue and Preparation

Choosing the venue also depends on the kind and number of intended participants. There should be a meeting room, changing rooms, and waiting rooms. Equipment needed to run the matches will depend on the number of courts.

4. Tournament and Competition Officers

Tournament Officers:

Honorary Chairperson (Meiyo Kaicho); Tournament Chairperson (Taikai Kaicho); Tournament Vice Chairperson (Taikai Fuku-kaicho); Advisers (Komon); Consultants (Sanyo); Tournament Organising Committee Chairperson (Taikai-iincho); Tournament Organising Committee Vice Chairperson (Taikai Fuku-iincho) etc.

Competition Officials:

Executive Committee Chairperson (Somu-iincho); Executive Committee Vice Chairperson (Somu Fuku-iincho); Executive Committee Members (Somu-iin); Competition Committee Chairperson (Kyogi-iincho); Competition Committee Vice Chairperson (Kyogi Fuku-iincho); Referee Director (Shinpan-cho); Court Managers (Court [Shinpan] Un'ei-shunin); Player Officials (Senshu-iin); Time Officials (Tokei-iin); Record Officials (Kiroku-iin); Marker Officials (Hyoji-iin); Scoreboard Officials (Saiten Keiji-iin); Equipment Inspection Officials (Keiryo Yogu-iin); Announcement Officials (Hoso-iin); Venue Officials (Kaijo-iin); Messengers

(Sokuho-iin); PR Officials (Hodo-iin); Results Officials (Sogo Seiseki Keisan-iin).
(3) Competition Officials
Reception; Clerk; Attendants; First Aid.

5. Tournament Finances

① Participation fees ② Subsidies ③ Donations

CHAPTER 2: Functions of Officers and Officials

(Tournament Officers)

1. Tournament Chairperson (Taikai-iincho)

The Tournament Chairperson is the highest authority in the tournament and is responsible for the following functions in overseeing the overall administration:

① Officially opening and closing the tournament.
② Directing the planning and operation of the tournament by taking the role of general supervisor.
③ Ensuring that the tournament events proceed smoothly. (This includes meeting with the various committee chairs and consulting with Shinpan-cho.)
④ Addressing any unforeseen problems that may arise during the tournament.
⑤ Convening a review meeting at the conclusion of the tournament, and recording any points that could be improved for future reference.
⑥ Must be present at all official meetings for Shinpan-in, Kantoku, and Competition Committee members.
⑦ Other matters that require attention.

2. Tournament Vice Chairperson (Taikai Fuku-iincho)

Assists the Tournament Chairperson.

(Competition Officials)

1. Executive Committee Chairperson (Somu-iincho)

Ensures that all activities proceed smoothly by overseeing all operations and coordinating with the head officials. The Executive Committee Chairperson will also liaise with the Referee Director (Shinpan-cho) and Competition Committee Chairperson (Kyogi-iincho) to administer the event.

① Create a plan of action based on the decisions made by Executive Committee to ensure that all the necessary tasks are completed efficiently.
② Direct officials in reception, ushers, and people in charge of looking after visitors.
③ Obtain progress reports from the various sub-committees to maintain overall cohesion.
④ Coordinate arrangements for the opening and closing ceremonies.
⑤ Ensure that trophies and certificates are organised.
⑥ Oversee the preparation of tournament facilities.
⑦ Arrange first aid stations.
⑧ Conduct meetings for Shinpan-in, Kantoku and Competition Officials, offering comments and guidance as required.
⑨ After registration, check if players are present or absent and make sure that the officials are aware of any changes.
⑩ Confirm the results of equipment checks.
⑪ Confirm the successful completion of preparations.
⑫ See to any other matters that require attention.
⑬ Receive report of Competition Officer attendance.
⑭ Confirm Shinpan-in attendance.
⑮ When an unforeseen emergency occurs (such as a natural disaster), must immediately consult with Competition Committee Chairperson and Shinpan-cho to decide the next course of action.
⑯ Announcement of the placings and winners.
⑰ Overseeing the tidy-up at the end of the tournament.
⑱ Overseeing the removal of court lines and so on at the conclusion of each competition.

2. Executive Committee Vice Chairperson (Somu Fuku-iincho)

Assists Executive Committee Chairperson.

3. Executive Committee (Somu-iin)

(1) General Affairs

① All matters concerning the running of the tournament.
② Coordinate with the Competition Committee and Officials (venue preparation, first aid, transportation and so on.)
③ Confirm the presence or absence of officers and officials.
④ Keep tabs of match progression.
⑥ Ensure that the concerned officials receive prompt notification of referee rosters and changes.

Shinpan-in Roster for Naginata Shiai		
Date:	Court No.	Shiai No.
Round No.	Entered by:	
Shushin		
Fukushin		

Shinpan-in Roster Changes				
Date:		Court No.	Match Nos. ~	Entered by:
Engi	Shiai	Original Shinpan-in	Change	
Shushin	Shushin			
1-Shin	Fukushin			
2-Shin	Fukushin			
3-Shin	X			
4-Shin	X			

(2) Meetings

① Set up meeting venues.
② Help with the running of all meetings.
③ Help with all aspects of the tournament. (Opening and closing ceremonies, accommodation, transportation, medical care etc.)

Examples of Opening & Closing Ceremonies

Opening ceremony

Start of the opening ceremony	Announcer	
"*Ichido Rei!*"	Announcer	
Official declaration for the start of the tournament	Tournament Chairperson	
National anthem		Make sure the tape or CD is ready
Returning trophies etc. from the previous tournament		Presentation of replica trophy
Chairperson's speech	Tournament Chairperson	
Congratulatory address	Guest	Ensure that the guest's position and organisation are confirmed beforehand
Announcement of congratulatory telegrams	Announcer	
Explanation of rules by the Chief Judge	Referee Director	
Competitor's oath	Inform the representative competitor in advance	
"*Ichido Rei!*"	Announcer	

Closing ceremony

Start of the closing ceremony	Announcer	
"*Ichido Rei!*"	Announcer	
Announcement of the results	Executive Chairperson	
Presentation of trophies	Recipients	Confirm the order of the presentation and recipients etc.
Closing remarks	Tournament Vice Chairperson	
Official declaration of tournament completion	Tournament Chairperson	
"*Ichido Rei!*"	Announcer	
Completion of the closing ceremony	Announcer	

4. Competition Committee Chairperson (Kyogi-iincho)

Ensure that the competition proceeds smoothly by overseeing all operations related to the matches, and coordinate with the chief officials to run the event without any delays.

① Confirming Contest Official numbers and staff allocations.
② Keeping tabs on all tasks that were decided at Executive Committee meetings.
③ Overseeing the marking of match courts and checking that all equipment necessary to run the matches is prepared.
④ Checking that everything is in place for the start of the tournament.
⑤ Be present at the Kantoku and Shinpan-in meetings and offer explanations when required.
⑥ Receive notification of *shiai-sha* absences from Executive Committee members.
⑦ Check the number of Competition Officials and where they are to be posted.
⑧ Confirm the presence of Competition Officials.
⑨ Explain the responsibilities, attitude, and points to take heed of to Competition Officials.
⑩ Coordinate and maintain communication with Executive Committee Officials, Shinpan-cho, and Executive Committee Chairperson.
⑪ Confirm the safety of the venue and well-being of the competitors.
⑫ Upon receiving notification of any accidents, immediately consult with the Tournament and Executive Committee Chairpersons to decide on appropriate action.

⑬ Confirm results and placings.
⑭ Supervise the venue clean-up after the tournament has been concluded.
⑮ Make a report on the activities of the competition officials.

5. Competition Committee Vice Chairperson (Kyogi Fuku-iincho)
Assists Competition Committee Chairperson.

6. Player Officials (Senshu-iin)
One head official (Shunin) and two or more staff.
① Guiding competitors. (Gathering and roll call.)
② Attaching ribbons to the back of *shiai-kyogi* competitors and around the waist of *engi-kyogi* competitors. Also check *zekken*, *bogu*, and attire of competitors, and whether the *naginata* have stickers authorising their use.
③ Guiding competitors to the court area before their match starts.
④ Collecting the names of the *shiai-sha* who will compete in a "Representative Match" (*daihyosha-sen*) from the respective Kantoku of each team, and promptly conveying the information to the officials.

Kantoku→Player Official→Scoreboard Official, Announcer, Shinpan-shunin

- Vigilantly check that the matches are running according to schedule.
- Do not make independent decisions even if there is a request from Kantoku or *shiai-sha* regarding a match.

Tournament Matches

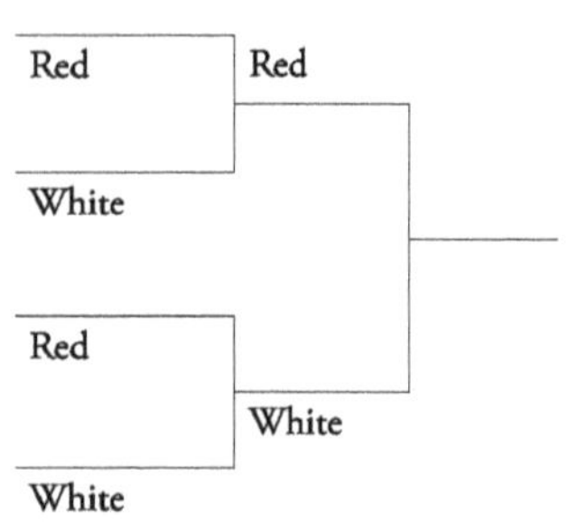

<table>
<tr><th colspan="2">1st Round</th><th colspan="2">2nd Round</th></tr>
<tr><td colspan="2">1–12</td><td colspan="2">1–11</td></tr>
<tr><td colspan="2">2–11</td><td colspan="2">12–10</td></tr>
<tr><td colspan="2">3–10</td><td colspan="2">2–9</td></tr>
<tr><td colspan="2">4–9</td><td colspan="2">3–8</td></tr>
<tr><td colspan="2">5–8</td><td colspan="2">4–7</td></tr>
<tr><td colspan="2">6–7</td><td colspan="2">5–6</td></tr>
<tr><td>Red</td><td>White</td><td>Red</td><td>White</td></tr>
</table>

7. Time Officials (Tokei-iin)
One head official (Shunin) and two or more staff.
- Start the stopwatch at exactly the same time as the commencement of the match.
- Blow the whistle and raise the flag as soon as the designated time expires.

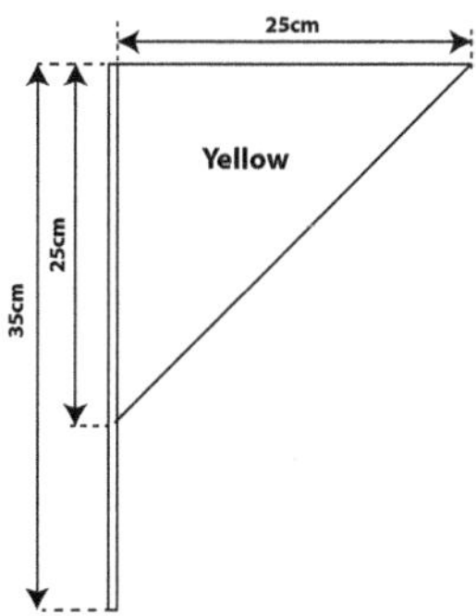

- Record the match time and the number of extensions (*encho*) in the appropriate form and convey the results to the Record Official.

(1) Shiai-kyogi

① When the Scoreboard Official (Saiten Keiji-iin) calls out the red player's name, the Time Official remains seated and raises the yellow time flag. The flag is lowered and the stopwatch started with the proclamation of "*Hajime*!" by Shushin.
② Time will be stopped with the pronouncement of a valid strike (e.g. "*Men ari*", "*Sune ari*" etc.) and "*Yame*" with the flag raised while remaining seated.
③ Time is restarted again and the flag lowered with the announcement of "*Nihon-me*", "*Shobu*", "*Hajime*", or "*Encho. Hajime*".
④ When the designated match time expires, the yellow time flag and blow the whistle.
⑤ When the match is temporarily stopped for other reasons, raise the flag to signal that the stopwatch has been stopped, and lower it when the match is restarted.

*Do no stop the watch for "*Wakare*" (separation of *shiai-sha*) as this is included in the overall match time.
* Time is not required for *fusensho*.

Shiai-kyogi Time Sheets

Shiai-kyogi Time Sheets

Kojin-shiai Time Sheet					
Date	Court No.	Round No.	Qtr-finals	Semi-finals	3rd Place Play-off
Team	Red		White		
Name					
Time	Mins.	Secs.	Encho x	Filled in by:	

Dantai-shiai Time Sheet						
Date:	Court No.	Round No.	Qtr-finals		Semi-finals	3rd Place Play-off
Team	Red			White		
	Sempo	Jiho	Chuken	Fukusho	Taisho	Notes
Time	Mins. Secs.	Mins. Secs.	Mins. Secs.	Mins. Secs.	Mins. Secs.	
Encho	x	x	x	x	x	Filled in by:

(2) Engi-kyogi

*Time is not recorded in the *hata-keishiki* method.

① In *saiten-shiki* (set or free forms), the time is recorded and conveyed to the Record Official.

② The designated time for *engi-kyogi* will be announced in the tournament outline.

③ The time for *engi-kyogi* begins as soon as one member of the pair of competitors puts one foot inside the court, and stops as soon as both step out of the court at the conclusion of the *engi*.

Engi-kyogi Time Sheet (Saiten-shiki)

Name	
Time	
Excess time	
Additional time	

8. Record Officials (Kiroku-iin)
One head official (Shunin) and two or more staff.

- Take care that there is no discrepancy between what is on the scoreboard and what is recorded on the sheet.
- If there are any mistakes or queries, promptly consult with the Court Shinpan-shunin to ensure that there are no hold-ups in the running of the competition. Ensure that your writing is legible, taking particular care with numerals.

(1) Shiai-kyogi

① Fill out the necessary information in the record forms before the commencement of the competition.
Record the progression of the recording.
② Be sure to record the kind and number of points scored as indicated on the scoreboard, the number of wins, and also the times from the Timekeeping Officials.

Symbols for Records

Symbol	Term	Symbol	Term
Ⓜ	Men	[1-Point Win]	Ippon-gachi
Ⓢ	Sune	[Draw]	Hikiwake
Ⓚ	Kote	[Abstention]	Kiken
Ⓓ	Do	△	Hansoku x1
Ⓣ	Tsuki	Ⓕ	Hansoku x2
Ⓡ	Hantei	[Default]	Fusensho
[Ext.]	Encho	[Expulsion]	Taijo

Record Sheet for Shiai-kyogi
Kojin-shiai (Individual matches)

Date:	Court No.	Match No.	Round No.	Quarter-finals	Semi-finals	3rd
	Team Name	Name	Match Result			Win/Loss
Red			Ⓣ Ⓜ		Hansoku x	O
White			△ Ⓢ		Hansoku 1 x	X
	Time: 4:35		Encho: 1 x			
Shushin:		Fukushin: Fukushin:				
Name of Recorder:		Name of Record Official:				

Team Match (5 players) (Daihyosha-sen)

Naginata Shiai-kyogi Record Sheet (5 Players)

Date:	Court No. Match No.		Round No.	Quarter-finals		Semi-finals		3rd place playoff	
Team		Sempo	Jiho	Chuken	Fukusho	Taisho	Wins	Points	Daihyo	Win 0 Loss X
Red	Name									
	Results	Hansoku x	Hansoku x	Hansoku x	Hansoku 2 x	Hansoku x	2	4	H x	X
		Ⓣ 1-Point Win	Ⓢ	Draw	△△	○○ Default				
White			Ⓜ △ Ⓢ		Ⓕ Ⓣ				Ⓡ	
		Hansoku x	Hansoku 1 x	Hansoku x	Hansoku x	Hansoku x	2	4	H x Encho x1 5:00	O
	Name									
Shushin:				Fukushin: Fukushin:						
Time		3:00	2:50	3:00	2:15		Filled in by:			
Encho							Record Official:			

Team Match (3 players) (No daihyosha-sen)

(2) Engi-kyogi

Naginata Shiai-kyogi Record Sheet (3 players)							
Date:	Court No.	Match No.	Round No.	Qtr-finals	Semis	3rd playoff	
Team		Sempo	Chuken	Taisho	Wins	Points	Win 0 Loss X
Red	Name				2	3	O
	Results	Hansoku x	Hansoku x	Hansoku x			
		△	Ⓜ	○ ○			
White		Ⓡ		Ⓢ Abstention	1	2	X
		Hansoku x	Hansoku x	Hansoku x			
	Name	Sempo	Chuken	Taisho			
Shushin:			Fukushin: Fukushin:				
Time		5:00	4:50	2:10	Filled in by:		
Encho		1 x	1 x		Record Official:		

Hata-keishiki

① Fill in necessary details before the contest starts.

② Record Shinpan-in decisions (number of flags given for red and white) as indicated on the scoreboard.

Saiten-keishiki

① Fill in necessary details before the contest starts.

② Record the results of the scoring and the time. Check the amount of time over or under the stipulated time and forward it to the Score Keeper officials.

Engi-kyogi Record Sheet

Date	Court No.	Match No.	Round No.	Qtr.	Semi	3rd
Team Name		Shikake-Oji			Points	Win O-X
Red		-			4	O
White		-			1	X
			Recorder:		Shunin:	

Engi-kyogi Score Record Sheet (Saiten-keishiki)

(3) Record Sheet

Records of each match should be distributed to Shinpan-cho, Competition

Committee Chairperson, Executive Committee Chairperson, and others who require the information.

<table>
<tr><td>Team</td><td></td><td>Group</td><td colspan="5">Open, University, High School, Other</td><td>Set / Free</td></tr>
<tr><td colspan="2">Shinpan-in / Competitor</td><td>Shushin</td><td>1-Shin</td><td>2-Shin</td><td>3-Shin</td><td>4-Shin</td><td>Points</td><td>Notes</td></tr>
<tr><td colspan="2"></td><td></td><td></td><td></td><td></td><td></td><td></td><td></td></tr>
<tr><td colspan="4">Name of Recorder:</td><td colspan="5">Name of Official:</td></tr>
</table>

<table>
<tr><td colspan="6">Scoring Card</td></tr>
<tr><td colspan="4">Group</td><td colspan="2">Event</td></tr>
<tr><td>Open</td><td>Univ.</td><td>High School</td><td>Other</td><td>Set</td><td>Free</td></tr>
<tr><td colspan="2">Name</td><td colspan="4"></td></tr>
<tr><td colspan="2">Free Engi
Difficulty
Composition
Riai</td><td colspan="4"></td></tr>
</table>

<table>
<tr><td colspan="6">Scoring Card</td></tr>
<tr><td colspan="4">Group</td><td colspan="2">Event</td></tr>
<tr><td>Open</td><td>Univ.</td><td>High School</td><td>Other</td><td>Set</td><td>Free</td></tr>
<tr><td colspan="2">Name</td><td colspan="4"></td></tr>
<tr><td colspan="2" rowspan="2">Scoring</td><td>Shushin</td><td>1</td><td>2</td><td>3</td><td>4</td></tr>
<tr><td colspan="5"></td></tr>
</table>

9. Marker Officials (Hyoji-iin)

One head official (Shunin) and two or more staff.

① Maintaining and checking the scoreboard.

② Marker Officials will be seated in front of the scoreboard on each court and convey the decisions of the Shinpan-in to the people inside the venue.

③ Marker Officials will raise the appropriate indication paddle as they stand up and show it to the front, sides, and then the front again.

④ In the case of *engi-kyogi*, either the red or the white paddle will be swiftly raised to accurately indicate the decision of the 5 Shinpan-in.

⑤ In the case of *shiai-kyogi*, Marker Officials will raise the appropriate paddle to indicate the point scored, *hansoku*, *ippon-gachi*, *fusensho*, *encho*, *hikiwake*, and *hantei* etc.

⑥ If Shushin's declaration or any other aspect is unclear, the official in charge (Shunin) should verify the decision immediately with Shushin.

Paddle Symbols

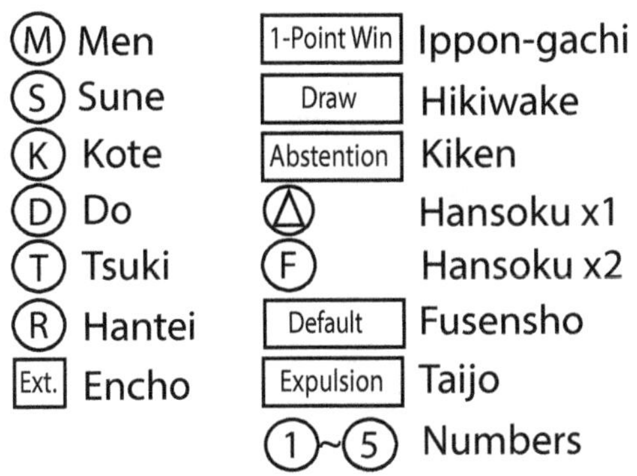

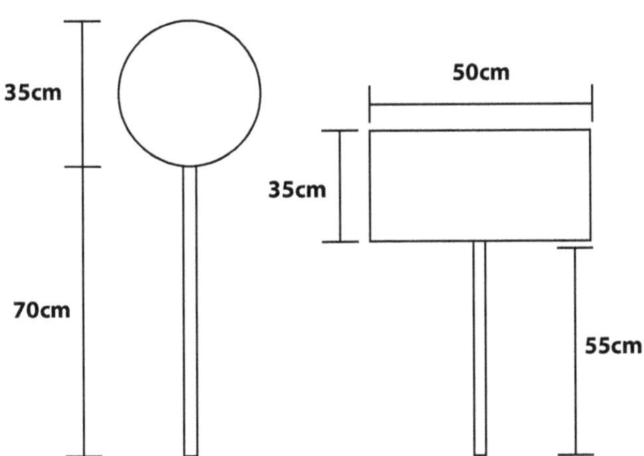

10. Scoreboard Officials (Saiten Keiji-iin)

One head official (Shunin) and two or more staff.

① Follow directions before the competition starts and Scoreboard Officials will attach the names of players and Shinpan-in on the board.

② Indicate the points that are scored during the match promptly and

accurately in accordance to Shushin's declaration.
③ There should be one double-sided scoreboard per court with the front showing the match in progress, and the back prepared for the next match. The back will be turned to the front at the same time as the Shinpan-in bow to the *shomen*.
④ *Engi-kyogi* (*hata-keishiki*) and *kojin* matches should be managed in the same way. The results of the previous two matches should remain on the board, but the rest removed promptly.
⑤ Summon the teams and players.

Scoreboard Symbols

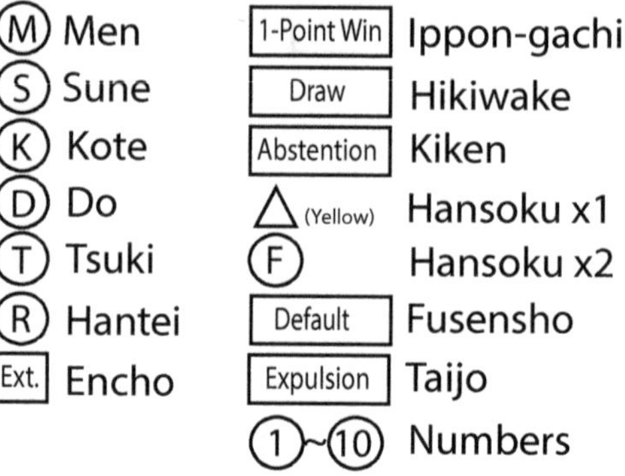

Scoreboard Markers

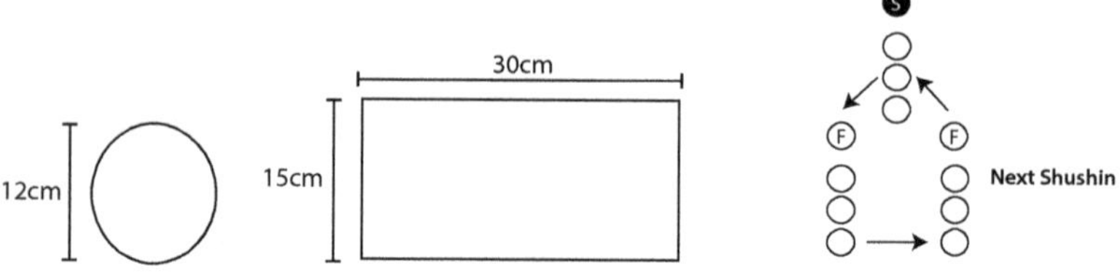

Appendix 3: Tournament Handbook

Shiai-kyogi (with daihyosha-sen)

Team		Sempo	Jiho	Chuken	Fukusho	Taisho	Wins	Pts	Daihyo	Win 0 Loss X
Red	Name									
		Ⓢ 1-Point Win	Ⓢ	Draw	△△	○○ Default	2	4		X
White			Ⓜ Ⓢ △		Ⓕ Ⓣ		2	4	Ⓡ	O
	Name								Daihyo	

Shushin: Fukushin: Fukushin:

Shiai-kyogi (without daihyosha-sen)

Team		Sempo	Chuken	Taisho	Wins	Pts	Win 0 Loss X
Red	Name						
		△	Ⓜ Ext.	○○	2	3	O
White		Ⓡ		Ⓢ Abstention	2	2	X
	Name						

Shushin: Fukushin: Fukushin:

Engi-kyogi

Name				
Red	③	①	⓪	
White	②	④	⑤	
Name				
Shushin:	1-Shin: 2-Shin:		3-Shin: 4-Shin:	

11. Equipment Inspection Officials (Keiryo Yogu-iin)
One head official (Shunin) and two or more staff.

① The length, weight and curvature, and *kissaki* cap (*tampo*) of the *naginata* used in *shiai* should be checked and the Equipment Inspection Form filled out and forwarded to the Executive Committee Chairperson.
② Required standards are stipulated in Article 8 of the "Shiai-kyogi Regulations".
③ Each competitor will have two *naginata* inspected. However, if the *naginata* is damaged during a match, the "Approved" sticker must be verified and another *naginata* inspected.
④ All *naginata* that pass the inspection will be certified with an "Approved" sticker. The seal should be attached to the top edge of the *naginata* where the *sendan-maki* meets the *e-bu.*
⑤ The blade and other parts of the *naginata* must be checked for safety.

Naginata Specifications
* The *sendan-maki* should consist of 15cm of white insulation tape with 1cm anchor tape on each end.
* The *kissaki* and *ishizuki* caps should be secured with clear tape for safety.

Equipment	Order	Section		Measurement
Weight	1	Overall weight		>650g
Scale (length)	2	*Sendan-maki*	Overlap	15cm
			Tape	17cm
	3	*Ha-bu*	*Sori*	2.2cm
			Length	50cm
	4	Total length		210~225cm
Kissaki-tampo gauge	5	*Kissaki*	Cap	2.6cm
			Length	5cm

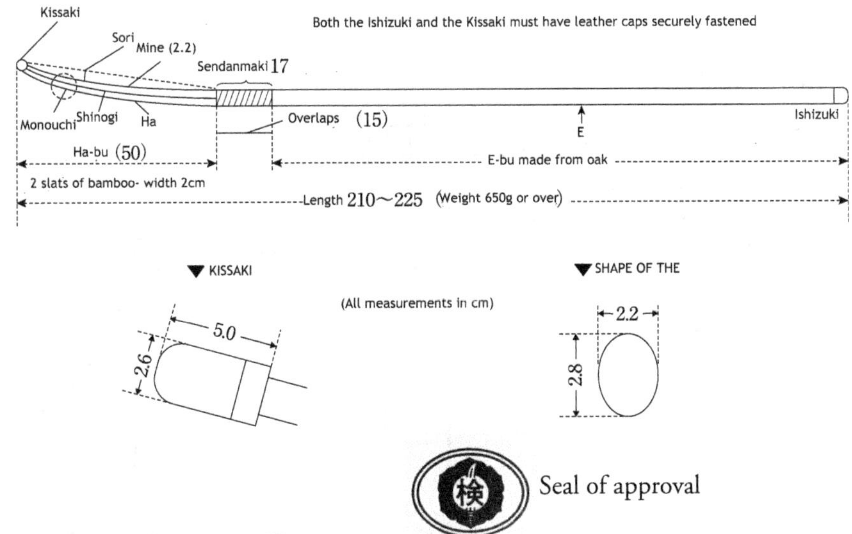

Naginata Inspection Form

Classification		Affiliation		Date of Inspection				Authorised by:	
Name	No.	Weight	Sendan-maki	Ha-bu		Kissaki		Total Length	Authorised by
				Sori	Length	Length	Cap		
	1								
	2								
	1								
	2								
	1								
	2								

12. Venue Officers (Kaijo-iin)

① Set up the venue.

② Set up the courts for *engi-kyogi* and *shiai-kyogi* in accordance with the program. In order to enable quick set, markers should be put in place on the floor to indicate where the start lines, centreline, Shinpan-in seats, player seats, *engi* waiting lines and so on will be marked.

③ Ensure the safety of the venue.

Venue Diagram

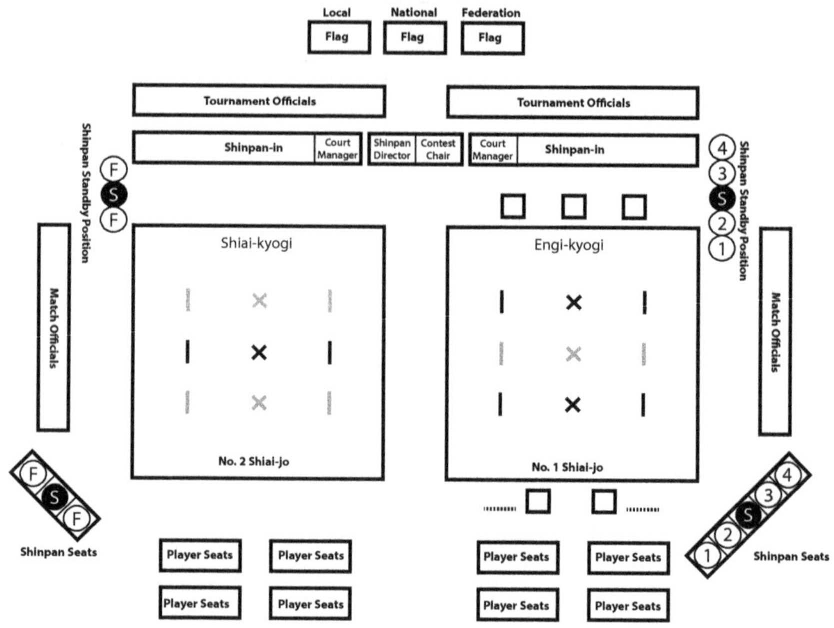

*In the case of two flags, the national flag should be on the left and the federation flag on the right.

CHAPTER 3: Other Matters

1. Zekken

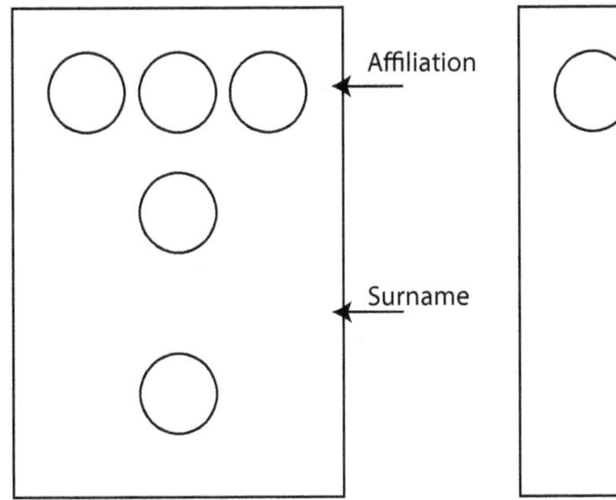

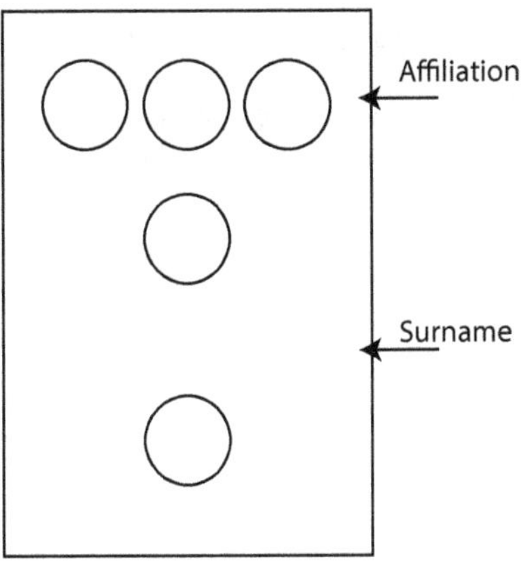

2. Ribbons (Tasuki)

① Red and white *tasuki* should be prepared.
② Each is 6cm wide and 130cm in length.

3. Lining Up and Starting Matches

(1) Shiai-kyogi (Dantai-sen)

① The two teams in the opening match, the match to decide 3rd place, and the final will line up as shown in Figure 1. In all other matches teams will line up as shown in Figure 2, in which the next teams to fight line up behind the finishing teams, and start with the command of Shushin. However, when the first teams for the opening match have lined up and the Shinpan-in are in position in each court, the Shinpan Director (Shinpan-cho) will signal commencement of matches. Shushin will start the matches thereafter.
② When lined up, the Senpo of the incoming teams and the Taisho of the outgoing teams should have their *naginata* in hand.
③ Kantoku will bow at the same time as the *shiai-sha* from their designated seats.

④ Each *shiai-sha* will raise their hand when called, and reply in a loud, clear voice. Both players line up at the start lines together.

*Players who contest the *daihyosha-sen* will line up in their original position.

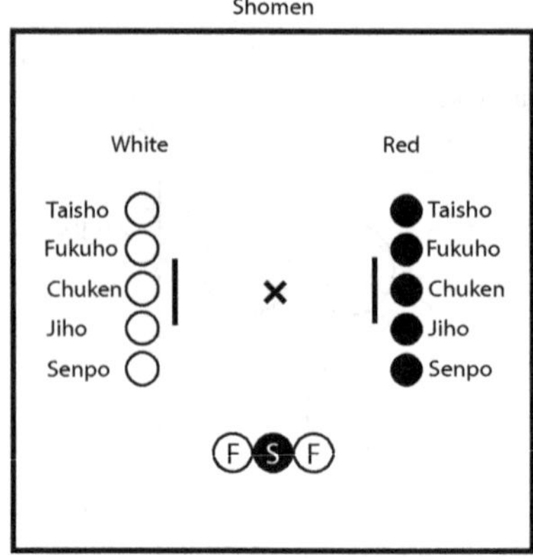

(Fig. 1)

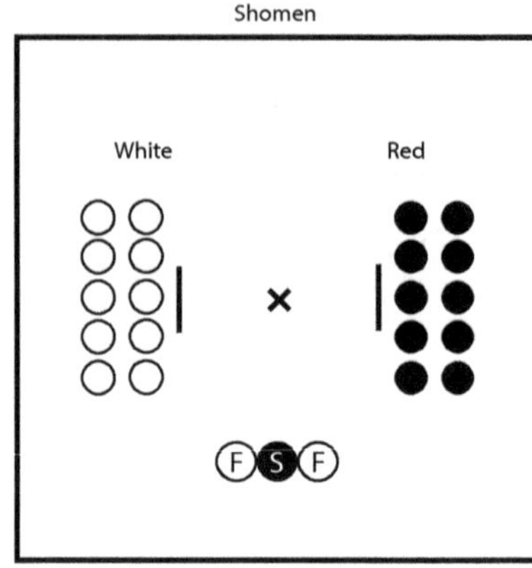

(Fig. 2)

(2) Engi-kyogi (Hata-keishiki)

① The teams in the first match proceed to the waiting line as the Shinpan-in enter the court (Fig. 3). When all competitors and Shinpan-in have assembled, Shinpan-cho will announce the commencement of the matches. The Shinpan-in will then take their seats, the competitors will proceed to edge of the court, and when the Scoreboard Officials call the name of the teams out, they will enter the court with the command of "*Nyujo*" and move to the start lines.

② Bow to the *shomen* with Shushin's whistle and perform the designated forms.

③ After *engi*, conduct a mutual bow, then bow to the *shomen* and exit the court. (Fig. 4.)

④ From the second match onward, the incoming teams move to the waiting line as the current match finish is in process, and then move to the edge of the court as soon as the Shinpan-in lower their flags.

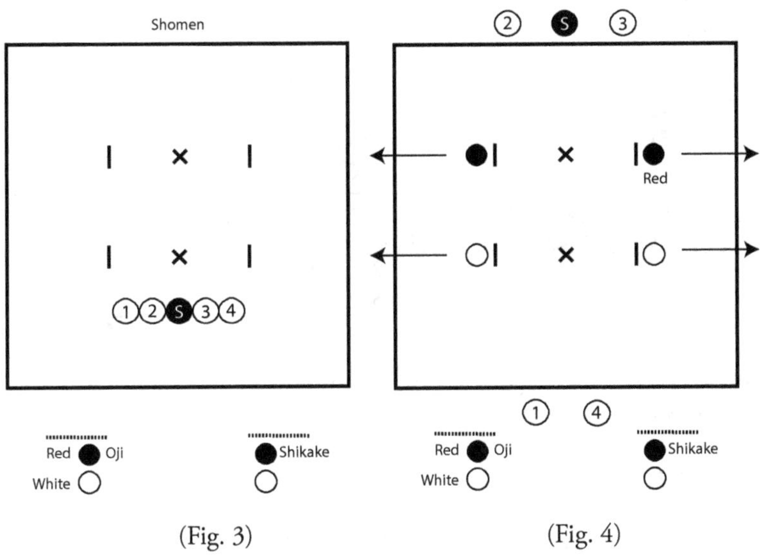

(Fig. 3) (Fig. 4)

4. Representative Matches (Daihyosha-sen)

① When the representative player is decided, the Kantoku will write the name down on the provided from and hand it to the Player Official.

Daihyosha-sen Form

Court No.	Round 1	Round 3	7th Place	5th Place	3rd Place
Match No.	Round 2	Quarter-finals	Play-off	Play-off	Play-off
Affiliation	Red		White		
Name					

5. Tournament Ladder Examples

Engi-kyogi

Shiai-kyogi Dantai-sen

(Daishyosha-sen)

Total Points / Total Wins

Shiai-kyogi Kojin-sen

1-Point Win

Ext.

6. League Matches

(1) Kojin-sen

	A	B	C	D	E	Wins	Points	Draw	Rank
A		X S''	△	X	△ S	0	2	2	5
B	(M'S'')		(S)	△	(M'M'')	3	5	1	1
C	△	X		(M'M'')	(S''K''')	2	4	1	2
D	(K)	△	X D	X	X	1	2	1	4
E	△ M	X	X S'	(S'S'')		1	4	1	3
Losses	2	0	1	2	2				
Points	4	1	3	4	5				

①B-E ②C-D ③A-E ④B-C ⑤A-D ⑥E-C ⑦A-C ⑧D-B ⑨A-B ⑩D-E
O Win X Loss △Draw

(2) Dantai-sen

①A-D ②B-C ③A-C ④D-B ⑤A-B ⑥C-D

	A	B	C	D	Wins	Winners	Points	Rank
A		(6/3)	(3/2)	X 1/1	2	6	10	2
B	X 0/0		(3/2)	X 1/0	1	3	4	4
C	X 2/1	X 1/0		(2/2)	1	3	5	3
D	(4/2)	(5/3)	X 1/1		2	6	10	1
Losses	1	2	2	1				
Losers	3	6	6	3				
Points	6	8	7	4				

For filling out the form for *dantai-sen*: <u>Total Points</u>
Total Winners

In the case of *daihyosha-sen*, the result is included in "Wins", but not "Winners" and "Points".

(3) Deciding Placings

①Highest number of wins
②Highest number of winners
③Highest number of points scored
④Least number of losses
⑤Least number of losers
⑥Least number of points scored against
⑦Highest number of draws

(This may be equal too, so decide what to do in this case before the tournament begins.)

Appendix 4

Kata Outline

Bow 30 degrees to the *shomen*. Then conduct a mutual bow from *tachi-maai* and assume *mugamae*. Take two steps forward from the left foot, and on the third step both step into *ai-chudan*, pull the left foot back and kneel down on the left knee (*orishiki*). The blade is turned to the right (not touching the floor) while another mutual bow is conducted. Turn the blade back again while bringing the right foot up level with the left as both stand up into *mugamae*. From the left foot take three steps back to the *tachi-maai*. The mutual bow from *orishiki* is conducted at the start and end of the *Kata*.

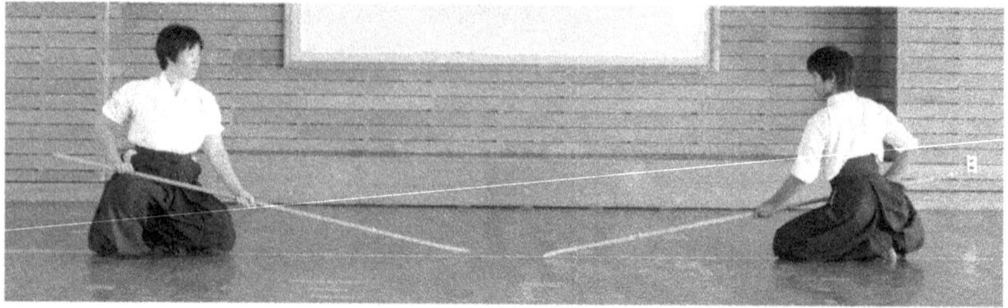

Mugamae: This is the *kamae* where the *naginata* is held on the right side of the body. Standing in *shizentai* (natural standing position) with the right hand holding the centre of the *e* (shaft), the left hand moves to grip the *naginata* just under the right hand and the *ha-bu* drops with the blade facing out and the *kissaki* covering the centreline of the body. The left arm comes across the body and the right hand grips the *naginata* from above. The *kissaki* is 10cm off the ground and the *monouchi* of the blade guards the centreline.

Appendix 4: Kata

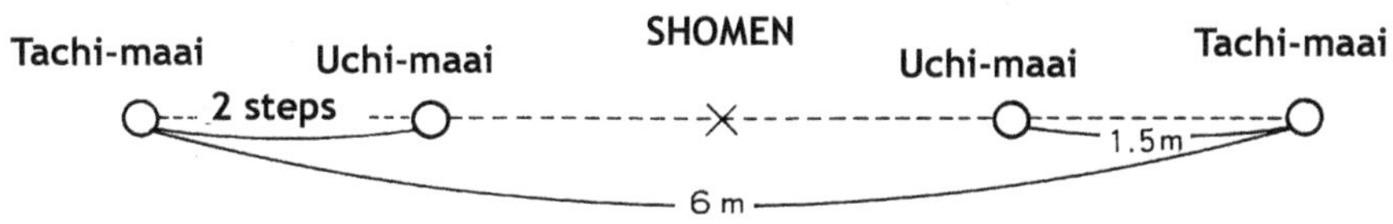

Uchi	Shi

Ippon-me

Uchi	Shi
(1) From *chudan*, take two steps forward with *ayumi-ashi* to enter the point of engagement, seize the opportunity and thrust to the solar-plexus while turning the blade to the left.	(1)' From *chudan*, take two steps forward with *ayumi-ashi* to enter the point of engagement, weaken the force of the *tsuki* by drawing the opponent's thrusting *naginata* diagonally downward to the left (*nayashi*) then thrusting it down with more force (*maki-otoshi*), following up with an immediate counter *tsuki* to the throat.
(2) *Zanshin*. Remaining alert, move back to the centre in *ai-chudan*, and draw the front foot back level with the back foot while assuming *mugamae*. Move back to the *tachi-maai*.	(2)' *Zanshin*. Remaining alert, move back to the centre in *ai-chudan*, and draw the front foot back level with the back foot while assuming *mugamae*. Move back to the *tachi-maai*.

Uchi	Shi
Nihon-me	
(1) From *hasso*, take two steps forward with *ayumi-ashi* to enter the point of engagement, seize the opportunity and cut *soku-men*.	(1)' From *gedan*, take two steps forward with *ayumi-ashi* to enter the point of engagement, then pivot on the back foot to spin around and face the opposite side as Uchi's *naginata* is knocked diagonally down (*haraiotoshi*).
(2) Using the momentum from the *haraiotoshi,* step forward with the left foot as the *naginata* is swung overhead (hands remain in the same position), and just as Uchi is about to move in for a follow-up attack, Shi makes a sweeping cut to *do*, and so Uchi is forced to move back out of the way.	(2)' Pivot to face the opposite direction with *fumikae-ashi* and make a sweeping cut to Uchi's *do* ending up with the right knee on the ground.
(3) *Zanshin*. Keeping distance, assume *chudan* (in *ayumi-ashi* or *okuri-ashi*).	(3)' *Zanshin*. Stand up and move back to the centre in *chudan.*

Uchi	Shi
Sanbon-me	
(1) From *chudan* take two steps forward with *ayumi-ashi* to enter the point of engagement, seize the opportunity and cut *sune*.	(1)' From *hasso*, take two steps forward with *ayumi-ashi* to enter the point of engagement, pivot on the back foot to spin around and face the opposite side while striking *sune*. Then, use the curvature of the blade (*sori*) to entwine then flick *Uchi's naginata* upward (*maki-age*) and cut *kote*.
(2) *Zanshin*. Move back to the centre in *migi-chudan*. Then spin the *naginata* around and into *mugamae* then returning to the *tachi-maai*.	(2)' *Zanshin*. Move back to the centre in *migi-chudan*. Then, spin the *naginata* around and into *mugamae*, then return to the *tachi-maai*.

Uchi	Shi
Yonhon-me	
(1) From *jodan* take two steps forward with *ayumi-ashi* to enter the point of engagement, seize the opportunity and cut *men*.	(1)' From *wakigamae*, enter the point of engagement, move back from the back foot to avoid the cut to *men*, then immediately step forward with the right foot and cut *men*.
(2) Step back from the back foot and receive the *men* cut with the blade, then force Shi's *naginata* down (*maki-otoshi*).	(2)' Use the momentum from the *harai*, and move forward to the diagonal left while executing *furi-kaeshi-sune*.
(3) *Zanshin*.	(3) *Zanshin*.

Uchi	Shi
Gohon-me	
(1) From *chudan* take two steps forward with *ayumi-ashi* to enter the point of engagement, *mochikae* and cut *do*.	(1)' From *jodan*, take two steps forward with *ayumi-ashi* to enter the point of engagement, then pivoting on the back foot spin around to face the opposite side and block the cut to *do* with the *ha-bu*. Then force Uchi's *naginata* down (*maki-otoshi*).
(2) Use the momentum from the *harai* and execute *furikaeshi-men*.	(2)' Pivoting on the back foot and turning to face the opposite side, knock *Uchi's naginata* down to the diagonal right (*uchiotoshi*), immediately pull the *naginata* in (*kurikomi*), and thrust to Uchi's solar-plexus with the *ishizuki*.
(3) *Zanshin*.	(3) *Zanshin*.

Roppon-me

Uchi	Shi
(1) From *chudan*, take two steps forward with *ayumi-ashi* to enter the point of engagement, and turning the *sori,* thrust to the solar-plexus.	(1)' From *mugamae*, take two steps forward with *ayumi-ashi* (left then right) to enter the point of engagement, then withdraw the left foot while catching (blocking) Uchi's thrust with the *ha-bu.* Then stepping forward with the right foot flick Uchi's *naginata* up (*makiage*) and assume *jodan* while pulling the right foot back again.
(1)" Using the momentum from the *maki-age*, move back and assume *jodan*.	
(2)' Move back and thrust out the *e-bu* (*kuridashi*) to block the cut to *sune*.	(2) Step forward with the right foot and cut *sune.*
(Uchi 3) Move back into *hasso*, and then step forward to cut *sokumen.*	(3)' Move back and receive the *men* cut with the *ha-bu*, and then take another step back while forcing Uchi's *naginata* down (*harai*).
(4) Use the momentum of the *harai* and execute *furikaeshi-men*.	(4)' Move back to the diagonal left and deflect the *men* cut (uke-*nagashi*), then step forward with the left foot and cut *men*.
(5) *Zanshin*.	(5) *Zanshin.*

Uchi	Shi
Nanahon-me	
(1) From *hasso*, take two steps forward with *ayumi-ashi* to enter the point of engagement, and make a big diagonal right cut to *men* stepping with the right foot then the left (*kesa-giri*). The cut should stop just below Shi's left shoulder, then assume *migi-hasso*.	(1)' From *hasso*, take two steps forward with *ayumi-ashi* to enter the point of engagement, draw the left foot back while pulling the *naginata* in (*kurikomi*), and protect the body with the blade.
(2) From *hasso* make a big diagonal left cut to men stepping with the left foot then the right (*kesa-giri*). The cut should stop just below the right shoulder.	(2)' Draw the right foot back and protect the body with the *e*.
	(3) Step forward with the right foot and cut *kote* from below ending up in *migi-wakigamae* (the blade is facing down).
(3)' Draw the left foot back and protect with the *e-bu*.	
	(4) Step forward with the left foot and cut kote from below ending up in *hidari-hasso*.
(4)' Draw the right foot back and protect with the *ha-bu*.	
	(5) Cut *men*.
(5)' Bring the feet together, block the *men* cut overhead with the centre of the *e-bu*, and then step out immediately with the left foot and cut *sune*.	
	(6) Move back and block the *sune* cut with the *e-bu*, *maki-age* up, *harai-otoshi* down, and strike *sune* while moving out to the right.

(7) Zanshin. Move back to the centre in *ai-chudan*. Kneel down and bow. Stand up into *mugamae* and move back to the starting position. Stand the *naginata* upright and conduct one more mutual bow.

(7) *Zanshin*. Move back to the centre in *ai-chudan*. Kneel down and bow. Stand up into *mugamae* and move back to the starting position. Stand the *naginata* upright and conduct one more mutual bow.

Appendix 5

Examination Questions

Possible Examination Questions and Answers

The is my personal translation of the revised *Naginata Handbook*, published by the AJNF for practitioners to study for the written section of *dan* examinations. I have taken the liberty of adding ***possible*** questions at the start of each entry. Most of the information required to write answers to these topics is contained throughout the pages of this book. Even though some of the questions overlap, it is expected that the candidate be able to answer with more detail as their rank advances. This appendix was included to give the practitioner a general idea of the kind of questions that will be in an examination. Also, given the rigid penchant of the AJNF to expect "verbatim" answers from their handbook, I highly recommend that you purchase the AJNF's somewhat under-publicised English version to study from. I hope that my unofficial rendition of the original Japanese text will serve to clarify a few points.

Shodan

1. Naginata and Reigi

Q: Explain the importance of reigi (etiquette, respect) in Naginata.
A: Just as in other budo disciplines, Naginata has always placed value on the ideal of showing respect to one's opponent or training partner at the start and at the end the engagement. Etiquette and protocols of courtesy are greatly emphasised in Naginata, not just in form but accompanied with genuine sincerity. It doesn't matter how skilled a person may be in the techniques of Naginata, to belittle opponents or act arrogantly runs counter to Naginata ideals. Interacting with others with respect and courtesy is not only expected in the environment where one trains, but also in the course of daily life. In this way, it is hoped that the practitioner can use lessons learned in Naginata to be a respectful and caring person.

2. Reiho

Q: Explain the various bows in Naginata.
A: *Reiho* means manners or protocols of etiquette. Practically speaking "*rei*" it is to bow, and bows are performed in Naginata to demonstrate humility. It shows esteem to others, and fosters a respectful mind and beauty in form.

Appendix 5: Examination Questions

There are two forms of *rei*: the standing bow (*ritsurei*), and the seated bow (*zarei*).

Ritsurei – The standing bow is conducted to training partners, opponents, and also the *shomen* of the dojo or venue. When bowing to the *shomen*, the upper body is inclined on an angle of 30° and 15° when bowing to one's opponent. Maintaining eye-contact, the left hand slides down the left thigh towards the inside. The *naginata* remains perfectly upright and does not move.

Zarei – When sitting down, the left foot is pulled back slightly and the left knee is placed on the floor followed by the right knee ("*saza-uki*" – sit down from the left, stand up from the right). The *naginata* is placed to the right with the blade facing outward and the *ishizuki* end about 30cm in front of the knee. The big toes overlap, the chin is pulled in, back straight, mouth lightly closed, and eyes looking straight ahead. Each hand is placed on the corresponding thigh, and the upper arms lightly touch the body. This sitting style is known as *seiza*. The hands slide down the thighs as the body bends forward, and come to a stop in front of the knees as the bow is made without splaying the elbows out. When standing, lift the toes up first so that they are perpendicular to the floor, turn the body slightly to the right to pick up the *naginata* with the right hand on the bottom and left hand on top. Then straighten up while standing from the right foot, and bring the left foot up level as you stand.

3. Naginata Parts and Construction

Q: Draw the Naginata and name its parts.

A:

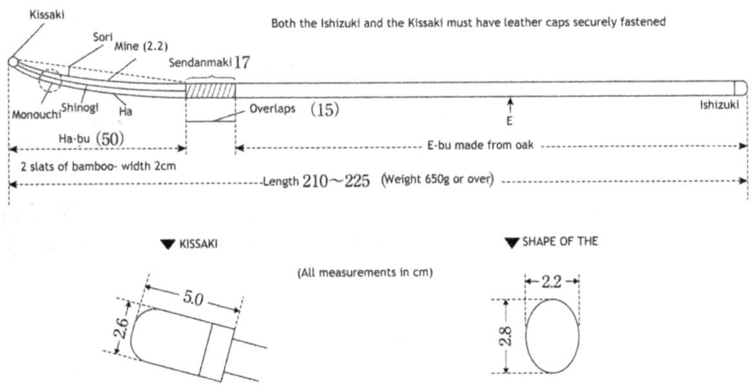

4. Tenouchi

Q: Explain the term tenouchi.
A: *Tenouchi* means grip. The *naginata* is gripped with the fingers and palms of both softly, and then tightened on impact when striking. The dispersion of power is equal in both hands.

5. Kiai and Hassei

Q: Explain kiai and hassei.
A: The name of the target (*datotsu-bui*) must be vocalised correctly with *ki* (energy) focussed in the lower abdomen area (*tanden*) when making a strike.

6. Shizentai

Q: Explain the term "shizentai".
A: *Shizentai* is the natural standing posture in Naginata, and should enable instant, unimpeded, and stable movement in any direction in response to the opponent's actions.

7. The Six Kamae

Q: Name the six kamae (stances) employed in Naginata.
A: *Chudan-no-kamae*; *Gedan-no-kamae*; *Hasso-no-kamae*; *Wakigamae*; *Jodan-no-kamae*; *Mu-gamae.*

8. Characteristics of the Six Kamae

Q: Explain the characteristics of the six kamae employed in Naginata.
A:

① ***Chudan-no-kamae*** (L&R) – *Chudan* forms the basis for all of the stances, and is suitable for moving off the mark or responding to the opponent's actions. It is beneficial for both attack and defence.
② ***Gedan-no-kamae*** (L&R) – The *kissaki* is lowered to offer protection while also applying pressure to the opponent's lower body, and enables response to their actions. This *kamae* is for beneficial for counterattacking.
③ ***Hasso-no-kamae*** (L&R) – In *hasso-no-kamae*, the *kissaki* is lifted up as the grip is swapped, and is primed to observe and attack any changes in the opponent.
④ ***Wakigamae*** (L&R) – The *ishizuki* is moved to the front. It is a stance that is useful for responding to change, and confusing the opponent.
⑤ ***Jodan-no-kamae*** (L&R) – The *naginata* is held overhead with

authority emanating from the *ishizuki* and a strong presence signifying the ability and will to attack at any moment. As it is an intimidating stance it is important to have a domineering attitude and apply pressure with *ki*.

⑥ ***Mu-gamae*** – In the "stance of no-stance", the *naginata* is held at the right side of the body protecting one's centreline in a state of *mushin* (no-mind).

9. The Correct Way to Assume Chudan

Q: Explain how to assume chudan-no-kamae.
A: *Chudan-no-kamae* forms the basis for all of the stances. The body should be side on (*hanmi*) with the *kissaki* in line with the centre of your body while pointing up at the opponent's solar plexus. The arms hang down naturally and hand width is the same as foot width at around two feet apart. The rear hand grips the shaft at a position leaving one forearm's length to the *ishizuki*, and is lightly placed on the inner thigh of the back leg. One must also be replete with energy and primed to apply pressure.

10. Types of Taisabaki

Q: What are the types of footwork used in Naginata?
A: Okuri-ashi; *Ayumi-ashi*; *Hiraki-ashi*; *Fumikae-ashi*; *Tsugi-ashi*.

11. Types of Suburi

Q: What are the various swings for striking in Naginata?
A: *Joge-buri*; *Naname-buri*; *Yoko-buri*; *Furikaeshi*.

12. The Objective of Suburi

Q: Explain the objectives of suburi?
A: The purpose of practising *suburi* repetitively is to learn to wield the *naginata* seamlessly with coordination, and also master the fundaments for striking (footwork, *tenouchi*, correct trajectory).

13. Correct Striking

Q: Explain what constitutes a correct strike.
A: Striking the target with precise trajectory (*hasuji*) and with the *monouchi* of the *naginata* in full spirit and good posture while vocalising the name of the target, and followed with continued alertness (*zanshin*).

14. Datotsu-bui Designations

Q: What are the names of the targets in Naginata?
A: *Shomen*; *Sokumen* (L&R); *Do* (L&R); *Inko*; *Kote* (L&R); *Soto-zune* and *Uchi-zune* (L&R).

15. Striking Methods

Q: Name the various striking methods.
A: *Furiage*; *Mochikae*; *Furikaeshi*; *Tsuki*.

16. Ways of Blocking

Q: What are the methods of blocking
A: Receiving with the *ha-bu*; Receiving with the *e-bu*.

17. The Characteristics of Uchikaeshi

Q: Outline the characteristics of uchikaeshi.
A: *Uchikaeshi* is a comprehensive training method that teaches the basic elements of striking such as breathing, *tenouchi*, *maai*, footwork, and so on. Being a predetermined striking sequence, Naginata practitioners of all levels can practise *uchikaeshi*, and improvement is made through continually executing strikes with precision.

18. Important Points in Uchikaeshi

Q: Explain the important points when doing uchikaeshi.
A:

① Turn and pivot the body adequately, and make sure that the overhead swings (*furiage*) and grip changes (*mochikae*) are executed with precision.

② Make sure that the trajectory of the blade (*hasuji*) is accurate.
③ The targets (*datotsu-bui*) should be struck correctly with the *monouchi* section of the blade.
④ The strike and body movement should be in sync.
⑤ The sequence of strikes should be made with one breath.

19. Types of Naginata Competition

Q: Outline the types of Naginata competition.
A: Naginata competitions include *shiai-kyogi* and *engi-kyogi*. In *engi-kyogi*, competitors perform Shikake-Oji or All Japan Naginata Kata. *Shiai-kyogi* consists of team matches (*dantai-sen*) and individual matches (*kojin-sen*).

Nidan

1. Happo-buri

Q: Explain the importance of happo-buri
A: In *happo-buri*, the *naginata* is swung freely without stopping in the eight directions of up and down (*joge*), diagonal from above (*naname*), horizontally from side to side (*yoko*), diagonal from underneath (*naname shita kara*) and overhead (*furikaeshi*). Through *happo-buri*, the practitioner learns the fundamentals of Naginata (footwork, *tenouchi*, sliding the naginata through the hands, etc.), and correct trajectory of the blade (*hasuji*).

2. Maai

Q: What are the different distances for engagement?
A: The distance between you and the opponent is called *maai*. It is important to always be aware of distance, and move to maintain an appropriate space to enable solid striking with the feet.

① *Uchima* – At this distance, one is able to strike the opponent by taking one step in, and avoid an attack by taking one step back. It is the most fundamental *maai* in Naginata.

② *Chikama* – This distance is closer than *uchima*. Although it is possible to step in and strike, it is also easy to be struck by the opponent from this distance, and is therefore dangerously close.

③ *Toma* – This distance is further away than *uchima*. It is difficult to reach the opponent with one step, but at the same time it is harder for the opponent to strike you as well. This makes it a safer distance to engage from, but it is also possible to strike the opponent by throwing oneself into the attack.

3. Zanshin

Q: What is zanshin?
A: *Zanshin* is the mental posture and physical readiness after making an

attack; to demonstrate *zanshin* means not letting one's guard down. This way, you can avoid leaving yourself open and being struck by your opponent. It also means that you are mentally and physically prepared to attack again at any time.

4. Categories and Names of Naginata Techniques

Q: Name the types of waza employed in Naginata.
A:

① *Shikake-waza – Harai-waza*; *fumikomi-waza*; *debana-waza*; *nidan-waza*; *sandan-waza*.
② *Oji-waza – Uke-waza*; *nuki-waza*; *haraiotoshi-waza*; *uchiotoshi-waza*; *makiotoshi-waza*; *ukenagashi-waza*.

5. Types of Shikake-waza

Q: Explain what shikake-waza is and the different types.
A: *Shikake-waza* is employed by initiating a movement, overcoming your opponent, and striking as soon as they become discombobulated. *Shikake-waza* includes the following techniques:

① *Harai-waza* – Striking after creating an opening in the opponent's defences by slapping their *naginata* to the right or the left.
② *Fumikomi-waza* – Using the various forms of footwork to position yourself to lunge in to make a strike with total conviction.
③ *Debana-waza* – Strike your opponent just as they start to move, or are about to attack.
④ *Nidan / sandan-waza* – A combination of two or three different techniques made in succession.

6. The Advantages of Renzoku-waza

Q: What are the advantages of striking continuously
A: Striking continuously in quick succession prevents your opponent from executing an attack, and the pressure creates openings in their defences.

7. Types of Oji-waza

Q: Explain what oji-waza is and the different types.
A: *Oji-waza* are techniques in which the *naginata* and body are used to nullify the opponent's attacks, followed immediately with a counterattack.

① *Uke-waza* – The opponent's attack is received with the *ha-bu* or *e-bu*

and followed immediately with a counterattack.
② *Nuki-waza* – Moving back or to the diagonal rear to dodge the opponent's strike, and then following immediately with a counterattack.
③ *Haraiotoshi-waza* – While moving away from the opponent's strike, use body movement in combination with the *ha-bu* or *e-bu* to deflect the strike down, and then follow immediately with a counterattack.
④ *Uchiotoshi-waza* – While moving away from the opponent's strike, use the *ha-bu* or the *e-bu* to strike the *naginata* down and follow immediately with a counterattack.
⑤ *Makiotoshi-waza* – As soon as you block your opponent's strike, use the curvature of the blade (*sori*) to flick the *naginata* down and then follow immediately with a counterattack.
⑥ *Ukenagashi-waza* – Receive and deflect the opponent's *naginata* and then strike.

8. Striking Opportunities

Q: Explain the optimal striking opportunities.
A:
① *Debana* – Just as your opponent is about to strike.
② As the opponent pulls back – Amidst the exchange of strikes when the opponent feels the pressure and steps back to create a safe distance.
③ At the end of a technique – At the end of an attack, or when the strike has failed.
④ As the opponent comes to a standstill – When the opponent's *waza* becomes disjointed and the movement stops.
⑤ As the opponent changes grip (*mochikae*) – The instant the opponent changes grip.
⑥ When the opponent breathes in.
⑦ When the opponent drops their guard and loses focus.
⑧ When the opponent becomes confused.

9. Kakari-geiko

Q: Explain how to do kakari-geiko.
A: In *kakari-geiko* one must actively execute many techniques in a nonstop attacking sequence against somebody of a higher skill level, striving to attack as much as possible for as long as one is physically and mentally able to continue.

10. The Benefits of Kakari-geiko

Q: Explain the benefits of doing kakari-geiko.
A: By attacking with all of one's might, one is able to learn correct breathing, distancing, striking opportunities, and footwork. Furthermore, one also hones technical ability and cultivate a strong spirit when striving to overcome a strong opponent by attacking continuously *in kakari-geiko.*

11. Gokaku-geiko

Q: Explain how to do gokaku-geiko.
A: *Gokaku-geiko* is a training method in which both sides do their best to score valid points on each other.

12. Mitori-geiko

Q: Explain the benefits of mitori-geiko.
A: *Mitori-geiko* is the act of watching other people train. Paying attention to the training method, attitude, techniques, and specialty *waza* of others is a useful way of developing one's own training and skills.

13. The Characteristics of Naginata

Q: What are the characteristics of Naginata?
A:

① Budo characteristics – Naginata is traditional Japanese culture in which one learns the differences and similarities between it and other sports.
② *Waza* characteristics – With technical improvement in Naginata, one learns how to use one's strength rationally with flexibility, agility, and delicacy.
③ Competitive characteristics – There are *engi-kyogi* and *shiai-kyogi* contests in Naginata. Retaining the characteristics of budo, Naginata can be studied throughout one's lifetime to fulfil a variety of objectives.

14. The Features of Naginata

Q: What are the features of Naginata?
A:

① Budo features – As a budo discipline, Naginata facilitates a deepening of concentration, focus in patterns of movement, appreciation of protocols of etiquette, and technical achievement.

② Technical features – Because the *naginata* is a long weapon, there are specific ways in which it is manipulated using movements such as *kurikomi*, *kuridashi*, *mochikae*, and *furikaeshi*.
③ Physical features – Side on stance (*hanmi*), body movement (shifting centre of balance), changing the direction the body faces (left and right), and so on are features that develop agility and good posture.
④ Competitive features – One can continue competing in Naginata for many years, and can participate as an individual or in a group to suit one's age and strength.

15. The Mindset for Training

Q: What attitude should one have when studying Naginata?
A: As a budo discipline, Naginata has evolved through a long historical process. In the modern age it is enjoyed as a competitive sport, but it is important that the budo aspects should be understood, and that it is learned and passed on correctly. The required attitude for the study of Naginata is as follows:
① *Reigi-saho*, or protocols of etiquette, are a way of showing respect to others, and it is important to carry that attitude into daily life.
② Learn correct Naginata techniques and the principles that underlie them.
③ Always engage in self-reflection with honesty and sincerity, and strive to achieve one's goals.
④ Through Naginata, learn the importance of acting in harmony with others and increase one's circle of friends.
⑤ Take care of one's health and maintaining a safe environment.

Sandan

1. The Necessity and Benefits of Warming Up and Cooling Down

Q: Why is it necessary to warm up before training, and cool down after?
A: It is important to warm up adequately to prepare the body and nervous system for the rigours of training. The purpose of doing preparatory exercises before training is to stimulate physical functions, in particular the heart and muscles, and to warm the body up. Stretching the muscles and improving blood flow increases heartbeat and body heat to facilitate smoothness in movement and decrease the possibility of injury in the course of rigorous exercise. These are the benefits of warming up. Also, it is important to cool down after training has finished. This will help alleviate accumulated muscle

fatigue and improve recovery, which will in turn help prevent injury.

2. The Value and Objectives of Kihon-dosa

Q: What is the importance of kihon-dosa?
A: *Kihon-dosa* are the fundamental movements in Naginata and form the basis for all *waza*. As one becomes more adept at *kihon*, it is easy to deviate from the correct method. *Kihon-dosa* must be practised with the feeling of relearning and fixing technique. *Kihon-dosa* is also very important for conveying correct Naginata technique to future generations.

3. Important Points When Instructing Uchikaeshi

Q: Explain the important points when instructing how to do and receive uchikaeshi.
A: Striking – Starting with correct *kamae*, strikes must be made without superfluous steps. The body should be pivoted adequately to the left and right in a smooth unbroken sequence of positive strikes.
Receiving – The receiver must take care to ensure that the *maai* is correct, and move carefully in time with the striker, turning the body adequately. The strikes must be blocked securely with the *monouchi* of the *shinogi* on the *ha-bu*, or the *e-bu*. Do not move to receive before the strike is initiated. For the *shomen* strike, keep the correct distance and pivot the body sufficiently to the side blocking the strike by keeping it off the centreline. With the *sokumen* strikes, pivot the body to the sides while going back, keeping the right distance, and block the strikes at the left and right *men* position. With the *sune* strikes, move the body back in the same way and block at the *soto-zune* position on the outside legs.

4. Tenouchi

Q: Explain what tenouchi is.
A: *Tenouchi* refers to the most efficient use of the palms, fingers and wrists in wielding the *naginata*. The shaft of the *naginata* is gripped lightly in the palms (as if holding onto eggs), and then tightened on the moment if impact when striking. An equal amount of power is in both hands.

5. Kiai and Hassei

Q: What is kiai and hassei?
A: Irrespective of whether or not *kiai* is vocalised, it is a spirited psychic equilibrium full of vigour and drive. *Hassei* refers to the correct vocalisation

of the target being struck which is generated from the build-up of energy in the lower abdomen (*tanden*), and has the effect of pressurising the opponent.

6. Hoshin

Q: What is hoshin?
A: In the context of Naginata, *hoshin* (literally "free mind") is the state of mind in which one is liberated from preoccupation and is able to liberally react to any situation without becoming distracted.

7. Shishin

Q: What is shishin?
A: *Shishin* (literally "stuck mind") is the state of mind in which one becomes preoccupied on something, rendering one unable to focus on the movement or intentions of the opponent. At the same time, the mind will also become restricted and slow at adapting to the changing circumstances. The body also stalls when the mind becomes stuck.

8. Kikentai-itchi

Q: Explain kikentai-itchi.
A: *Ki* is spirit, *ken* refers to the *naginata*, and *tai* is body or physical posture and movement. *Itchi* is the coalescence of all of these factors.

9. Hikitate-geiko

Q: What is hikitate-geiko?
A: *Hikitate-geiko* is a sparring training method in which seniors or instructors help their charges get ahead. The junior practitioner is encouraged to attack and the senior adjusts the distance and striking opportunities to suit, making sure that the attacker does so with gusto and is able to demonstrate the best of their abilities. This training method is effective for nurturing mental and physical strength. The senior receives the strikes in a way that it does not seem intentional. That way the attacker feels what it is like to score a palpable strike, and understands the principles leading to success. It is important to be skilled at encouraging the junior to strike by subtly creating openings appropriate for their level.

10. Gokaku-geiko

Q: What is gokaku-geiko?

A: This is a training method in which people of comparable skill try their best to score techniques on each other as if competing in a match. They judge the validity of the points themselves. Instead of relying on specialty techniques, the aim is try as many different *waza* and combinations. Respect must be shown to training partners, and acknowledgement given every time one is struck successfully. It is important to have this attitude to try and develop one's technical ability and as a person.

11. The Benefits of Naginata Training

Q: Explain the psychological and physical benefits gained from studying Naginata.

A: *Psychological Benefits*

① *Reigi*

Rei is a bow or feeling of respect to one's opponents. One nurtures a cooperative and humble attitude through training with partners to develop technical proficiency and forge the body and mind.

② *Kiryoku*

Kiryoku is the force of will and energy. Naginata is rich in terms of movement and techniques, and through the process of mastering them, one's powers of concentration and judgment are enhanced. Fortitude and stamina are increased through continuous training.

Physical Benefits

① Increased strength

Naginata involves comprehensive physical exercise which improves blood flow and increases metabolism, and overall fitness. Physical strength and balance is naturally augmented through continued training.

② Training with correct posture improves good physical equilibrium and begets beautiful carriage.

③ Naginata training works out both the left and right sides of the body. Also, as it is practised with a partner, it helps cultivate the ability to react nimbly to any action with vim and vigour. Continued training in Naginata promotes vitality.

12. Fudoshin

Q: What is fudoshin?

A: *Fudoshin* is the state of mind which does not become agitated. The mind does not succumb to surprise, fear, doubt, or hesitation (*kyo-ku-gi-waku*) through pressure applied by the opponent. The mind remains unfettered and able to react calmly to the opponent's movements.

13. Interpreting the Official Concept of Naginata

Q: Explain the meaning of the "Concept of Naginata".
A: "The concept of Naginata is to foster people harmonious in body and mind through training in its techniques."

- "Concept" – The highest philosophical meaning of Naginata. In other words, "What is Naginata?"
- "Naginata" – The "Way" of Naginata, or its ultimate objectives.
- "Through training in its techniques" – The actual practical study of Naginata. Honing one's ability and understanding of the techniques and spirit of Naginata.
- "Harmonious in body and mind" – A synergy of physical and mental attributes, this means balance in both aspects of one's development with a character imbued with virtues such as richness, beauty, propriety, cheerfulness, health, clarity, and certainty.
- "Foster people" – To nurture individuals who are able to contribute to the greater good.

14. The Objective and Mindset for Studying Naginata

Q: State the objectives and required mindset for studying Naginata.
A: Naginata is a traditional form of Japanese athletic martial culture which has evolved through history. There have been many changes in its form over the centuries until the present day which have successfully reflected the educational needs and values of the times. The objective of studying Naginata is to foster people harmonious in body and mind through training in its techniques.

15. The Right Attitude

Q: State the right attitude or mindset necessary for studying Naginata.
A:
① Learn correct Naginata technical principles, and strive to develop one's morality.
② Be a dignified person worthy of respect in one's daily deportment.
③ Always seek improvement, and be full of positivity.
④ Study ways of improving one's technical and instructional ability, and demonstrate those skills when teaching.
⑤ Always be cognizant of the health and safety of self and others.

16. Important Points When Instructing Naginata

Q: What points should be taken heed of when instructing Naginata?
A:

① Keeping the essence of Naginata in mind, aim and plan to teach to an appropriate level in accordance with the learner's age (level of development), ability, and objectives. Devise a teaching methodology suited to the learner, and teach systematically and methodically.
② Instruct in a way that the learners are enthusiastic to continue of their own volition ensuring that they improve as they go.
③ Emphasise the basics when instructing. This applies to teaching techniques, and ideally includes schooling students comprehensively in etiquette and appropriate behaviour.
④ The more one practises the higher the rate of improvement in terms of learning the techniques, so the more the better. The easier techniques and movements of Naginata should be taught first, and increase in difficulty incrementally.
⑤ Be mindful of safety.

- Think of safety before and after training, and arrange contact information in the case of an emergency.
- Ensure that the fitness of learners is understood, and classes are taught with their wellbeing firmly in mind.
- Keep the training environment and equipment in order.
- The instructor must also look after her or his own health.

Yondan and Godan

1. The Meaning of Shiai and Keiko

Q: State the meaning of competition and keiko.
A: The term *keiko* literally means to "consider antiquity". Antiquity in this context is referring to past teachings, and even the *men* strike you have just made has been and gone. In other words, everything happens must be considered and reflected on in the course of one's study. Other words are also used in reference to *keiko* such as "practice" and "training". These terms, comparatively speaking, place more emphasis on the physical aspects rather than the spiritual. Traditional Japanese arts and budo have always used the term *keiko* to denote its study. This is an indication of the depth of the arts, and the nobility of the paths associated with them. *Shiai* is the Japanese word for match, and literally means "to test each other". In other words, this it is a contest to ascertain the aggregate of one's continuous learning of techniques

and manner in Naginata.

2. The Three Unforgivable Openings

Q: What are the "three unforgivable openings"?
A: There are three optimal striking opportunities that should not be missed when striking:

① Just as the opponent's *waza* is about to manifest (*debana*).
② When the opponent has been blocked.
③ When the opponent's *waza* has come to an end.

3. Striking Opportunities

Q: What are the striking opportunities in Naginata?
A: There are various striking opportunities, and of particular importance are the "three unforgivable openings": Just as the opponent's *waza* is about to manifest (*debana*); when the opponent has been blocked; When the opponent's *waza* has come to an end. Others include:

① When retreating.
② When stopped.
③ When changing grip (*mochikae*).
④ When breathing in deeply.
⑤ When the "four illnesses" (*shikai*)—fear, surprise, doubt, hesitation—arise.
⑥ When the mind experiencing doubt (*kogishin*) while executing a *waza* arises.
⑦ When *kyo* appears after avoiding *jitsu*. (When the opponent is on their guard, this state is referred to as "*jitsu*" (real), and there is no opening to strike. However, when they lose their focus, this is called a state of "*kyo*" (hole), giving rise to many openings.)

4. Striking Opportunities and 'Invitations' (Sasoi)

Q: Explain Striking opportunities and what is meant by "inviting" an opponent?
A: *Striking opportunities*:

- The three unforgivable openings (*debana* or *degashira*, when the opponent is blocked, when the *waza* is finished).
- Avoiding *jitsu* and striking at *kyo*.
- Fluster the opponent and strike.
- When the opponent has come to a standstill.

- The moment that a state of *kogishin* arises.
- When the opponent breathes in or when the "four illnesses" (*shikai*) arise.

Inviting the opponent

When pitted against an opponent who is also looking for striking opportunities in your defences, 'invite' them to strike by consciously feigning an opening.

5. The Three Sen

Q: Explain the significance of the "three sen".

A: To take *sen* is to seize victory by suppressing the opponent's movement the instant it begins. There are various interpretations of *sen*, but generally there are said to be three:

① *Sensen-no-sen*

Just as the opponent's *waza* is about to take form, nip it in the bud and defeat it before it can fully manifest. When two protagonists face off and are intent on striking each other, this is the first *sen*. When the opponent tries to strike *men* or *kote*, this is counted as the second *sen*. Sensing the opponent's *sen* and striking before it bears fruit is the *sen* of the first two *sen-sen* (*sensen-no-sen* – moving earlier in anticipation of your attacker's intentions).

② *Senzen-no-sen*

As the opponent sees an opening and attempts to strike, turn it against them with *suriage*, *kaeshi*, or *nuki-waza* and so on. When two protagonists face off and are intent on striking each other, this is the first *sen*. Countering their attack before it is successful comes before the second *sen*, which is why it is called *sen-zen* (before) i.e., the *sen* before the second *sen*. *Senzen-no-sen* is also called just *sen*.

③ *Sengo-no-sen*

Striking the opponent's attack down or dodging it and then counter-striking immediately after as their momentum is compromised. *Sengo-no-sen* is also called as *go-no-sen*.

These explanations elucidate the mental aspects of *sen*. In Miyamoto Musashi's treatise *Gorin-no-sho*, there is a practical explanation of the three *sen* in the section titled "Three methods to forestall the enemy".

> The first is to forestall him by attacking. This is called *ken-no-sen* (to set him up). Another method is to forestall him as he attacks. This is called *tai-no-sen* (to wait for the initiative). The other method is when you and the enemy attack together. This is called *tai-tai-no-sen* (to accompany him and forestall

him). There are no methods of taking the lead other than these three. Because you can win quickly by taking the lead, it is one of the most important things in strategy. There are several things involved in taking the lead. You must make the best of the situation, see through the enemy's spirit so that you grasp his strategy and defeat him. It is impossible to write about this in detail.

6. Adjusting Maai

Q: Explain the importance and method of controlling distance.

A: The distance (*maai*) between you and the opponent is the same. Nevertheless, even though the spatial distance is the same, one can make that distance beneficial depending on the *kamae* and the way the *kissaki* is manipulated. An old teaching states that the best distance is one that seems close for you, but distant for your opponent. In order to control the *maai*, the technical ability of you and your opponent is pivotal. It is important to know the opponent's strategy and ability. When you face your opponent, you have to perceive their physical condition, *kamae*, spirit, and how they try to adjust distance to suit their style. In order to do this, you must have a firm understanding of the principles of engagement, and also nurture your perception and ability to sense and make instant judgments through training.

7. Heijoshin

Q: What is heijōshin?

A: *Heijoshin*, is a human being's natural, inherently calm state of mind. When suddenly faced with something frightening, people tend to freeze and lose composure. One also becomes agitated and loses confidence when confronted with the great unknown. *Heijoshin* is to remain calm and collected regardless of the circumstances. In this way, irrespective of what happenings or problems occur in the course of one's daily activities, dealing with it with a placid mind that does not become perturbed or clouded by emotion, and fostering the courage to act confidently in the face of adversity is vital for success in any social undertaking.

8. Kigurai

Q: What is kigurai?

A: Years of training in which one develops their moral outlook, forges the body and masters the techniques of Naginata will manifest into an air of dignity and authority. This cannot be achieved overnight. It requires considerable effort over time to purge oneself of malevolent thoughts, and be able to discern between good and bad without being preoccupied with winning or losing. To improve as a human being who is indomitable in body and spirit, and who exudes absolute self-belief when facing an opponent in a state of no-mind (*mushin*) is achieved only after years of rigorous training. The special aura of elegance that emanates from within is called *kigurai*.

9. Kogishin

Q: What is kogishin?

A: *Kogishin* refers to a hesitating mind that inhibits one's ability to make and follow through on decisions. The phrase is thought to originate in the old saying "Foxes are cautious by nature". "*Ko*" means fox, and "*gishin*" means doubt or apprehension. Once one becomes apprehensive, one starts to second guess the opponent. "If I strike *men*, my opponent will get my *sune*…" While worrying about this prospect, other openings will become apparent to the opponent, and one's hesitation will result in one's demise.

10. San-sappo

Q: What is san-sappo?

A: To "kill" the opponent's "weapon", "*waza*", and "*ki*" to create an opening.

① To kill the opponent's *naginata* means to suppress it, or employ techniques such as *maki-harai* to render it ineffectual. This is essentially killing the threat of the opponent's *kissaki*.

② To kill the opponent's *waza* is to take the initiative (*sen*) and apply constant pressure without affording them the opportunity to attack. That way, the opponent will not be able to execute any *waza*.

③ To kill the opponent's *ki* is to keep up the momentum of "killing" or threatening to kill their *naginata* and *waza* and overcome them mentally with your own vigour and determination. This will make the opponent afraid and unable to move, opening the way for a successful strike. Creating panic in the opponent's mind is what is meant by "killing their *ki*". To kill means to close the opponent down and not let them demonstrate their capabilities. Even shutting down just one of the three will result in striking chances.

11. Suki, Kan, and Kyojitsu

Q: Explain suki (opening), kan (instinct), and kyojitsu (replete and empty).

A:

① *Suki* means opening. There can be openings in the mind, *kamae*, and movement. An important point in Naginata is to not succumb to any mental weaknesses and to keep one's *kamae* straight and steadfast to protect any targets from the opponent's probing *naginata*. Then, jump on any opening that is revealed by coaxing the opponent into making a move.
② *Kan* is the pre-emptive ability to be already attacking as the opening is revealed. In other words, it is to trust one's instincts. *Kan* is as quick as a reflection in the mirror, which means to read things before they transpire with acute sensibility.
③ *Kyojitsu* is made up of two contrasting glyphs. *Jitsu* refers to the situation in which one's opponent is mentally primed, and is in no way complacent. *Kyo* is the opposite of *jitsu*, and refers to "holes" in the opponent's mental or physical posture. In other words, a state of *jitsu* means the opponent is guarded, and *kyo* is when the opponent has dropped her guard. *Jitsu* will clash with *jitsu*, and both sides will be worse for wear. If *kyo* attacks *jitsu*, *kyo* will be soundly defeated. In this way it is important to be able to identify *jitsu* and *kyo* in your opponent, and mask it in yourself. You must avoid the opponent's *jitsu* and strike at their *kyo* state. Just as the shape of the ground controls the way the water flows, you must also control the opponent and not allow them to attain victory. This requires planning and training. Also, when the opponent is about to strike, this will become evident in their movement as they launch into the attack. Remember that their *jitsu* is aimed at the target they are attempting to strike, and the rest of them is full of holes ready to be picked off. Ride the *kyo* as they start to attack. That is basically the small movement as they prepare to launch. Or, their hesitation (*kogishin*) as they contemplate whether or not to strike is another *kyo*. Or, when they come to a standstill, or when they are hurried and their technique comes to a head. These are all scenarios where *kyo* arises. (Another interpretation suggests that *jitsu* is the substance and *kyo* is the void. In other words, showing the void to entice the opponent into the *jitsu*.)

12. Shikai

Q: What are the "four illnesses" (shikai)?
A: *Shikai* are the "four illnesses" of the mind: *kyo* (fear), *ku* (surprise), *gi* (doubt), *waku* (hesitation). These are mental states that must be avoided in Naginata.

Kyo-ku – Surprise and fear. One must remain calm and collected regardless of the opponent one faces. However, if the opponent is physically domineering, for example, is particularly aggressive, is famous for how strong she is, or has a bizarre *kamae*, it is easy to become surprised or afraid.
Gi-waku – Doubt and hesitation. When facing an opponent who is steadfast and looking as if she is ready to pounce, is she trying to entice you, or is she afraid? Or, if you see an opening, is it really a striking chance, or is it a trap? These conundrums result in doubt and hesitation. Not knowing where to strike or what *waza* to use, or suddenly having a change of heart when you are about to attack and are unable to make crucial decisions and follow through are fatal weaknesses. Such debilitating thoughts often arise, but must be avoided in *keiko* at all costs. It will result in their confidence falling away, enthusiasm dropping off, and prevent you from successfully executing techniques. This in turn makes you open to attack and will lead to defeat.

13. Shu-ha-ri

Q: Explain the process of study using the terms shu, ha, and ri.
A: Traditionally, the study of the arts was premised on three stages known as "*shu-ha-ri*". In this process, "*shu*" (protect, abide by) is the first step in which the adept abides by the teachings of the master or senior practitioners. The student must not do things as they see fit. Once something is learned, it is difficult to unlearn, which is why it is crucial to thoroughly learn correct *kihon* from the beginning. In this sense, the notion of *shu* is very important, and students must strive to learn correctly based on proper theory.

"*Ha*" means "to break", but implies exceeding or leaving, or even forgetting. So, after learning all you can in the *shu* stage, you forget that, and break away to enter the *ha* stage. Using the fundamental techniques that the student was taught in the *shu* stage, the student tests them and learns how to apply them in various situations, and ultimately improves on them. In order to do this, the student tests his or her skills in matches and other situations, and adapts the techniques as required, but still in accordance with the teachings and fundamentals that they learned from their teacher in *shu*.

Ri is to separate. This includes becoming independent of the master, and all objectives held in the *ha* stage and entry into a higher realm where one's own style is created. It is a realm in which principles are mastered and technical mastery underpinned by this, seeking a mental state of with total clarity and forming one's own art.

14. Sei-chu-do and Do-chu-sei

Q: What is sei-chu-do and do-chu-sei?

A: It is exceedingly difficult to explain the intricacies of the spiritual or psychological factors underlying technical matters. For example, when you strike the opponent you have to move. The preparatory movement is small and then it leads into the strike at the revealed opening. At that point, all thoughts and desires have left the mind, and the body acts out your accumulated efforts in training to execute the technique and take it to completion. The mind is serene like a moon rising above the peak. If the mind gets carried away with the execution of the technique, the opponent will sense this movement and stop it in its tracks with a counterstrike. The harder the technique the more serene the mind must be. This is represented by the phrase *do-chu-sei*—serenity in movement.

Opposite to this, when facing an opponent and are probing intently to identify openings to attack, the body remains steadfast and still, but the mind is a flurry of activity looking to identify any opportunity to capitalise on. If this appears evident to the opponent in any way through physical signs, they will manoeuvre to counter or avoid being struck, so the intensity and determination to strike must be masked. The interior is vibrant but the exterior must appear calm. This is what is meant by *sei-chu-do*—movement in serenity. In Miyamoto Musashi's *Gorin-no-sho* this idea is explained as follows:

> Meet the situation without tenseness yet not recklessly, your spirit settled yet unbiased. Even when your spirit is calm do not let your body relax, and when your body is relaxed do not let your spirit slacken. Do not let your spirit be influenced by your body, or your body be influenced by your spirit. Be neither insufficiently spirited nor over spirited. An elevated spirit is weak and a low spirit is weak. Do not let the enemy see your spirit.

15. A Thorough Knowledge of "Jutsuri"

Q: Explain what jutsuri is, and its importance in the study of Naginata.

A: *Jutsuri* are technical principles learned through training that encompasses overall theory. *Jutsu* refers to technique and has form, whereas *ri* means principle and generally has no form. There is no technique without principles, and no principles without technique. The coming together of technique and theory is called *riai*. *Waza* that do not have a theoretical underpinning are ineffectual, and will go nowhere. One will not improve regardless of how much effort is made if that effort is not premised on proper theoretical principles. Knowing theory facilitates the correct acquisition of techniques, and entry into the path of correct Naginata. Not only this, it is also requisite for self-perfection. *Jutsuri* can be divided into the following branches:

Technical Aspects	Mental Aspects	Training Method / Teaching Method
Body (Fundamental strength–muscular power, stamina, flexibility) Technique (Technical skill – Naginata *waza*, understanding the rules)	*Kokoro* (mind) – Attitude to training; Flow of tradition (*Munen-muso* [Unfettered mind], *Meikyo-shisui* [serene frame of mind])	Instruction – (Systematic instruction, scientific instruction, Naginata's competitive aspects)

To acquire knowledge in these aspects of Naginata requires plenty of training and experience in various situations in teaching, refereeing, and so on.

16. The Mindset of a Naginata Instructor

Q: What is the required mindset for a Naginata instructor.
A:

① An instructor must teach with a detailed understanding of, and in accordance with the "Concept of Naginata". Therefore, an instructor must continually strive for self-perfection through technical and instructional improvement and ongoing self-reflection.
② Research the requirements for an instructor and teach in a methodological fashion.
③ Beginners should be taught in an encouraging manner making sure that their interest does not wane. More advanced students should be made cognizant of theoretical matters so that they gain a higher understanding of the essential principles of Naginata. Questions and doubts that are raised by students should be answered conscientiously in accordance with their level of advancement.
④ Have a proper management system in place for the following:
(1) Health and safety

(2) Equipment

(3) Dojo or training environment

17. Basic Strength Needed in Naginata

Q: Outline the basic strength needed in Naginata.
A: Technical capacity is defined by a balance of physical strength, technical skill, and mental strength. Even if one is technically skilled, this ability will be impossible to demonstrate adequately without physical strength. Physical strength can be divided into the following components.

Physical Strength	
Resistance	**Action**
Resistance against bacteria, drugs, dirt. Resistance against excessive humidity, high and low pressure, acceleration, oscillation etc.	Power; stamina (muscular and cardiovascular); conditioning (agility, balance, delicacy); flexibility (joints).

To excel at Naginata and its techniques requires the building up of various kinds of strength through the process of training. This, must be coupled with technical improvement and mental strength to demonstrate even more power.

18. The Difference Between Naginata and Other Sports

Q: Outline the differences between Naginata and other sports.
A: Just as with other sports, Naginata is an excellent form of exercise which fosters stamina, perseverance, good manners, courage, decisiveness, and spiritual development. One of the characteristics of Naginata is the stress placed on the mental aspects. The following is a list of characteristics that define Naginata.

① It has a long history and tradition.

② It places considerable emphasis on etiquette.

③ It demands emotional control and facilitates mental or spiritual development.

④ It seeks the development of the aesthetic ideals of excellent posture and attitude, grace, heartiness and presence.

⑤ From the perspective of exercise, Naginata has the following characteristics:

(1) As correct posture is emphasised, the practitioner naturally develops

and maintains good carriage.

(2) Naginata employs movement on both sides of the body it is excellent for developing and maintaining a balanced physique.

(3) Naginata is an activity that can be continued throughout one's life, and studied by people all ages. It is the perfect lifelong sport.

19. Propagating Naginata

Q: How can Naginata be effectively disseminated?
A: The instructor should have ideas of how best Naginata can be spread in the community.

20. The Virtues Cultivated Through Naginata

Q: What virtues can be cultivated through the study of Naginata?
A:

- Righteousness (*seigi*) – Through the study of Naginata, the practitioner is able to review and correct the way they think, rectify their attitude and the way they act and by learning principles of propriety. This in turn nurtures the virtue of righteousness.
- Honour (*renchi*) – Through training, the practitioner learns consistency in what is right and what is wrong, and learns to place value on integrity without thinking about personal gain. The practitioner works for the betterment of others and develops a sense of shame.
- Courage (*yuki*) – By throwing heart and soul into training without fear requires that one build confidence and courage.
- Decorum (*reisetsu*) – As Naginata begins and ends with *rei*, the practitioner learns the importance of decorum and propriety, and to respect other people.
- Discipline (*kokki*) – Discipline is nurtured through learning to subdue the "four illnesses" (*shikai*) and forging the mind and body in *keiko*.
- Perseverance (*nintai*) – Participating in the various training methods in Naginata will take the practitioner to his or her limits, both physically and mentally. Breaking through personal limitations enhances one's ability to persevere.

21. Naginata versus Kendo

Q: What are the characteristics of Naginata compared to other disciplines (kendo)?

A:

① Because the *naginata* is long, it is advantageous from further away.
② The *naginata* is able to be shortened (*kurikomi*) or lengthened (*kuridashi*).
③ *Waza* can be executed from the right or the left with *mochikae*, and the side-on stance is used from both sides giving Naginata multiple directions for attack. This can confuse the opponent.
④ The blade (*ha-bu*), shaft (*e-bu*), and *ishizuki* can be used in attack.
⑤ Naginata includes both the inside and outside *sune* on both legs as a target. In this way, Naginata has many target areas, the naginata is versatile and dynamic in its usage, and techniques can be executed from a distant *maai*. All of these factors make the naginata advantageous when pitted against other disciplines (kendo.)

Examination Questions from a Previous Era

The following is a list of the kinds of questions that used to feature in *dan* examinations. There is considerable overlap with what I have introduced above, but there have been some changes made to the *shodan-sandan* group. I have included these for reference.

Shodan

1. Explain why you started Naginata.
2. Explain the significance of *reigi* (etiquette) in Naginata.
3. Explain the method of performing *zarei* (seated bow) and *ritsurei* (standing bow).
4. Explain the structure of the *naginata*.
5. Why is warming-up necessary before training?
6. Explain the benefits of *kangeiko* (mid-winter training) *shochu-geiko* (mid-summer training).
7. Explain *shizentai*.
8. Explain the five *kamae* used in Naginata.
9. Explain how to do *chudan-no-kamae* correctly.
10. Explain the different types of *tai-sabaki* (*ashi-sabaki* footwork) utilised in Naginata.
11. Explain the *datotsu-bui* (targets) in Naginata.
12. Explain the different types of *suburi* (*happo-buri*).
13. What is meant by “close *maai*” (*chikai-maai*)?
14. What is *zanshin*?

15. Explain the differences between *kakari-geiko* and *gokaku-geiko.*
16. Explain important points when putting *bogu* on.
17. Explain the various competitive events in Naginata.
18. How many metres apart are the start lines in *shiai-kyogi* and *engi-kyogi*?

Nidan

1. Explain the important factors for improving at Naginata.
2. Explain the characteristics of Naginata.
3. Explain the correct attitude required when training in Naginata.
4. Explain the mental and physical benefits gained through training in Naginata.
5. Explain the concept of "*fudoshin*" (immovable heart).
6. Explain the characteristics of *chudan-no-kamae.*
7. Explain striking opportunities.
8. Explain striking methodology and the different ways for executing techniques.
9. Explain the importance of *uchikaeshi.*
10. Explain the method of *uchikaeshi*, and the benefits.
11. Explain the points which require care when doing *uchikaeshi.*
12. Explain the various kinds of *shikake-waza* and *oji-waza.*
13. Explain *shikake-waza.*
14. Explain *oji-waza.*
15. Explain the various different types of Naginata techniques.
16. Explain striking opportunities (*mittsu no yurusanai tokoro*—three unforgivable acts).

Sandan

1. Explain *tenouchi.*
2. Explain the importance of *kiai* and *hassei* (shouting while striking).
3. Explain the "*mittsu no yurusanai tokoro*" (three unforgivable acts—striking opportunities).
4. Explain the benefits of *mitori-geiko* (watching others train).
5. Explain the things that can be learned by being struck.
6. Explain *hoshin* (being liberated from tenacious thoughts or preoccupation, thus enabling effectiveness and concentration).
7. Explain the dangers of *shishin* (preoccupation with something).
8. Explain correct striking methodology.
9. Explain the characteristics of the five *kamae.*
10. Explain the significance and objectives of practising *kihon-dosa* (basics).
11. Explain the objectives of practising *suburi* (practise swings).

12. Explain the fundamental moves in Naginata (Including bowing, footwork, striking etc.)
13. Explain the benefits of *renzoku-waza* (combination techniques).
14. Explain *shikake-waza.*
15. Explain the meaning of *ki-ken-tai-itchi.*
16. Explain the importance of *maai* (distance).
17. Explain the importance of the concept of *ken-tai-itchi* (attack and defence as one).
18. Explain striking opportunities.
19. Explain what constitutes a valid strike (*yuko-datotsu*).
20. Explain the importance of *kakari-geiko.*
21. Explain the different types of *keiko.*
22. Explain the ideal mindset for engaging in matches.
23. Explain what an ideal match would be.
24. Draw and explain the court used in *engi-kyogi.*
25. Explain what constitutes a *hansoku* (foul play) in *shiai.*
26. Explain the responsibilities of Shinpan (Referees).
27. Explain the significance of having three *shinpan* to judge a match.
28. Explain *mugamae.*
29. Outline the characteristics of the martial "Way" of Naginata.
30. Explain the criteria necessary to be able to sit the *yondan* examination.
31. Explain the *shinpan-ki* (refereeing flags).
32. Illustrate the positions of Shinpan in *shiai-kyogi* and *engi-kyogi.*
33. Explain the positioning and composition of Shinpan in matches.

Yondan & Godan

1. State the official "Concept of Naginata" and analyse it in your own words.
2. Explain the objectives of studying Naginata, and the required attitude.
3. Explain the benefits to be gained from studying Naginata.
4. Explain the benefits of warming-up before training, and those of cooling down properly afterwards.
5. Explain *maai.*
6. Explain the concept of *kigurai.*
7. Explain the concept of *heijoshin.*
8. Explain the meaning of *shiai* and *keiko.*
9. Explain the virtues nurtured in the individual through training in Naginata.
10. Explain the concept of *kogishin.*
11. Explain the meaning of *san-sappo.*
12. Explain the meaning of *suki, kan, kyojitsu.*
13. Explain *shikai* (the four illnesses).

14. Explain the concept of *shu-ha-ri.*
15. Explain the techniques (*waza*) of Naginata.
16. Explain *mittsu-no-sen.*
17. Explain the concept of *sei-chu-do*, and *do-chu-sei.*
18. Explain points which require attention when teaching Naginata.
19. Explain points which require attention when teaching *uchikaeshi.*
20. Explain the responsibilities of the officials of *Engi-kyogi.*
21. State your opinions in regards to the propagation of Naginata.
22. Write about the importance of having knowledge of *jutsuri* (technical conceptual components of Naginata).
23. Explain the attitude required of an instructor.
24. Explain the basic physical attributes required to do Naginata.
25. Explain the differences between Naginata and other sports.
26. Explain striking opportunities and coaxing the opponent into initiating an attack.
27. Explain the differences between the *naginata* and other weapons.
28. Explain the required attitude of Shinpan.
29. Explain the "Tournament-method of conducting matches.
30. Explain the "League-method" of conducting matches.

APPENDIX 6

INF CONSTITUTION

Chapter 1: General Provisions

(Name)

Article 1: This organization shall be called the International Naginata Federation. (Hereafter referred to as "INF".)

(Membership)

Article 2: INF shall consist of National Naginata Organizations, each of which exclusively represents one nation in Naginata. (Hereafter referred to as "Affiliate".)

(Headquarters)

Article 3: INF shall have its Headquarters in the country to which the President belongs. The Secretariat shall be located in the country to which the Secretary General belongs.

(Language)

Article 4: INF's official language shall be English, and its official technical terms shall be Japanese.

(Character)

Article 5:INF shall be a non-profit organization for overseeing Naginata. It shall be non-political and not permit any discrimination on account of race, religion or other factors.

(Registration)

Article 6: Each Affiliate shall register with INF headquarters or with its Secretariat.

Chapter 2: Purpose and Activities

(Purpose)

Article 7: INF shall develop and promote Naginata on a global basis and foster mutual trust and friendship among Affiliates through Naginata.

(Activities)

Article 8: INF shall engage in the following activities to achieve the purposes outlined in Article 7:

(1) To organize World Naginata Championships
(2) To promote Naginata worldwide
(3) To establish international rules of Naginata matches
(4) To establish standard rules for examination of Naginata Kyu/Dan and review of Shogo
(5) To establish international rules for examination criteria of Shinpan-in
(6) To organize seminars and study meetings
(7) To procure equipment and teaching materials for Naginata
(8) To exchange information and publish bulletins

(9) To undertake other projects to achieve the purposes outlined in Article 7

Chapter 3: Affiliation, Dismissal, Withdrawal

Article 9: The procedures for affiliation with, dismissal and withdrawal from INF shall be defined in the "Separate Detailed Regulations".

Chapter 4: Organization

(General Assembly)

Article 10: The General Assembly shall be the highest deliberative organ of INF, having the power to deliver decisions on the appointment of Directors, amendments to the constitution, the annual budget and financial reports, as well as reports on championships and other projects and all other matters of importance to INF.

Article 11: The President shall call a General Assembly every four (4) years. The President may convene an Extraordinary General Meeting when necessary.

Article 12: The General Assembly shall consist of no more than two (2) representatives delegated by each Affiliate and INF Officers (excluding Auditors), and shall be chaired by the President. If an Affiliate's Chairperson cannot attend, another representative may attend with a letter of temporary appointment signed by the Chairperson of the Affiliate. An Officer may appoint another Officer as proxy to exercise his/her voting rights, in which case a letter of proxy signed by the Officer shall be submitted in advance.

Article 13: Each Affiliate and each Officer (excluding Auditors) shall have one (1) vote. Provisional members may attend the General Assembly as non-voting observers.

Article 14: A quorum at the General Assembly shall be a majority of members in accordance with the stipulations in Article 12. A resolution shall be passed by a majority vote of the members present. In the case of a tie, the Chairperson shall cast the tie-breaking vote.

Article 15: Affiliate representatives may attend the General Assembly accompanied by a personal interpreter.

(Board of Directors)
Article 16: The Board of Directors shall make decisions based on the resolutions passed by the General Assembly. The Board may make decisions on all emergency matters. However, they must obtain ratification on such decisions at the following General Assembly.

Article 17: The Board of Directors Meeting shall be called by the President once every year and extraordinary meetings as necessary. An annual report of its activities shall be provided to each Affiliate.

Article 18: The Board of Directors shall consist of the Officers designated in Article 20 (excluding Auditors), and shall be chaired by the President. An Officer may appoint another Officer as proxy to exercise his/her voting rights, in which case a letter of temporary appointment signed by the Officer must be submitted in advance.

Article 19: A quorum at the Board of Directors Meeting shall be a majority of the members. A resolution shall be passed by a majority vote of the members present, and the Chairperson shall have a casting vote.

Chapter 5: Officers

Article 20: INF shall consist of the following Officers:

President	1
Senior Vice President	1
Vice President	3 or less
Executive Director	1
Director	(As defined in the "Separate Detailed Regulations")
Secretary General	1
Auditor	2

(Election)
Article 21: (1) The President shall be elected at the Board of Directors Meeting and the election results shall be reported at the General Assembly.
(2) Vice Presidents shall be appointed by the President, and the appointments shall be reported at the General Assembly with the approval of the Board of Directors. The President shall appoint one Senior Vice President among the Vice Presidents approved by the Board of Directors, and the appointment

shall be reported at the General Assembly.
(3) Directors shall be appointed at the General Assembly in accordance with the procedures outlined in the "Separate Detailed Regulations". However, when there is any change during the term of service, a replacement may be assigned with the approval of the Board of Directors.
(4) An Executive Director shall be elected by members of the Board of Directors, and the election shall be reported at the General Assembly.
(5) The Secretary General shall be appointed by the President, and the appointment shall be reported at the General Assembly with the approval of the Board of Directors.
(6) The Auditors shall be assigned at the General Assembly but shall not hold positions as Officers.

(Function)
Article 22: (1) The President shall represent INF.
(2) The Vice Presidents shall assist the President and conduct their duties in accordance with the "Separate Detailed Regulations". If the President is unable execute his/her duties, the Senior Vice President may temporarily replace the President.
(3) The Executive Director shall manage and supervise the activities of the Board of Directors.
(4) The Directors shall observe the regulations and faithfully execute their duties as Board members.
(5) The Secretary General shall carry out administrative functions for INF.
(6) The Auditors shall undertake the audit of all financial and other matters.

(Term)
Article 23: (1) The term of office for all Officers shall be four (4) years, and they may be reappointed.
(2) If an Officer's position is filled by a replacement, the term of the successor shall be the remaining term of the predecessor.

(Advisor)
Article 24: An Advisor(s) may be appointed for the Federation.
(1) Advisor(s) shall be commissioned by the President with the consent of the Board of Directors.
(2) Advisor(s) shall be consulted on matters that the President thinks are necessary.

Chapter 6: Technical Committee

Article 25: The Technical Committee shall be supervised by the Vice President designated by the President based on Chapter V, Article 22-(2). The Technical Committee shall consist of an appropriate number of members and review technical matters related to Naginata at the President's request.

Article 26: Technical Committee members shall be commissioned by the Board of Directors. A Chairperson shall be designated by the President when the Vice President in charge of the Technical Committee is vacant. The term of office of Committee members shall be the same as that stated in Article 23.

Chapter 7: Finance and Accounting

(Finance)
Article 27: The administrative expenses of INF shall be financed from affiliation fees, annual membership fees, contributions, subsidies and other income.

(Affiliation and Membership Fees)
Article 28: Affiliation fees and membership fees shall be determined at the General Assembly.

Article 29: Failure to pay annual membership fees for three (3) years or more without just cause may result in disqualification from participation in Championships or other events, depending on the decision of the Board of Directors.

(Fiscal Year and Financial Settlement)
Article 30: The financial year of INF shall commence on April 1st and end March 31st of the following year. The financial and business report on the fiscal year shall be completed within three (3) months of the end of each fiscal year, and shall be sent immediately to each Affiliate. However, the General Assembly may approve the reports for four (4) fiscal years collectively.

Chapter 8: Amendment of the Constitution and Dissolution

(Amendment of the Constitution)
Article 31: Any amendment to the Constitution must be approved at the General Assembly by an affirmative vote with a two-thirds (2/3) majority in accordance with the stipulations of Articles 12 and 13.

Chapter 9: Dissolution

(Dissolution)
Article 32: Resolution to dissolve INF must be approved at the General Assembly by an affirmative vote of two-third (2/3) of its members. In the event of dissolution, all remaining assets and funds shall be allocated to all Affiliates at an appropriate ratio.

APPENDICES

Article 1: (For Article 8-1)
The World Naginata Championships shall be held every four (4) years. The venue, date and the host organization shall be determined at the General Assembly. The program details and budget shall be decided by the Board of Directors based upon the host organization's proposal.

Article 2: (For Article 11)
In urgent cases, a vote of the General Assembly may be made in writing with the President's agreement. In such a case, the details of the process and substance shall be reported at the next General Assembly Meeting.

Article 3: (For Article 17)
In urgent cases, a vote of the Board of Directors may be made in writing with the President's agreement. In such a case, details of the process and substance shall be reported at the next Board of Directors Meeting.

SEPARATE DETAILED REGULATIONS

1. INF OFFICIAL LANGUAGE

Set forth below are the regulations pertaining to official language use in the INF as stipulated in Chapter 1, Article 4.

Although the official INF language for general correspondence is designated as English and Japanese for technical terms, exception may be made in the case of seminars and promotion examinations. Other languages may be used depending on circumstances. However, in principle, the method of written examinations and INF examinations should be conducted in accordance with the stipulations for taking INF Dan Examinations.

(Language)
Article 4: INF's official language shall be English, and its official technical terms shall be Japanese.

2. PROCEDURES for AFFILIATION to INF

Set forth below are the procedures for affiliation to INF in accordance with Chapter 3, Article 9 of the Constitution.

1. Procedure:
(1) A recommendation in writing by an Affiliate shall be required. However, in the case of Europe-Africa zone, the national organization shall first become a member of the European Naginata Federation (ENF).
(2) The application shall be filed in writing.
(3) Judgment

a. The Review Committee shall be convened by the President.
b. The Committee members shall consist of a minimum of five (5) persons, including the Secretary General and a representative from the Zone concerned, nominated by the President and others nominated from among Vice Presidents and Directors.

(4) The result of this review shall be reported to the Board of Directors.
(5) The affiliation shall be approved at the General Assembly following the result of the Board of Directors.

2. Matters for Deliberation

(1) Organization

a. Statute, Rules, Regulations etc.
b. President and other Officials.
c. Date of foundation.
d. Population of registered members.
e. Number of members with Kyu/Dan grades.
f. Number of Dojo (training halls) and practice sessions.

(2) Position in the sports world of that country.

a. The position of the athletic organization, if any, to which the applying Naginata organization is affiliated.

(3) History of the development of Naginata in the country.

3. Manner of Affiliation

Depending on the conclusions of the Committee, INF has the right to validate the affiliation as:
(1) Permanent member.
(2) Provisional member, limited to the term for one (1) year or more.

3. PROCEDURES FOR EXPULSION AND WITHDRAWAL

Set forth below are the procedures for expulsion or withdrawal of an Affiliate from INF, in accordance with Chapter 3, Article 9 of the Constitution.

1. Request for Expulsion

(1) Any member organization may file a request with INF for expulsion of an Affiliate.
(2) The request shall be made in writing, with reasons clearly stated.

2. Procedures for Expulsion

(1) The President shall organize an Investigation Committee.
(2) The Committee members shall be appointed by the President.
(3) The Investigation Committee shall provide the President with a report on the results of its investigation.
(4) Expulsion shall be approved at the General Assembly following the result of the Board of Directors.

3. Cause(s) for Expulsion
(1) Payment default of Annual Membership Fees for three (3) years or more without good reason.
(2) Insufficient promotion of Naginata and poor leadership.
(3) Taking inappropriate advantage of Naginata for commercial purposes.

4. Procedures for Withdrawal
(1) The Affiliate shall file an application for withdrawal from INF.
(2) The Board of Directors shall first validate the application.
(3) Finally, the General Assembly shall validate the withdrawal.

4. RULES FOR APPOINTMENT OF DIRECTORS

Set forth below are the rules for the appointment of the Directors of the Board of INF, in accordance with Chapter 5, Article 21-(3).

1. The Director shall represent the Zone where he/she belongs to.
2. One (1) Director shall be assigned from each Zone and any Zone having ten (10) or more Affiliates can assign two (2) Directors.
3. Director(s) shall be assigned from the following four (4) Zones. The Board of Directors shall decide which Zone an Affiliate belongs to in cases of ambiguity.
   - Asia Zone
   - Europe-Africa Zone
   - Oceania Zone
   - Pan-America Zone
4. Japan may currently nominate three (3) Directors.
5. The Director(s) appointed to represent a Zone must have the nationality of one of the countries in the Zone concerned.

5. FUNCTIONS OF VICE PRESIDENTS

Set forth below are the functions of the Vice President in accordance with Chapter 5, Article 22-(2).

1. Each Vice President shall be charged with a specific function indicated by the President.
2. INF has the following four (4) functions for Vice Presidents:

(1) General Affairs
(2) Finance
(3) Technique
(4) Promotion and International Coordination

3. The Senior Vice President shall be in charge of General Affairs and supervise the Secretariat of INF.
4. The Vice President in charge of finance shall supervise INF accounts and inspect the financial situation in order to ensure stable administration, as well as study to ways to procure extra contributions and subsidies.
5. The Vice President in charge of Technique shall supervise the Technical Committee.
6. The Vice President in charge of Promotion and International Coordination shall investigate effective means for the promotion of Naginata worldwide, and supervise mutual cooperation, partnership and solidarity among INF member countries and people who practice Naginata.
7. Each Vice President can seek assistance from Director(s) to execute these functions.
8. These functions can be modified when necessary depending on the conditions or situations surrounding INF.

6. DUTIES OF DIRECTORS

Set forth below are the duties of the Directors in accordance with Chapter 5, Article 22-(4).

1.The Director shall give guidance in the Zone from which he/she has been assigned, based on the resolutions passed at the Board of Directors Meeting, and shall make the greatest possible efforts to implement any resolutions.

2. The Director shall make all possible efforts to understand the conditions in each country in their zone and work to promote and develop the activities of INF.

3. When the Director(s) is required to assist the Vice President they shall assiduously execute their tasks as directed.

END

APPENDIX 7
GLOSSARY OF NAGINATA TERMS

Glossary of Naginata Terms

A

aite
Opponent or partner.

ai-uchi
Striking simultaneously.

AJNF
All Japan Naginata Federation (Zen Nihon Naginata Renmei).

ashi-sabaki
Footwork. Examples include *okuri-ashi*, *ayumi-ashi*, *hiraki-ashi*, *tsugi-ashi*, *mae*, and *ato*.

atarashii naginata
The "new" post-war style of Naginata, which was created as a sport and for use in the education system.

ato
Move back.

ayumi-ashi
Footwork used for going forward and backward. When moving forward start with the right foot first and move four steps forward. When moving back, start with the left foot first and take four steps back.

B

bōgu
The protective armour worn by Naginata practitioners. It consists of the *sune-ate* (shin protectors), *men* (head gear), *kote* (gauntlets), *dō* (chest protector), and *tare* (waist protector).

bokken
Wooden sword.

bokutō
Wooden sword.

budō
The martial Ways of Japan.

chūdan-no-kamae
A stance or *kamae* which is considered the basis for all *kamae*, and is the most suitable for offence and defence. The body faces sideways and the *naginata* is held horizontally with the *kissaki* slightly raised and pointed at the opponent's centreline.

chūi
A warning verbal warning.

counting
Ichi, ni, san, shi, go, roku, shichi, hachi, kyū, jū (1~10).

D

dan
Grade used in Naginata. (*shodan, nidan, sandan, yondan, godan* 1st~5th *dan*).

datotsu
A strike or thrust made to specified targets on the opponent.

datotsu-bō
A small staff used as a target for students to practise the various strikes.

datotsu-bu
Striking section of the *naginata*.

datotsu-bui
Valid striking points or targets.

dō
The protective plastron for the mid-section of the body which is a valid target.

dōjō
Training hall.

dō-uchi
A strike to the mid-section of the body.

E

e-bu
The wooden shaft of the *naginata*.

e-harai
A technique in which the *e-bu* is used to sweep away the opponent's *naginata*.

Edo period
(1603-1868). Also referred to as the Tokugawa period.

enchō
Time extension. Up to three *enchō* may be allowed before the match is decided by *hantei* (Referees' decision).

engi
A demonstration of *kata* or prearranged moves. *Engi-kyōgi* refers to *Shikake-ōji* or *Kata* matches.

F

fukushin
A Sub Referee. Two Sub Referees assist the Head Referee in deciding points and fouls in a match.

fumikae-ashi
Footwork used for changing the direction that the body is facing on the spot when striking or counter-attacking.

fumikomi
Lunging in to strike.

furiage-men-uchi
An attack in which the attacker swings the *naginata* directly overhead and then makes a strike to the centre of the opponent's *men*.

furiage-kote-uchi
An attack in which the attacker swings the *naginata* directly overhead (to a lesser degree than for *men-uchi*) and then makes a cut to the wrist.

furiage-sune-uchi
A strike to the shin in which the attacker swings the *naginata* overhead and then brings it down on an angle to strike the *sune-ate*.

furikaeshi
An overhead strike which starts from *chūdan-no-kamae*. The *naginata* is spun overhead and brought down to strike the target. The circular motion makes it a representative technique in Naginata.

G

gedan-no-kamae
A *kamae* used mainly for defence and then counterattack. The *kissaki* is lowered and kept in line with the body's centreline. The *kissaki* is approximately 10cm from the floor. The *ha* should be facing up, and the *ishizuki* should be at the back with the rear hand held at ear height.

gōgi
Referee consultation.

H

ha / ha-bu
The *naginata* blade section.

hachimaki
See *tenugui*.

hajime
"Begin". This is called by Shushin to start a match.

hakama
The "split skirt" worn during *keiko*. It is made of cotton or synthetic fabrics and is navy blue or black in colour.

hanmi
Side-on posture.

hansoku
A penalty incurred after committing a foul. The accumulation of two *hansoku* results in 1 point (*ippon*) for the opponent.

hantei
A decision made by the referees when the match cannot be decided by points. The winning point is awarded to the player who exhibits greater skill in offence and defence, posture, manner, and has the least number of fouls.

happō-buri
Warm-up exercises performed at the beginning of *keiko*. Examples include *jōgeburi* (vertical), *naname-buri* (diagonal), *yoko-buri* (horizontal), *naname-buri shita-kara* (diagonal from below), and *furikaeshi* (overhead).

hara
The lower-abdominal region.

harai-waza
Techniques used to ward off an attack. The *sori* or curvature of the blade is typically used to sweep or knock the opponent's *naginata* away. The *e-bu* can also be used (see *e-harai*).

hassō-no-kamae
An offensive stance in which the *naginata* is held upward and slightly on a diagonal. The *ishizuki* is near the mid-thigh region and in line with the body's centre, and the upper hand grips at ear level. The *ha-bu* faces toward the opponent.

hidari
Left (direction).

hidari kamae
Kamae (stances) in which the left foot is forward. For example, *hidari-chūdan* refers to *chūdan-no-kamae* in which the left foot is in the front.

hidari-(ni)-hirake
A command to move to the left.

hikiwake
A draw.

himo
Cords used to tie the *bōgu* and *hakama*.

hiraki-ashi
Footwork used when avoiding a strike or responding. When moving to the left, step with the left foot and follow with the right. Move to the right with opposite stepping order.

hyōji-iin
The Marker Officials responsible for indicating the referee's decisions.

I

igi
A formal protest lodged to the Shinpan-cho or Shinpan-shunin.

INF
International Naginata Federation.

inkō
The throat, and target for a *tsuki* attack.

ippon
One point.

ippon-gachi shōbu-ari
"Victory decided by a single point". An announcement made by Shushin after a victory has been decided by a single point.

ishizuki
The butt end of the *naginata.*

ishizuki-tsuki
A thrust to the throat or side of the body using the *ishizuki* end of the *naginata*. This technique is currently prohibited in matches, but is utilised in Shikake-ōji, Kata, and matches against kendo.

J

ji-geiko
Free sparring.

Jikishin Kage-ryū
One of the predominant traditional styles of Naginata. Training in the traditional styles centres on *kata* repetition of the *naginata* versus other weapons such as swords, daggers and so on. Many Naginata practitioners train in a traditional style as well as the modern sports version.

jōdan-no-kamae
This *kamae* is considered the most aggressive stance. The *naginata* is held horizontally overhead with the *ishizuki* forward and aligned with the body's centreline. The *ha* is facing upward at the back.

jōgai
A foul incurred when a player steps out of bounds.

K

kakari-geiko
Attack practice.

kamae
Fighting postures or stances. These include *chūdan-no-kamae*, *jōdan-no-kamae*, *gedan-no-kamae*, *wakigamae*, *hassō-no-kamae*.

kata
Set forms. The All Japan Naginata Federation has a set of official *kata*

consisting of 7 forms.

katana
A Japanese sword.

keiko
Training.

keiko-gi
Training jacket.

ken-tai-itchi
Attack and defence as one.

ki
Energy which enables the functioning of body and mind.

kiai
Spirited psychic equilibrium full of vigour and drive.

ki-ken-tai-itchi
Striking with the spirit, *naginata*, and body in unison.

kihon (-dōsa)
Basics or fundamentals of Naginata.

kissaki
The tip of the *naginata* blade.

koshi-ita
The back panel on the *hakama*.

kote
The wrists or the protective gauntlets. Left and right *kote* are valid striking targets in competitive matches.

kuridashi
Pushing the *naginata* out.

kurikomi
Pulling the *naginata* in.

M

maai
The spatial distance or interval between opponents. *Tōi-maai* (*tōma*)=long distance; *uchi-maai* (*uchima*)=striking distance; *chikai-maai* (*chikama*)=close distance.

mae
Forward movement.

makiotoshi-waza
Use of the *sori* to flick the opponent's *naginata* downward, taking away their power to attack, and then following quickly with a strike.

Meiji period
1868-1912.

men
The protective mask. It is a valid striking target.

men-uchi
A strike to the head.

migi
Right (direction).

migi-(ni)-hirake
A command to move to the right.

migi kamae
Kamae in which the right foot is forward. For example, *migi-chūdan* refers to *chūdan-no-kamae* in which the right foot is in the front.

mitori-geiko
Watching training.

mochikae
Changing *kamae* or grip.

mochikae-sokumen-uchi
Alternating strikes to the left and right *men*.

mochikae-sune-uchi
Alternating strikes to the left and right shins.

monouchi
The part of the *ha* or *e* in which the targets must be struck with to be considered valid.

motodachi
Training partner who receives attacks, or who takes the role of instructor.

mune (mine)
The upper (concave) surface of the blade.

N

naginata
A weapon consisting of an ovate wooden shaft measuring approximately 6-8 feet in length with a curved blade on the end of it. The blade measured between 1 and 3 feet, and was sharpened on one side (the convex side). Also, the martial art in which this weapon is used.

naginata-ka
A practitioner of *naginata*. This term is seldom used.

nuki-waza
Techniques used to avoid (rather than block) an opponent's strikes.

O

obi
The belt or sash worn around the waist underneath the *hakama*. It measures

approximately 2-3 metres in length (enough to wrap around the body twice and tie at the back) and is made of bleached cotton.

ōji-waza
Counter techniques.

okuri-ashi
The footwork used when striking, and for moving in all directions.

R

rei
A bow of respect. Mental preparedness is required from the start to the finish of the bow. If bowing to the *shōmen*, the angle should be 30 degrees. The back should be kept as straight as possible when bowing. If bowing to an opponent, then an angle of 15 degrees should be used while maintaining eye contact at all times. The feeling of respect for one's opponent must be maintained at all times.

ritsurei
Standing bow

ryū / ryūha
Martial schools or traditions.

S

saiten keiji-iin
Scoreboard officials keep track of scores, match time, and the number of valid points and fouls.

san-bon-shōbu
A three point scoring method used in matches.
sayū-dō-uchi
Strikes to both the left and right sides of the body (*dō*).

sayū-sokumen-uchi
Strikes to both the left and right sides of the head (up to 30 degrees either side

of the centre of *men*).

sayū-sune-uchi
Strikes to both the left and right shins.

seiza
The formal sitting (kneeling) position. The knees should be approximately five inches apart (for men), and together for women, with the two big toes crossed (or touching) at the back.

seme
Applying pressure on the opponent and probing for openings.

sendan-maki
The section of the *naginata* at which the *ha-bu* is attached to the *e-bu*. This joint is held firmly in place by wrapping it several times with white plastic tape.

sensei
Teacher

senshu-iin
Player officials who call the players out onto the court. The *senshu-iin* also inspects the player's equipment ahead of time to make sure that all is in order so that no delays occur.

seri-ai
Engaging at close quarters.

shiai (-kyōgi)
Competitive matches.

shidō
Instruction, guidance, direction.

shikake-ōji
Eight movements and *waza* into prearranged sequences. The attacker is called *shikake*, and the defender is *ōji*.

shikake-waza
Offensive techniques.

shinogi
The side of the *naginata* blade.

shinpan
Referee.

shinpan-shunin
The Court Manager. It is the Court Manager's responsibility to act as an assistant to the Shinpan-cho (Referee Director) when there are more than two courts in use at the same time.

shinpan-chō
The Referee Director. The Shinpan-cho's responsibility is to make sure that the match rules are abided by.

shizentai
Natural standing position. *Shizentai* enables quick reaction to the opponent's movements, and is a free and stable posture.

shōbu-ari
"Victory decided". All matches end with Shushin declaring either "*shōbu-ari*" or "*hikiwake*" (draw).

shōgō
Ranks awarded after *godan* in the order of Renshi, Kyōshi, and finally Hanshi, which is the highest possible rank in Naginata.

shōmen
The centre of the face or head. This word also refers to the altar or sacred place in the *dōjō*.

shushin
The Head Referee.

soku-men-uchi
A strike 30 degrees to the left or right of *shōmen*.

sori
The curvature of the *naginata* blade.

sōtai
The position held by two opponents who are facing each other in *shizentai* 4 metres apart.

suki
Weakness or opening.

sune
The shins. Valid striking target in competitive matches.

sune-ate
Shin protectors.

sune-uchi
A strike to the shins.

T

tachi
Sword.

taijō
An ejection from a match.

taisabaki
The footwork used to move the body and when striking.

tare
The waist protector.

te
The hand

Tendo-ryū
One of the predominant traditional styles of Naginata. Training in the traditional styles centres on *kata* repetition of the *naginata* versus other

weapons such as swords, daggers and so on. Many Naginata practitioners train in a traditional style as well as the modern sporting version.

tenouchi
Grip or use of the hands to manipulate the *naginata* when striking.

tenugui
A protective head wrap worn underneath the *men*. It absorbs sweat and prevents chafing.

tokei-iin
The Time officials in a match.

tsugi-ashi
Footwork used when striking from a distance or when you want to reduce the *maai* quickly.

tsuki
A thrust with the *kissaki* or *ishizuki*. Thrusting to the throat in *shiai* is prohibited until age eighteen. *Ishizuki tsuki* is prohibited.

U

uchikaeshi
A basic *kihon* exercise for repetitive striking of *men* and *sune*.

wakare
Command to separate.

wakigamae
A *kamae* in which the *naginata* is held horizontally with the *ishizuki* forward and in the centreline of the body. The *ha* faces outwards at the back.

waza
Technique.

Y

yame
Stop.

yūkō-datotsu
A valid strike or thrust.

Z

zanshin
Maintaining physical and mental alertness after attacking.

zarei
Bowing from the *seiza* (seated) position.

zekken
Name patch attached to the front panel of the *tare*.

Zen Nihon Naginata Renmei
All Japan Naginata Federation.

Bibliography

AJKF, *Japanese-English Dictionary of Kendo*, AJKF, 2000

AJNF, *Naginata Handbook*, 2013

Sports V Course: Shin-Naginata kyoshitsu, Taishukan Shoten, 2003

Amdur, Ellis, "The Development and History of the Naginata", *Journal of Asian Martial Arts* Vol. 4. No. 1, 1995. Via Media Publishing

"Women Warriors of Japan", http://www.koryu.com/library/wwj1.html

Bennett, A. C., *Kendo: Culture of the Sword*, Berkeley: University of California Press, 2015

Bottomly, I., *Arms and Armor of the Samurai: The History of Weaponry in Ancient Japan*, NY: Crescent Books, 1996

Conlan, T., *State of War: The Violent Order of Fourteenth Century Japan*, Ann Arbor: Center for Japanese Studies, University of Michigan, 2003

Friday, K., "Off the Warpath: Military Science and Budo in the Evolution of *Ryuha Bugei*" in Bennett (ed.), *Budo Perspectives*, Auckland: KW Publications, 2005, Chapter 15.

Futaki Ken'ichi, Irie Kohei, Kato Hiroshi (eds.), *Budo*, Tokyo: Tokyodo Shuppan, 1994

Hurst, G. C., *Armed Martial Arts of Japan*, New Haven: Yale University Press, 1998

Ishigaki Yasuzo, *Gekkenkai shimatsu*, Tokyo: Shimazu Shobo, 2000

Irvine, G., *The Japanese Sword: the Soul of the Samurai,* Trumbell: Weatherhill, 2000

Kajihara Masaaki and Yamashita Hiroaki (annot.), Tokyo: *Heike monogatari*, Tokyo: Iwanami Shoten, 1991–1993

Kinoshita Hisanori, *Kenpo shigoku shoden*. Tokyo: Taiiku to Supotsu Shuppansha, 1985

Kodansha, *Budo hokan*, Tokyo: Kodokan, 1975

Knutsen, Roald, M., *Japanese Polearms*, London: Holland Press, 1963

McCullough, Helen, C., (trans.), *The Tale of the Heike*, Stanford: Stanford University Press, 1988

Monbusho, *Zenkoku shihan gakko-cho kaigi-yoko*, Monbusho Futsu Gakumukyoku, 1911

"*Zenkoku chuto-gakko ni okeru kyudo naginata ni kansuru chosa*", Monbudaijin Kanbo Taiiku-ka, 1937

Nakabayashi Shinji, *Budo no susume*. Tokyo: Nakabayashi Shinji Sensei Isakushu Kankokai, 1987

Nakamura Tamio, "The History of *Bogu*", (translated by Alex Bennett) in *Kendo World* Vol. 1 No. 1, 2001

Kendo jiten, Tokyo: Shimazu Shobo, 1994
"*Kindai naginata shoshi*" in *Kindai Naginata meicho senshu* Vol. 8. Tokyo: Hon no Tomosha, 2004
Oya Minoru, "Central Issues in the Instruction of Kendo: With Focus on the Inter-connectedness of Waza and Mind" in Bennett (ed.), *Budo Perspectives*, Auckland: KW Publications, 2005, Chapter 11.
Sakakida Yaeko, Tsuyama Katsuko, *Atarashii naginata: shido no tebiki*, Kyoto, Taiiku no Kagakusha, 1960
SCAP, *Political Reorientation of Japan, September 1945 to September 1948*; Report. Contributors: Supreme Commander for the Allied Powers. Government Section—Publisher: U.S. Govt. Print. Off, Washington, DC.

About the Author

Alexander Bennett Ph.D.

Alex Bennett was born in 1970 in Christchurch, New Zealand. He graduated from the University of Canterbury in 1994. He received his Doctoral degree from Kyoto University in 2001, and another from the University of Canterbury in 2012. After working at the International Research Centre for Japanese Studies, and then Teikyo University, he is currently employed as Professor at Kansai University's Department of International Affairs. Alex is Vice President of the International Naginata Federation, International Committee member of the All Japan Kendo Federation, Director of the Japanese Academy of Budo, and also represents NZ Kendo as the Head Coach. He is co-founder and Editor-in-Chief of *Kendo World*, the world's only English language journal dedicated to kendo, and holds the grades of Kendo Kyoshi 7-dan, Iaido 5-dan, Naginata 5-dan Tankendo 3-dan, Jukendo 3-dan, Jikishin Kage-ryu Kenjutsu 3-dan. He has competed successfully in international competition in Naginata and Kendo, taking second place in the World Naginata Championships in July, 2011, and leading the New Zealand National Kendo Team to the top 8 in the world at the 15th World Kendo Championships. Recent publications include *Kendo: Culture of the Sword* (University of California Press, 2015) and *Hagakure: The Secret Wisdom of the Samurai* (Tuttle, 2014).

www.arekku.nz

www.ingramcontent.com/pod-product-compliance
Lightning Source LLC
Chambersburg PA
CBHW060315100426
42812CB00003B/787